Theban Plays

Sophocles

Theban Plays

Translated, with Introduction and Notes, by

Peter Meineck and Paul Woodruff

Hackett Publishing Company, Inc.
Indianapolis/Cambridge

Printed in the United States of America

22 21 20 19   4 5 6 7

For further information, please address:
  Hackett Publishing Company, Inc.
  P.O. Box 44937
  Indianapolis, IN 46244-0937
  www.hackettpublishing.com

Cover design by Brian Rak and Abigail Coyle
Interior design by Meera Dash
Composition by William Hartman

Excerpt from "Do Not Go Gentle Into That Good Night," by Dylan Thomas, from
The Poems of Dylan Thomas, copyright © 1952 by Dylan Thomas. Reprinted
by permission of New Directions Publishing Corp. In Walford Davies and Ralph
Maud, eds., *Collected Poems, 1934–1953* (London: Dent, 1993). Reprinted by
permission of the publisher.

Library of Congress Cataloging-in-Publication Data
Sophocles.
    [Selections. English. 2003]
    Theban plays / Sophocles; translated with introduction and
notes, by Peter Meineck and Paul Woodruff.
        p. cm.
    Includes bibliographical references.
    Contents: Antigone—Oedipus tyrannus—Oedipus at Colonus.
    ISBN 0-87220-586-X (cloth) — ISBN 0-87220-585-1 (paper)
    1. Sophocles—Translations into English. 2. Antigone (Greek
mythology)—Drama. 3. Oedipus (Greek mythology)—Drama.
4. Thebes (Greece)—Drama. I. Meineck, Peter, 1967–.
II. Woodruff, Paul, 1943–. III. Title.

PA4414.A2 M45 2003
882'.01—dc21   2002038790

ISBN-13: 978-0-87220-586-4 (cloth)
ISBN-13: 978-0-87220-585-7 (pbk.)

Contents

Preface   vi

Introduction   ix
    Sophocles and the Composition of the Plays   ix
    Athenian Theatre and Performance   xii
    Antigone   xvi
    Oedipus Tyrannus   xxxv
    Oedipus at Colonus   liii

Suggestions for Further Reading   lxxii

Note on the Translations   lxxv

Acknowledgments   lxxvi

Theban Royal Family Tree   lxxviii

Antigone   1

Oedipus Tyrannus   61

Oedipus at Colonus   125

Endnotes   208
    A. *Antigone*   208
    B. *Oedipus Tyrannus*   211
    C. *Oedipus at Colonus*   212

Appendix: Hegel on *Antigone*   214

Selected Bibliography   217

Preface

The first of the three Theban plays, *Antigone*, was written in the glory days of Athens while the Parthenon was being built. Then came *Oedipus Tyrannus*, probably staged after Athens had gone to war with the Spartan alliance and had been struck by a fearful plague. And, last of all of Sophocles' plays, *Oedipus at Colonus* was written in the twilight of the Athenian empire and staged after its author's death. More than thirty years passed between the writing of the first and the last of these three plays, yet they are often read together. And why not? They are Sophocles' most famous plays, they have common themes, and they follow one family through a cycle of disasters.

Do not think of them as a trilogy, however, for Sophocles did not write them to be performed together. They are not anything like the plays in the *Oresteia* of Aeschylus, which follow a distinct, tight chain of events from bloody beginning to peaceful resolution and were written to be seen together as presenting an almost continuous story in which one play shows the cause from which spring the actions of the next, and in which the final play brings the cycle to a resolution.

If we saw the Theban plays in the order of the stories they tell, we would not find—and should not look for—a similar chain of causes. Each play is complete in itself, presenting the causes of its own action in its own terms. We would see Oedipus first as the mature ruler of Thebes (*Oedipus Tyrannus*), a ruler with a terrible secret who is, at the same time, a man who takes pride in his talent for bringing what has been secret into the light. In the second play (*Oedipus at Colonus*), we would see him as a homeless old man, reduced to begging for a place to sit—and die—on sacred ground near Athens, but also as a man who brings a blessing to the Athenians, a hero who will have the powers of a god. And what brought this situation about? Nothing in the first story prepares us for Oedipus' extraordinary death. The last play would be an anticlimax; here we would see Oedipus' daughter Antigone daring the wrath of the king in order to give proper burial to her outlawed brother. In itself, this is a splendid play, but it does nothing to resolve the family drama except to kill off most of its survivors. If these three stories have a resolution, it is in *Oedipus at Colonus*, but what this play resolves is far grander than the story of this family. Oedipus himself has become an enormously powerful figure in this last play: his presence throughout the action, seated on the forbidden ground he has chosen, which the gods have chosen for him, concentrates in one man great themes of the sacred and the profane, of the acceptance and denial of mystery, and of the violence that destroys peace and the violence that sustains it.

Perhaps some details from the plays would allow our seeing them in narrative order. *Oedipus at Colonus*, for example, alludes to the issue of burial. Also, the characters show some consistency across the plays. Oedipus is prone to explosions of fierce and fatal anger, as we see in the two plays that bear his name. Antigone loves her brother in both of the plays in which she has a part. Creon uses sneaky arguments in the two Oedipus plays and shows a fondness for cliché in both *Antigone* and *Oedipus at Colonus*.

Both of the translators of this volume, however, want to emphasize the independence of these plays from one another. Each play stands alone, brilliantly. Sophocles' style as a playwright—so far as we can tell from the surviving texts—requires independence. Sophocles seems to know intuitively that theatre is most gripping when it represents human *action*—people actually doing things they choose to do—rather than events that lie outside of choice. That is why we see no deus ex machina here, no god brought in to force an ending on a play. The gods may be at work behind the scenes (as the chorus believe), but what we see on stage has been, for the most part, brought about by human actions that we have also seen on stage. The dreadful curse, for example, the one that Oedipus carries at the end of *Oedipus Tyrannus*, is a curse he himself called down on the king's murderer early in the play. Of the three great tragedians—Aeschylus, Euripides, and Sophocles— Sophocles is closest to humanism in his way of writing plays, and this humanism leads him to construct discrete dramas that link human effects directly to human causes. His devotion to the gods shows itself outside his plots: in the beauty of his choral lyrics, in the pious reserve with which he treats the actions of the gods, and in the dignity of his own extraordinary life.

The first two sections of the Introduction present what is known about the life of Sophocles and the performance of ancient

plays; those sections can be reasonably objective. I prepared the
first section, which examines Sophocles' life. Peter Meineck's
experience in producing ancient Greek plays gives him special
authority on performance, and he is the author of that section.

The plays themselves call for a more personal response. In
introducing the three plays, one after the other, I have made no
attempt to hide my own responses to them. You who read this
book are probably not a scholar of Sophocles. Neither am I. What
I know about the plays comes from many years of caring about
them, as well as from an acquaintance with the scholarly literature. Neither of us has any reason to pretend to be objective. For
my part, I have tried to distill for you the wisdom of the scholars
without hiding my own opinions. In reporting the points on
which scholars disagree, I have tried to give you the tools and the
impetus to form your own judgments on the main issues. For
your part, I ask you to try to care about these plays, as well as
about what the characters and the action mean to you. Argue
about them with your friends. But above all, allow yourself to be
moved by them. Sophocles knew more about intense feelings
than any other playwright in European history. He was never
afraid of feelings, and he could express them with overwhelming
power.

PAUL WOODRUFF
SEPTEMBER 2002

Introduction

Sophocles and the Composition of the Plays

Sophocles was born about 495 B.C.E. at Colonus, just outside the city of Athens, and lived until about 405. During his long life, he celebrated the naval victory of the Greek allies under Athenian leadership at Salamis (in 480), served as an official at the zenith of the Athenian empire, survived the great plague, and saw the shadows closing on Athens as the Spartans neared victory in the Peloponnesian War. In midlife, Sophocles heard the sophists, who brought to Athens their professional art of persuasion and their challenges to the old order. Meanwhile, he knew of the beginnings of medical science that were starting to question religious teachings about sickness and healing.

Sophocles was born about fifteen years after the last tyrant ruled in Athens. Athenian democracy came to full flower during his youth, and in his old age it almost collapsed under the pressure of war and right-wing revolution. His themes belong partly to his own time—attacks on traditional reverence by intellectuals or tyrants—and partly to all time, or at least to all human time.

In 468, Sophocles first competed in the festival of tragic plays, and he won against Aeschylus. Sophocles was the most successful Athenian playwright of the fifth century, composing 120 plays and winning 20 victories. This is an extraordinary record, since each victory represented the success of three tragic plays. Sad to say, only seven complete tragedies survive, and we know little about the others aside from fragmentary evidence. Even about the surviving plays we do not know as much as we would like. We know virtually nothing about the circumstances under which they were produced.

From the surviving plays, which were evidently the most admired, we can hazard some generalizations about Sophocles' beliefs and interests. More than any of his contemporaries, and especially in *Oedipus Tyrannus*, he is fascinated by the enduring question of what it is to be human in a world that does not bend itself to support human ambitions. His patriotic sentiments as an Athenian are especially evident in *Oedipus at Colonus*. We do not know how strongly he felt about the democracy in Athens, but we can tell from his plays that he was resolutely opposed to tyranny.

His attitude to the intellectual revolution of his time must have been complex. Two things were especially widespread in what is called the "new learning": the art of persuasion, which came to be known as rhetoric, and various programs to explain natural and human events without reference to the gods. Sophocles displays the art of persuasion; we see it in Creon's defense in *Oedipus Tyrannus*, for example, and in his debate with Haemon in *Antigone*. In these contexts, those who practice the art are not good, and they do not succeed. So Sophocles cannot have been bowled over by the new fashion for rhetoric.

In other areas, Sophocles took the new teachings to heart; he seems to have adopted a godless explanation for human progress (as we see in the first stasimon of *Antigone*): human beings invented their own culture, for better and worse. His treatment of the events that he brings to the stage is especially interesting; he generally does not use a deus ex machina, and he almost never relies on divine intervention to make a human event plausible. The speech of Heracles at the end of *Philoctetes* is an exception, but since it comes from the same actor who has been playing the wily Odysseus, who has merely exchanged one mask for another, Sophocles has given us an opportunity to imagine an entirely human turn behind the final twist in the play.[1] The end of *Oedipus at Colonus* is another exception: we are given no natural way to understand how a blind cripple is able suddenly to stand and lead a procession offstage.

In spite of the humanism implied in his dramaturgy, Sophocles was a deeply religious man, and religious in ways that do not have clear modern analogues. His principal value in the plays— in these three especially—seems to be the reverence that his stage tyrants neglect. This has two related components. Sophocles' reverent choruses recognize (1) that they are human, with limited knowledge and power, and (2) that crossing into sacred space has

---

1. I owe the point to Peter Meineck, who found, through producing the play, that audiences did indeed suppose that Heracles was yet another of Odysseus' manipulative disguises.

serious consequences.[2] I will return to these themes in discussing the individual plays.

The Athenians must have admired the man as much as they adored his writing, since they made him a treasurer in 443 and a general, with Pericles, in 441. At the city's moment of greatest need, after the disaster of 413 in Sicily, the Athenians turned to Sophocles as one of the ten advisers empowered to see them through the crisis. After his death they honored him with cult as a hero in his own right.[3]

Dating the Plays

The only play of Sophocles for which we have a firm date, *Philoctetes*, was produced in 409. Otherwise, dating is uncertain, but scholars generally place *Antigone* at about 441[4] and *Oedipus Tyrannus* some time later, probably shortly after the plague years in Athens. As a working hypothesis, we may accept the period 428–5 for the first production of *Oedipus Tyrannus*.[5]

As for *Oedipus at Colonus*, we know when it was produced but not when it was written. The production took place after the res-

2. In my book on reverence (2001), I expanded on the first theme—the recognition of the human—at the cost of the second—the recognition of the sacred, i.e., that which human beings should neither touch nor tread on.

3. He had been "the Receiver" of the cult of Asclepius, having opened his home to the god of healing and providing the first altar in his own house in 420, when the Asclepius cult was inaugurated in Athens. On the significance of Sophocles' role in cult, see Lowell Edmunds, *Theatrical Space and Historical Place in Sophocles' Oedipus at Colonus* (Lanham, Md.: Rowman and Littlefield, 1996), pp. 163–8.

4. According to an ancient summary of the play, Sophocles was made general after his success with *Antigone*; the expediton for which he was responsible most likely occurred in 441–0. See Griffith 1999, pp. 1 ff., for a discussion of this period in Athenian cultural history. (Full references not given in notes appear in the Selected Bibliography.)

5. The plague struck in 430–29 and recurred in 427–6. Bernard Knox argues for dating the production of *Oedipus Tyrannus* (OT) in 425 B.C.E., after the second outbreak (when Athens did consult the oracle) and before the production in 424 of Aristophanes' *Knights*, which may echo lines from OT. The case for this date is not proved, and scholars withhold judgment; still, Knox's date is, in our opinion, the most likely of those that have been suggested (Knox, 1956).

toration of the democracy in Athens, in 401, four years after the death of the playwright. Ancient sources tell us that Sophocles wrote the play at the very end of his life, but these are very late sources and have not persuaded all modern scholars. It is too natural a hypothesis that a play about a very old hero was written by a very old writer. Some modern scholars think that the play was written about the same time as *Oedipus Tyrannus*, others around 411, when an oligarchic coup in Athens made special use of Colonus. Some think that the play was written in stages and that only the final draft was written in Sophocles' last years. Some ancient sources tell us that Sophocles' sons brought him into court, asking for the management of his property on the ground that the old man was senile. But the poet proved the clarity of his mind by reciting from *Oedipus at Colonus*, which he was then composing (probably in 407). Some scholars think that Sophocles introduced the episodes concerning Oedipus' sons after this date, but most readers in recent years prefer to interpret the play as an organic whole.[6]

Athenian Theatre and Performance

Each play was conceived and staged for only one performance, along with two other tragic plays by the same author that may or may not have been related in theme or subject, followed by a brief satyr-play. Performances were held in broad daylight in the Theatre of Dionysus on the southeast slope of the Acropolis in Athens. The Theatre of Dionysus of the mid-fifth century B.C.E. was a large, open-air structure that took advantage of the natural slope of the Acropolis to accommodate a huge raked auditorium known as the *theatron* (seeing place). This seating area consisted mainly of wooden benches, with perhaps some marble seating for dignitaries in the front rows, and it could accommodate between 15,000 and 25,000 spectators, making it the largest public structure in the city of Athens.

The Festival of Dionysus itself was a multiday event financed by the city in celebration of the god of wine, revelry, and the

6. The best defense of reading the play as a unified whole is still Reinhardt's chapter (1947/79). Tanner (1966) supplies a helpful review of the evidence, along with a strong argument for taking scenes bearing on Polynices as later interpolations by Sophocles.

theatre, but it was also a prime opportunity for politics: civic functions and ceremonies took place at the festival alongside cult practice and theatrical performances. The performances were competitive; victory was declared for the author of the three-play set that was judged the best. There is much debate among scholars as to the composition of the audience and, in particular, as to whether women attended the theatre during this period. It seems that the bulk of the audience consisted of adult male Athenian citizens. The judges for the dramatic competition certainly would have been men.

The audience sat around three sides of a large, flat playing space called the orchestra, which was traditionally the performing area for the chorus, though there is reason to believe that the actors playing the named roles also may have used this space at certain points in the play, such as when Jocasta (in *Oedipus Tyrannus*) makes an offering at the altar that stood at the center of the orchestra (line 911 ff.). On the upstage edge of the orchestra was a low, raised wooden stage about three feet high and probably only a few feet deep, with a small set of steps. This low playing area allowed the principal actors to dominate the performing space and to be clearly seen and heard from all parts of the *theatron*.

The stage itself stood in front of a low, wooden scene building, the *skene*, probably no more than ten feet in height, with an upper level (which does not seem to have been used in any of Sophocles' Theban plays) and a large central doorway dominating the strongest visual position of this performing space, upstage center. The actors entered the stage either through this doorway, from behind the *skene* directly onto the stage or from one of the two side entrances (known as *eisodoi*) that ran into the orchestra from left and right. An actor entering from an *eisodos* would be seen by a large proportion of the audience as he traveled up the slight slope prior to emerging into full sight. Sophocles makes repeated dramatic use of these long entrances when the prolonged physical entrance of the actor is used to generate dramatic excitement.

Only three actors were employed in a performance for speaking parts; in addition to these, an unregulated number of mute actors wearing masks took the parts of attendants, guards, or (rarely) major characters in scenes in which they do not speak. All the performers were male. The three-actor rule led to some interesting effects of doubling. In *Antigone*, for example, the actor playing Antigone might also have played Haemon and Tiresias, so that Creon's antagonists all would have had one voice, though this actor would have worn a different mask for each role. In *Oedipus Tyrannus*, the role of Oedipus was probably a solo performance, while Creon, Tiresias, and the Corinthian may have been played by a second actor, and the roles of the Elder, Jocasta, the Herdsman, and the Messenger fell to the third actor. *Oedipus at Colonus* seems to require a fourth speaking actor in the last scene, but perhaps a silent actor took Ismene's part at the end, while the third actor switched masks from Ismene to Theseus.

The cast of each play included a chorus of twelve young men (possibly fifteen in later plays) recruited and trained specifically for the production. The chorus leader was assigned the bulk of the dialogue, but the whole chorus sang and danced the choral passages and remained onstage throughout the play usually as a dramatic reactive force to the events unfolding. In *Oedipus at Colonus*, however, the chorus takes a more active role, making real threats and promises and affecting the action.

What marks the plays as poetry is not rhyme (ancient poetry almost never used end rhyme) but figurative language, wordplay, assonance, alliteration, and, above all, meter. The meter is a matter of syllable length, so that each line is like a string of quarter notes and eighth notes arranged in a special sequence. The dialogue and speeches are written to be spoken, in iambic meter (short-long). The choral odes (the parodos, or entry-song, and the stasima that divide the scenes) are written to be sung, in a variety of complex meters, to the musical accompaniment of a drum and a reed instrument called the *aulos* (usually translated as "flute"). These odes are composed of pairs of metrically identical stanzas called strophes and antistrophes. In addition, several passages for chorus, or chorus leader, are neither strophic nor iambic; for example, *Antigone* lines 155–62 are written to be chanted by the chorus in a rhythm of anapests (short-short-long). There are also a few strophic passages for a single voice, such as the solos for Antigone (806–82) and those for Creon (1261 to the end). (Commentaries on the Greek texts usually lay out the metrical forms of all the non-iambic passages.)

The characters wore a distinctive theatrical costume of a long-sleeved long robe and a tragic mask. No fifth-century masks survive today, since they were probably constructed of lightweight perishable materials, such as linen, cork, or wood. But representations of tragic masks do exist on vase paintings of the period, and with some caution we can assume that the masks were whole-faced with a soft skullcap (*sakkos*) and realistic hair. The masks were slightly larger than life, though not grotesque, and there is certainly no evidence for any kind of megaphone mouth or other speaking device. The superb acoustics of the fourth-century theatre of Epidaurus in the Peloponnesus proves that classical-theatre architects were able to use the natural acoustic qualities of the hollowed-out hillside.

The mask is a vital element of Greek drama, and it seems that the actors never performed bare-faced. Performing in a mask does dictate a certain style of acting: the performer must face the front or make no more than a three-quarters turn, and must stand back on the raised stage while speaking. Otherwise, the voice will be lost to a majority of the audience, and the mask will not be visually engaging and therefore will seem offstage. Gestures would have been more pronounced and precise than in modern acting without masks, and since the performers have no peripheral vision, their movements and relationships to each other onstage would have been highly stylized. This result does not imply that the Greek tragic mask could not convey a whole range of emotions. On the contrary, a mask manipulated correctly becomes a blank canvas to be painted by each audience member's individual imagination, and here the shared experience of drama between performer and audience member is at its most powerful.

Set and props were minimal but nevertheless vitally important in Greek tragedy. The *skene* probably was not decorated specifically for any given production, but the doorway was often invested with an important dominant stage presence. In *Oedipus Tyrannus* the doorway denotes the entrance to the palace of the house of Cadmus and is used to superb dramatic effect throughout the entire play. In *Oedipus at Colonus* it may have remained stubbornly closed until the very end when the doors finally open to represent the entrance to the secret sacred place where Oedipus meets his mysterious death. Sophocles would also have utilized the spatial relationship of orchestra and stage, skillfully blocking his actors to take maximum advantage of the opportunities that this physical relationship offered. It is not hard to imagine Oedipus sited magnificently on the raised stage at the start of *Oedipus Tyrannus* and then at the end of the play stumbling into the orchestra, the chorus backing away from him while Creon takes the dominant position on the stage in front of the doors upstage center. In *Oedipus at Colonus*, the sacred space where the hero first takes his seat would have been clearly marked off by the awe-stricken reluctance of other characters to cross into that space.

Stage properties also formed an important part of Sophocles' dramatic arsenal. In his *Philoctetes* the bow of Heracles is important as the focus of the play, and in *Ajax* the sword of Hector plays a deadly role. In both Oedipus plays, the primary prop is less discernible from the text and yet vital to the play: Oedipus' walking stick (clearly shown in all images of Oedipus that have come down to us from ancient artists). As the first play unfolds, we hear how he uses this stick because of a childhood affliction induced by his parents and how this physical manifestation of his lameness was the actual instrument that he used to kill Laius. At the play's end, we see this potent symbol as the cane of a blind man, a poignant reminder that ancient Greek tragedy was as much a visual as an aural experience and that Sophocles was a master at blending the two. In the second play, the stick is a constant reminder both of Oedipus' blindness and of his potential for violence.

Antigone

I have been in love with Antigone since I first encountered the play that bears her name. The ideas to which she gives voice are interesting and important, but this young woman is captivating—the character that Sophocles created for this play, Antigone, daughter of Oedipus, Antigone who gives up everything to put right something she believes is wrong. I confess my passion at the outset because it explains why I may not succeed in writing objectively about the play. In what follows, however, I will attempt to show why some scholars think that her original audience must have condemned her as a bad woman, and I will do my best to bring out the good qualities in her antagonist, Creon. But in the end, like Creon's son who plans to marry her, I want to spit in the old man's face. Creon was sensible, fair-minded, and public-spirited, as are many patriarchal figures. But he does not know how to listen to anyone he considers inferior. Teachers who are advisers to young adults know from sad experience that a parent like Creon can drive sons and daughters to acts of violence against themselves. The kindness that does not listen can be lethal.

To my surprise, however, students often prefer Creon to Antigone, and I have to admit that they have a point. Antigone is no better at listening than her uncle, but he has an excuse she does not have. Creon is facing the greatest danger that could befall a city in ancient Greece—civil war. Nothing does more harm in any society than civil conflict, which affects every part of life, destroying not just governments but also families and the moral character of individuals. This particular civil war is especially disturbing because it exposes Creon's city to destruction by external enemies. No wonder Creon concludes that his city is like a ship in stormy weather: if no one puts a strong hand to the steering oar, the ship will capsize or sink. Creon is right about many things. And, by the end of the play, he does reveal some capacity for listening.

The original audience probably did not sympathize strongly with either Antigone or Creon. The play is open-ended enough that people probably responded in various ways. What we know of the history of ideas suggests not only that typical Athenians would have found things to like in both characters but also that both would have troubled Athenian viewers too much for them to take sides. Although this audience probably wavered, as do the chorus during the play, they ultimately would have known that the gods were against Creon, but the audience had no reason to infer that the gods therefore supported Antigone. We moderns tend to rush to judgment because we don't know what the ancients understood around 442–1 B.C.E. when the play was probably first produced. But Sophocles' audience had heard the background of his story already, and they knew the danger of civil war. So let's begin by reviewing the state of affairs in Thebes before the sun rises on the opening scene of the play when the citizens of Thebes will rejoice, and the battlefield, littered with bodies of dead warriors from both sides, will not have begun to smell.

What Happened before Sunrise

Yesterday, to the horror of the people, a traitor brought an outside enemy down upon the whole city of Thebes. The threat of destruction by fire and sword was very real. Had battle gone against the people of Thebes, the victors might have led women and children into slavery from their burning homes, passing the corpses of their massacred husbands, fathers, sons, and brothers.

But Thebes has been saved. Its citizens now breathe freely, though they have not forgotten the terror.

Who brought this terror against Thebes? It was Polynices, one of two sons of Oedipus, the king who had married his own mother after killing his father, not knowing that they were his parents. When Oedipus was disgraced, Polynices and his brother, Eteoclês, were too young to rule, so their uncle Creon served as regent. After they had reached mature years, the brothers were willing to let Creon rule at first, in order to shield the city from the curse that followed their family. But then they fell to quarreling over which of them would hold a tyrant's power in Thebes. As the elder, Polynices laid claim, but he was violently ousted by his younger brother, Eteoclês. In exile, Polynices sought refuge in the powerful city of Argos, where he enjoyed the support of the king and married the king's daughter.[7] After mustering a mighty army, in a fury against Eteoclês and thirsty for the blood of his own people, Polynices led an army from Argos against his homeland. Thebes was victorious, but the cost was high for the royal family. Before the battle, Creon's elder son, Megareus, was sacrificed to ensure success for Thebes. And in the battle, Antigone's two brothers died, each one with the sin of fratricide on his head. They had killed each other.

As the play opens, power has been returned to the young men's uncle, the former regent Creon, a man so suited to the throne that his very name means "ruler." Now that he has taken charge, Thebes should be safe. Besides, a wedding is in the air, though we will not hear of it until well into the play. Creon's only surviving son, Haemon, is engaged to marry Antigone, one of Oedipus' two daughters. Antigone and her sister, Ismene, are now the only surviving children of Oedipus' family. This marriage will tie up loose ends by keeping two of the three surviving young royals in the ruling family. All should be serene.

The Athenian audience, however, would have expected trouble in Thebes. They were steeped in epic tales of this city's tormented myth-history. Antigone represents the last generation of a family that, according to myth, carries a fatal curse. Thebes will not rest easy while any member of this family remains alive

---

7. This version of the story comes from *Oedipus at Colonus*, 365–81 and 1291–1307. Sophocles seems to have been the first to make Polynices elder.

within its boundaries. The tale of Antigone's private action against Creon was not well known, but every Athenian knew a different story about unburied dead. In this version, Creon leaves the whole Argive army unburied; then Theseus brings an army from Athens to defeat Thebes and bury the Argive dead. Athenians took great pride in the victory of Theseus, so they would have found this play surprising: no Theseus, no glorious role for the army of Athens. (On the old version, see Griffith 1999, pp. 4–12, and Else 1976.) Besides, Thebes represents many things that Athens is not (see Zeitlin 1990). Athens is a democracy; Thebes favors authoritarian forms of government—monarchy in myth, oligarchy more recently. Athens stood against the imperious Persian invaders fifty years before this play was produced; Thebes shamefully supported the Persian invasion. Athens welcomed Dionysus and his worship at the first opportunity, but (according to myth) Thebes initially rejected him. And Dionysus is held to be the god of joy who presides over the festival of plays in which Antigone is staged.

Conflict

In the opening scene, we learn that Creon has decided to reward the brother who defended Thebes but to impose a penalty on the other brother. Whereas Eteoclês will receive a noble funeral, Polynices will have the punishment that is common for traitors—no burial at all, on pain of death for anyone who attempts to inter the body. Creon had every reason to suppose that he was on safe ground in making this decree. He was making a fair distinction between the two brothers, one that is more or less in keeping with accepted practice.

To be denied the full ritual of burial is shameful, a grievous penalty for a traitor and his family. Normally, however, the body of a slain traitor would not be left as carrion for wild dogs and vultures. Sometimes relatives were allowed to give it a burial outside the city, or sometimes the body was thrown into a pit or into the sea. Either of these methods, while leaving the sting of shame as a penalty, would save the land from the pollution of rotting flesh. Although well known in Athens and elsewhere, the non-burial of traitors raised a number of problems. The unburied dead would be shamed and unable to rest in their assigned places. Their family would carry shame as well, for having left one of the most important family obligations unfulfilled. The land on which the corpse was left would also be affected not just by the unpleasantness of rotting flesh but, of more importance, by what the Greeks called miasma—the pollution, a kind of implied curse that spreads over a land that has not treated its dead with propriety. Besides, the gods of the Underworld, principally Hades, are entitled to have the dead in their domain. To keep the dead above ground and to send the living below ground—both of these are affronts to the gods below.

That is why Antigone has decided to shoulder the responsibility of burying her brother Polynices. In this she goes beyond what is normally expected of women. But there is no man left in the family, aside from Creon, whom Antigone now sees as an enemy. In such a case, a woman could be expected to take on a masculine role. And so the drama unfolds, as a determined young woman falls foul of an unmovable king. This troubled city, Thebes, is not yet free of conflict; violent death is not yet finished with this doomed family. In fact, the king will lose his son, his wife, his niece, and his throne, all in one terrible day.

Antigone stirs the modern imagination like no other play that has come down to us from the ancient world (Steiner 1984). Even today, discussions of the play rapidly become arguments between women and men, between young people and older ones, between religious folk and defenders of secular reason. All of these conflicts and more come to a head in the collision of young, powerless, passionate Antigone against her uncle, the mature, powerful, initially coldhearted Creon.

Religion, ethics, and even politics are at stake. Antigone sides with divine law against the king's decree. Her gods—such as Hades—are beneath the earth. Creon, on the other hand, speaks for order and respect at the human level. But he is not godless. His god is in the sky—thunder-wielding Zeus—and Creon has only contempt for those who worship the lord of the Underworld, Hades.

Ethically, uncle and niece promote different virtues. Creon tries to enforce a rational sort of justice that takes no notice of family ties and that seeks to preserve the health of the city-state (polis) above all. So Polynices, born as Creon's nephew, becomes his uncle's enemy, through subsequent actions that trump original ties of kinship—according to Creon. Antigone, by contrast, is committed totally to reverence, and nothing matters more to her than the particular obligation that she has with a person naturally, by birth. These ties mean far more to her than justice between her brothers; more than the city-state; more, even, than family ties such as marriage, which are chosen under human law and not given to her at birth.

Politics do not interest Antigone, but her resistance to Creon must have been welcome in democratic Athens. Creon is king, sole ruler of Thebes, and he has the character of a tyrant. Antigone stands for values she shares with many of the common people: family, ceremony, and, especially, the duty of a family to bury its dead.

The politics of burial at the time *Antigone* was written were turbulent with crosscurrents. The democratic leadership of Athens was trying to reduce the role of women in public mourning and to curb the excesses of the rich in funeral displays; this attempt was part of a broader strategy that tried to put loyalty to the city ahead of the family and the extended family ties that were represented in burial rituals. On the other hand, funeral ceremony was of the utmost importance to ordinary Athenians, who took great pride in their claim to have forced Thebes to bury the Argive dead.

We cannot know how active such political concerns were in the minds of Sophocles' audience. In any case, those concerns belonged to Athens, not Thebes, and at the time of performance rather than in the mythic past. But the Theban myth-story is political enough, at least as Sophocles shapes it: Antigone's refusal to obey Creon, though not part of a democratic uprising, will bring on the final catastrophe for the royal family, proving to the survivors that leadership must be tempered by advice from those who are led.

Interpretation

Truly, there is a conflict in this play to suit every interest, and *Antigone* has fascinated intellectuals as a drama of ideas. Philosophers love this play and sometimes treat it as if it were a treatise on philosophical ethics in disguise. While historians are fascinated by the light it sheds on the history of ideas, anthropologists are intrigued by its treatment of gender and family issues. Literary critics remind us that *Antigone* is poetry of spectacular beauty, as well as a drama constructed with extraordinary care. There is room for all of these approaches and more in reading this play, but keep in mind that none of them has led to general agreement. The play is still open. The scholars have left each reader and each member of the audience a wide scope for interpretation. This Introduction will give you the basic tools you need to arrive at your own view; if you want to know more, consult the Suggestions for Further Reading section (page lxxii) or the Selected Bibliography (page 217).

The early 19th-century German philosopher G. W. F. Hegel prized the play as "that supreme and absolute example of tragedy." He held that Antigone and Creon both serve moral powers that are valid in themselves—family love and the law of the state, respectively. But both characters, Hegel thinks, fail to recognize that these powers are two parts of the whole "moral substance" (Paolucci 1962, p. 325). So Creon and Antigone go wrong in being one-sided, and they may go wrong in particular actions they take as well. When Hegel writes of a synthesis of opposing powers, he does not mean to imply a relaxation of tension. The conflict that Antigone faces will destroy her and the ethical world of which she is a part, because both sides belong to what is right. True, Antigone's conflict will be superseded by a modern one, but the conflict between family and state lives on in ethical consciousness, never to be resolved in itself, and it continues to move the Spirit. So a Hegelian synthesis is not one of perfect harmony (see the Appendix, page 214).

Nussbaum argues against too harmonious a synthesis; in her view, the conflict between Creon and Antigone cannot be resolved, and this difficulty is not a bad thing:

> We are asked to see that a conflict-free life would be lacking in value and beauty next to a life in which it is possible for conflict to arise; that part of the value of each claim derives from a special separateness and distinctness that would be eclipsed by harmonization. That, as Heraclitus put it, justice really is strife: that is, that the tensions that permit this sort of strife to arise are also, at the same time, partly constitutive of the values themselves. (1986, p. 81)

Another family of interpretations depends on the history of ideas. Scholars in this group think that an Athenian audience would have solved the conflict with ease. From what we know of common Athenian moral values in the period, some argue that the audience would have felt from the first scene that Antigone was a bad woman; others contend that the audience would have taken her side even before the play began (see later, page xxv). Some historical scholars take more balanced views. Perhaps, for example, the audience would have rejected both antagonists— Creon as an autocrat and Antigone as an incestuous product of an accursed and incestuous royal family. Both may be seen to be responsible for the catastrophe (Griffith 1999, p. 29). So the historical approach has not led to any greater consensus than has the philosophical.

Readers with more literary interests focus on imagery and characterization. The imagery of the play is dazzling and confusing, especially in the choral odes; still, it forms a pattern that is useful in understanding the play (Goheen 1951). Characterization is a very thorny issue. Virtually every scene shows us a character doing something that runs against our initial expectations; this tendency is so strong that some critics have thought that Sophocles paid no attention to consistency of character. For example, Haemon establishes himself at the start as a dutiful and respectful son:

> I am yours, Father. You set me straight,
> Give me good advice, and I will follow it.
> No marriage will weigh more with me,
> Than your good opinion. (635–8)

But before his exit, he is arguing furiously with his father:

> Talk, talk, talk! Why don't you ever want to listen? (757)

Was he lying when he said he respected his father? Has he changed during the scene? Was he forced by his father's suspicions to take on new attitudes? Or is he an inconsistent character? On this point, too, there is no firm consensus. My view (influenced by Reinhardt 1947/79) is that the characters are forced to change under the pressure of events, with the result that the play is highly dynamic. The characters are moving targets, morally speaking; therefore, in the final analysis, we cannot simply take sides on moral grounds. We love Haemon or we hate him; but, from this viewpoint, we can't justify our preference any more than could an Athenian audience. The ancients believed, along with the chorus, that a person's judgment can be shaken by the madness Zeus sends, and that to be so shaken is more sad than blameworthy:

> . . . once a house is shaken by the gods,
> Then madness stalks the family without fail,
> Disaster for many generations.
> It is like a great salt wave
> Kicked up by foul winds from Thrace, . . . (583–7)

If Zeus shakes these characters off course, however, he does so indirectly. Onstage, we see that they are changed by each other and by the terrible pressures under which they must decide what to do. And as one person changes, another must change in response. Creon grows more and more suspicious once he hears of the illicit burial, under the fear of resurgent civil war, and Haemon must react to those rising suspicions with increased independence. When Creon calls his son "a woman's toy, a slave"— and does so in public (756)—he is delivering a deadly insult. No wonder calm, rational Haemon flies into a rage.

Call this the "moving target" theory: whatever else it conveys, the play warns against moral complacency. In *Antigone*, people are tested beyond their limits with catastrophic results. For such a catastrophe, who is to blame? According to the chorus, Zeus is in control:

> O Zeus! Who could ever curtail thy power? (604)

So ask the chorus, knowing that no one, not even a lesser god, can stand against Zeus. Onstage, however, it is not Zeus but Creon who drives his son crazy. No surprise in that; fathers often drive their sons crazy. The scene makes sense for any audience, whether or not they agree with the chorus that Zeus is pulling strings from behind the scenes. Either way, the outcome is intensely sad.

Setting aside quarrels about interpretation, all parties agree that Sophocles is a master dramatist. *Antigone* is a brilliant stage piece built around human conflicts that carry three people to their deaths and threaten two others. It is a play of characters, all of whom matter as people to their audience. Sophocles draws characters so powerfully that we care about them from their first entrances, are touched by them, and come to like them—yes, even Creon.

Besides, the language of the play is ravishing, never dropping to the bare painstaking diction of a debate about ideas. The chorus of elders burst upon us from the start with a breathtaking ode to victory. The poetry that Sophocles has given the chorus to sing throughout the play is beautiful beyond a translator's art; yet its images are so concrete and so striking that no translator who carried them honestly across the divide from Greek to a modern language could fail to convey their imaginative power.

Poets were free to give new shape to old myths. Sophocles chose to retell the old story of the unburied dead (page xix earlier) in personal terms. It's not the whole army of Argos that is unburied; it is only Polynices (but see lines 1080–3). And the burial is achieved not by the whole army of Athens under Theseus, as in the old myth, but by one young woman, Antigone, who is engaged to marry the son of the king. As far as we know, Sophocles invented this variant on the myth for just this play; the resulting collisions of niece and uncle, son and father, are far more intense theatrically than the clash of armies, which could not be shown onstage. By this change, Sophocles has enabled his characters to touch our sympathies beyond what is usual in ancient Greek tragedy. They move us because they are moved by each other; each one follows a great passion, but each one shifts under our eyes as one passion enters the force field of another.

Antigone cares about her brother and worships the gods below. Creon cares about his city and the principle of hierarchy that he thinks sustains it. Haemon and Ismene are passionate about Antigone. The Watchman cares about his own life. The chorus are exuberant over Thebes' victory, Tiresias is bitterly upset at the pollution that blocks his sacred tasks, and the Messenger is grieved at the fall of the family he serves. Eurydice is said to reveal her furious anger at Creon. We are caught by these many passions, and we are tempted to share them, but we are troubled by the changes that each character's passion seems to undergo.

Characters

The name *Antigone* comes from the Greek for "born" and "against," and Antigone was plainly born for trouble. She is so passionate about her cause that at the start she does not seem to care if it leads her to death in place of marriage. But Antigone's assurance gives way to grief as she approaches death. Isolated in her new understanding that the elders of Thebes do not support her, she mourns her own death.

The list of charges that critics have made against Antigone is long. She leaves her home in the dark before dawn to conspire with her sister, and such activity in the dark is forbidden to women. She takes on burial, which is men's work. In a play intended for a male audience, she does not accept male authority, and she threatens the order of the city by violating an order of the king. She prefers burial to marriage, and a brother to a husband, perhaps because she has an incestuous longing to lie in the embrace of her brother beneath the ground (line 73). Aside from her devotion to her dead brother, Antigone is harsh and unloving, cruel to Ismene, and thoughtless of Haemon. Her justifications for burying her brother are not consistent with each other: first an appeal to a general unwritten law about burial, then a claim about her particular obligation to her brother. Antigone is vulnerable on both points. The unwritten law against non-burial exists in her imagination; the concept of unwritten law was unheard of before Antigone, and in any case it is legal to leave traitors unburied. Some critics have attacked her argument from a particular relationship as having nothing to do with serious morality—which, most modern philosophers have agreed, must follow universal imperatives. So run the charges against Antigone.

Many scholars have agreed with Goethe, who said that the motive stated for Antigone in lines 904–20 is "quite unworthy of her, which almost borders on the comic." The great English scholar Sir Richard Jebb agreed that the lines were unworthy of Sophocles; along with many other scholars, he treats the lines as spurious.

Defenders of Antigone, however, defend these difficult lines as well (Cropp, Neuburg, Murnaghan, and others). One of the most interesting defenses (Foley 1996) shows how Antigone's reasoning fits the particular situation in which she finds herself; her moral reasoning is similar to that which Carol Gilligan defends in her book In a Different Voice. According to Gilligan, men in western cultures typically prefer reasoning from general abstract principles of the kind Creon and Haemon use, and they tend to disregard or to scorn the kind of moral reasoning that is based upon particular relationships, which she believes is common among women.

Perhaps some of the charges against Antigone are true, but it is surely wrong to blame her for being harsh and unloving. In ancient Greek culture, the man desires the woman, not the other way around. As Antigone is not yet married to Haemon, she has no obligation to him, aside from that of a cousin. (This situation alone may explain the exclamation "O Haemon, dearest," if it is hers at line 572, which uses the expression for family-feeling, not sexual love.) As for Ismene, Antigone tries to save her life by leaving a distance between them. Although her words are harsh, we know how painful they are to Antigone (551), and her intention may be to save a life. Her love for Polynices is, indeed, troubling in view of the incestuous history of her family; she is, after all, the daughter of her own half-brother. In this, as in other aspects of the play, we must remember that however much we may love Antigone, she belongs to a family that bears a curse. As for her decision to bury her brother, this is incumbent on her as a family member, since Creon has declined the responsibility. If she plays the part of a man, it is because no one else in the immediate family is left to do so.

The most striking features of Antigone are her unique approaches to law and to love. Antigone obeys a law that she says belongs to

> the gods' unfailing,
> Unwritten laws. These laws weren't made now
> Or yesterday. They live for all time,
> And no one knows when they came into the light. (456–9)

We do know, however, that no surviving text older than *Antigone* refers to such a concept of unwritten law. The concept probably comes into the light in the fifth century along with increasing awareness of potential conflicts between human law (*nomos*) and nature (*physis*). With these oft-quoted lines, Antigone inaugurates the tradition of natural law in European thought. For Hegel, the lines carry even more significance; they acknowledge "the absoluteness of the right" (see the Appendix, page 214).

For Antigone, love has mainly to do with family relationships forged at birth. Only once is a word implying erotic love associated with her, but that use occurs when Ismene tells Antigone that she loves the impossible (line 90). Elsewhere Antigone's words for love connote the reciprocal relationship that binds family and friends together. (On Antigone's love and friendship, see Blundell 1989.) Her most famous speech about love must be read with care:

I cannot side with hatred. My nature sides with love. (523)

Her point is that no one has enemies by birth; by nature, one is tied only to family. On the whole, her love appears to be hard-headed, unsentimental, and traditional. But her longing for her brother is remarkable:

I will have a noble death
And lie with him, a dear sister with a dear brother. (72–3)

The verb "lie with" has sexual connotations in Greek, just as in English, and this usage may have sent a shock through the original audience.

The name *Creon* means "ruler." Creon's devotion to rational order and evenhanded justice grows darker as his suspicions of conspiracy grow: we see him looking more and more like a tyrant as the play progresses. He is not ambitious, however, and his passion is not for himself or his own power, but for the principle of hierarchy without which he thinks the city will founder, like a ship in a storm with no captain at the helm.

The dreadful threat of civil war lies upon him; when he hears that his edict against the traitor has been violated, his suspicions begin to multiply and his judgment deteriorates. He is obsessed with two ideas, both of them wrong: that the city is like a ship at sea in a storm and that the people around him are swayed by money. The ship-of-state image is a common trope, but an autocratic one, used mainly by enemies of democracy. It is true that a ship needs the firm hand of a captain and that the captain must make decisions without calling a meeting of the crew; but the democratic people of Athens felt strongly that their city needed only elected leaders, or leaders appointed by lot, who would listen to voices from the people. Creon is a very poor listener, as his son rightly points out.

Money is a red herring. None of Creon's antagonists care about money. They care about what is right and about him and his family, and some of them care about the city. But Creon's suspicions blind him, and he misjudges one person after another—the Watchman, Ismene, Haemon, and Tiresias. His career is a living illustration of power subverting good judgment.

And yet Creon does yield, unlike Antigone, who has shown consistently the grand rigidity of her doomed father. Twice Creon listens, though he seems to have a delayed reaction both times. He hears the chorus's plea for Ismene and spares her life because he has heard Antigone's plea, much earlier, to recognize Ismene's innocence. He also heeds the chorus about Tiresias, after the seer departs. Then Creon takes the advice that he had earlier received from Tiresias too late, of course; still, he shows that he is not an unyielding tyrant. In the end, we must see that he went wrong, but we must also pity him. Although some critics are contemptuous of his lament, I found it quite moving. He has no reason to mourn at length: we have heard the long dirge that Antigone sings to herself, felt the pity expressed by the Messenger, and readied ourselves for the play to end when Creon's dead wife is wheeled through the great doors onto the stage.

Ismene will surprise us more than anyone else in the play. When we first hear from her, she seems numb, unable to call up any feelings about the future, and passive in the face of events. She is afraid to break the law, afraid of death, and unwilling to challenge male authority:

> How horrible it will be to die outside the law,
> If we violate a dictator's decree!
> No. We have to keep this fact in mind:
> We are women and we do not fight with men. (59–62)

If women are to resist men, Ismene can imagine their doing it only in secret (84). In this, she conforms to what men expected of women at the time; she also takes on an attitude that common people adopt to separate themselves from the dangerous ambitions of rulers:

> My mind
> Will never aim too high, too far. (67–8)

She conforms in other ways as well to the ancient Greek male concept of the feminine. But, in the end, she tries to share Antigone's punishment:

But these are your troubles! I'm not ashamed;
I'll be your shipmate in suffering. (540–1)

No, please! You're my sister: Don't despise me!
Let me die with you and sanctify our dead. (544–5)

Now she has forgotten her advice against resisting male authority; now she argues against Creon. Ismene is the first to mention the planned marriage between Antigone and Haemon, probably delivering the audience a surprise (568). It may also be she who breaks out with a brief, fond address to Haemon: "O Haemon, dearest" (572) in protest against Creon's attitude toward the marriage.

What has given Ismene the courage to take on Creon in this way? Perhaps it is her unswerving love for her sister, which parallels Antigone's love for Polynices. Perhaps, also, she is reacting to Creon's rush to judgment, his unreasoning conclusion that Ismene is Antigone's accomplice (531–5).

The *Watchman* is the only common man or woman to speak in this play, and he is not afraid to speak his mind—even to talk back—to Creon. In speaking his mind, he shows up the aristocratic chorus of elders, so that his voice must have delighted and amused the democratic audience of Athens. When Creon reveals how much he has been troubled by the news, the Watchman replies:

So where's it biting you? On your ears or in your mind? (317)

Surely the playwright expected a laugh on this line. And elsewhere, in his outspoken concern for his own life, the Watchman is antiheroic to the point of comedy. He is, nevertheless, a man of refinement. He knows the conventions in poetry and drama for messengers, and he is clever enough to make fun of them on his first entrance:

I can't say I am out of breath.
I have not exactly been "running on light feet." (223–4)

His account of the arrest of Antigone is poetic, however, and charged with strong images:

She gave a shrill cry like a bird when she sees her nest
Empty, and the bed deserted where her nestlings had lain. (424–5)

But we should keep in mind that messengers in ancient tragedy often speak in heightened language that takes them out of character. The Watchman is here taking on the voice of a messenger; in speeches such as this, the origins of ancient drama in narrative poetry come close to the surface.

The name *Haemon* carries an echo of the blood that is spilled behind the scenes in this play. Haemon changes under our eyes from dutiful son to rebellious youth (a pattern familiar to parents of young adults). I discussed the change earlier (page xxiii), but more needs to be said here about Haemon as we first know him. He is remarkably like his father. His main speech is the same length as Creon's, and, like Creon's, it is based on large generalizations about government and good judgment. Like his father, Haemon steers clear of addressing the moral issue of burial versus non-burial. He does, however, put his finger on exactly what is wrong with Creon—his rigidity and his inability to listen to opinions he does not share.

Athenian audiences would have been shocked by the sight of a son arguing with and making threats against his father; this may have been enough to turn them against the young man. But the speech Creon takes to be a threat (751) is actually a promise of suicide, and the arguments Haemon gives would have been admired, on the whole, by tyranny-hating Athenians. So the audience may have remained sympathetic to Haemon throughout this scene. The real horror—Haemon's taking a sword to his father—is yet to come. Even then, he has been driven mad by the lethal combination of anger at his father's insults and grief for the woman he loves.

Tiresias, the blind prophet, is never wrong and almost never believed in tragic drama. In this play, for once, he is believed, but too late. Only he, aside from Antigone, dares to address non-burial. Like Ismene and Haemon before him, he is stung to anger by Creon's suspicions and changes from a distraught diviner to a furious old man who tells a piece of the future he had planned to hold back—the death of Haemon.

The *Messenger* vividly tells what cannot be shown onstage, with all the art of a storyteller. On the whole, he speaks for the poet as narrator in this play, but he has his own views and delivers his own commentary on the disaster that has fallen upon the first family of Thebes. He is the only character who is not changed by circumstances in the play.

The presence of *Eurydice* is brief and to the point. She is the suffering audience for the Messenger, and she provides the perspective from which we can feel the full horror of her son's death. Her change will take place offstage when she rails at her husband and calls him "Childkiller."

The *Chorus* consists of twelve or fifteen men who have been summoned by Creon to serve as his Council of Elders. As a group, they sing and dance the choral odes. Their leader, however, speaks for them when the chorus enter into dialogue with the main characters. They defer to Creon at the outset (211–4), but they show more independence of judgment as the play progresses. When they do venture to give advice to the king, he usually takes it. They influence the course of the plot by these means on two occasions: by saving Ismene from execution (770) and by persuading Creon to follow the advice of Tiresias (1091–4). But they are cautious on the whole and reluctant to take sides ("Both sides spoke well," line 725). Their attitude toward Antigone is puzzling: they think her as mad as her father, impetuous, stubborn, and wrongheaded (471–2, 853–6, 875, 929–30). But they recognize that she has chosen a path that leads to glory:

> . . . when you die, you will be great,
> You will be equal in memory to the gods,
> By the glory of your life and death. (836–8)

They admire her without taking her side, and this behavior makes them appear weak and uncertain. The chorus are even more puzzling in the odes; each ode presents its own problems.

The parodos, or entry-song (lines 100–54), is a hymn of jubilation. The ode begins by praising the sun, proceeds to recognize the power of Zeus, and ends by turning to Bacchus (Dionysus), the god of wine and dance. This shifting focus, unusual in such an ode, promises us a wild ride from the chorus and a turn to Dionysus toward the end of the play.

The First Stasimon (lines 332–75) is known as the Ode to Man. It is the most famous of Sophocles' choral poems. From the first line, the ode is ambiguous: "There are many things that are *deinos*," the Greek term meaning both "wonderful" and "terrible." Ambiguities continue to pepper the lines—for example, the word translated "character" in line 357 may also mean "anger"—and the meaning of the ode in context is uncertain. The chorus are condemning someone, but whom? Creon? Antigone? the human race? or the male gender? Why does this come now, after Creon has made his decree and had it ratified by the chorus? We are left to draw our own conclusions.

The premise of the ode comes from a theory that was new at the time Sophocles wrote: that humankind found its own means of survival without help from the gods. This humanist theory was probably taught by various sophists and philosophers of the period such as Protagoras and Democritus. (For a review of such theories, see Guthrie 1971, pp. 60–84; for the imagery of the ode, see Segal 1981.) Curiously, the chorus deliver this theory with a mixture of pride and terror. It is wonderful to count up the many things human beings have invented, but it is horrible to contemplate the effects of their inventions on the sacred earth and the wild beasts that roam upon it:

> For he is Man, and he is cunning.
> He has invented ways to take control
> Of beasts that range mountain meadows:
> Taken down the shaggy-necked horses,
> The tireless mountain bulls,
> And put them under the yoke. (347–52)

The fear of Man implicit in these lines is one that a modern environmentalist could share; but it goes further, because the metaphor of putting wild beasts under the yoke bears on both political and gender relations. The yoke is a common image for marriage in ancient Greek poetry, and Creon has already used the yoke as an image for his authority as king (293). The dark turn at the end of the ode comes as a shock: man (the gender is clear on this point) may have tamed animals and women, but he has not tamed death, and disaster awaits those who are wicked.

In the Second Stasimon (lines 582–625), the chorus sing of the power of *atê*. Now that Creon has condemned Antigone and Ismene to death, the chorus sing to this power that is both madness and the destruction that follows on madness; *atê* is sent by Zeus as a punishment to the family of Labdacus (Antigone's ancestor—see the Theban Royal Family Tree, page lxxviii). While the chorus must be referring to the madness of Antigone and Ismene at one level (561–2), the Athenian audience must have felt that this was odd. They knew that Antigone was doing the right thing, exactly what Athens did in the other version of the myth, when the city sent its army to bury the Argive dead. And Athenians took great pride in this myth. So, perhaps, the madness has infected Creon, and this, at a deeper level, is the meaning of the ode. (On the ode, see Else 1976; on the pride of Athens, see Bennett and Tyrrell 1990.)

The Third Stasimon (lines 781–800) is an ode to sexual love, which may startle a modern audience unused to the ancient Greek poetic tradition of fearing love as evil. Before Plato, ancient Greece's most famous love poet, Sappho, set the tone for writers on love:

> It's love again! Limb-loosener, he makes me shake,
> The bitter-sweet, the impossible creeping thing!
>   (Fragment 130, my translation)

In Sophocles' ode, the madness is apparently Haemon's; his father has plainly accused him of having been unmanned by love of a woman (746, 756). But as always, other meanings are lurking beneath the surface. Haemon's plea was to family-feeling and justice, not love (741, 743), and the character first associated in the text with love is Antigone, who loves the impossible (90) and seems to cherish an odd kind of love for her brother.

The Fourth Stasimon (lines 944–87) is beautiful and puzzling. This evocation of myths of death and premature burial is meant to provide comfort to Antigone as she is led to her death down the long ramp leading to the plain outside the city. She hears it all; it is what she has from her people in place of a marriage hymn. Creon might hear it as well; if so, his presence could dampen expressions of sympathy from the chorus.

The Fifth Stasimon (lines 1115–54) is sung at the terrifying crisis of the play. Creon has hurried off in the desperate hope of righting the wrong he has done; but now the chorus sing an ecstatic hymn to Dionysus, recapturing the mood of the parodos with its final invocation. They pray for protection (1134), for healing (1143) and, most beautifully, for the blessing of dance (1146–54). They will be interrupted by the Messenger with ghastly news. So why this hymn of praise and supplication? Why now? Again, we are left to draw our own conclusions, but the beauty of the ode is itself a comfort to reader or audience at this harsh moment in the play. Keep in mind that Dionysus was believed to preside over the theatre in which this play was performed and that the final expulsion of Antigone's accursed and autocratic family will be a healing for Thebes.

Oedipus Tyrannus

The king of Thebes finds that he has brought plague and pollution to the land that he rules: he has killed his father, and he has been making children with his mother. No story is more familiar to modern readers, and yet Sophocles delivers it to us with dramatic power that does not fade. I remember reading *Oedipus Tyrannus* for the first time when I was twelve. The translation was called *Oedipus Rex*, and I found it in my father's study. What astonished me at the time was that I read the play through to the end, even though I knew that the main action—the murder and sex—was already over before the play began, even though I knew that the play would end badly for the hero. The stories I liked at the time were chains of events full of surprises for a reader, which led through heart-stopping difficulties to a triumph for the hero. So how could I have been fascinated by this play, when I knew from the first page that every moment brought the hero closer to a miserable discovery?

More than forty years later, I am still unsure how to explain the power of this play. When I came to do my part in this translation, I had long been accustomed to the surprising thought that representing extreme suffering can give pleasure to an audience. But I was not prepared to be as badly shaken by the play as I was. Before three-quarters of the lines are spoken, Oedipus knows the full truth, as do we all, and there is nothing left to happen but his inevitable departure from Thebes. Still, that long final quarter of the play is riveting. We do not pull back as we see the irascible tyrant becoming a voluptuary of horror, "flowering in his torment" (Reinhardt 1947/79, p. 130).

The power is in the emotions, above all. The traditional elements of plot, character, diction, argument, spectacle, and song—all are present in this play, but all are on a tight rein, so that they may serve to make a clear and direct impact on the feelings of the audience. Sir Richard Jebb, the greatest Sophocles scholar of his day, was pleased to find that the novelist George Eliot had been reading Sophocles. When he asked her how the poet had influenced her, she replied, "in the delineation of the great primitive emotions." Jebb noted this response with particular delight, because he had already written in his private diary that he found Eliot to be "the modern dramatist (in the large sense)" most like Sophocles and that Sophocles had affected her work "probably *in the outlining of the first emotions*" (Jebb's emphasis).[8]

Sophocles does not make his task easy. His main character, though admirable in many ways, is not altogether likable in the early scenes and grows more self-centered and prone to swift anger as the action unfolds. As for action, there is precious little onstage. The main events are long past, and such events as are current—Jocasta's suicide and Oedipus' self-blinding—occur offstage after the truth has come out.

The main event of the play is discovery: Oedipus finds out who he is and knows that his hard-won glory has been a mask for misery. True, long before the play began, he had solved the riddle of the Sphinx by recognizing his own human species—the animal that may go on two, three, or four legs, and is slowest on three. The three-legged human of the riddle is failing in old age, walking on two legs and a cane. So this riddle brings to mind weakness and mortality—human features that Oedipus must understand as applying to the species but does not see in his own case. Probably he had thought of himself as outside the common sort of humanity since he was a child, because he was more intelligent than most and perhaps condemned by his lameness to walk on three legs—that is, with a cane—from infancy.[9] Once he learns what he has done, however, he must learn who he is, and that the deep meaning of the riddle is as true of him as of anyone. Then he knows, and we too have a chance to know who we are. The elders of his city, who have been entertaining various false hopes, now recognize that Oedipus stands for them all. Human happiness is at best an illusion. They ask,

> Does anyone, anyone at all
> Harvest more of happiness
> Than a vacant image,
> And from that image fall away? (1189–92)

---

8. Caroline Jebb, ed., *Life and Letters of Sir Richard Claverhouse Jebb* (Cambridge: Cambridge University Press, 1907), pp. 155–6. The incident is briefly cited in Lloyd-Jones's introduction to Reinhardt (1947/79, p. xx).

9. Many vase paintings show Oedipus leaning on a spear, staff, or cane, possibly the weapon used against Laius (*LIMC* 1981, vol. 7, pp. 1–15).

Oedipus stands for them all, but he will carry a unique burden when he leaves the city. We believe, but are not told at this point, that Oedipus will take the plague with him and that the city that formerly enjoyed his rule will breathe a sigh of relief at his exit.

This is one of many reversals: from hope to bane of the city, from king to scapegoat, from father to son, from healer to source of disease, and from the great knower to the thing known. And now this powerful ruler, who retains the habit of demanding obedience from all around him, will come to see himself as an outcast, an untouchable.

The play has been understood in a number of ways: as a tragedy of destiny, as a tragedy of character, or as a tragedy of complexity. How far we go along any of these lines is measured by our understanding of Oedipus himself, his life, and his character. At the time the play begins, everyone takes him to be a foreigner in Thebes, whose success against the Sphinx and brilliant marriage have made him a popular and trusted ruler of the city. I will begin, then, with a few words about early versions of the Oedipus myth, then review the other characters, and end by returning to hard questions about Oedipus, his fate, and his character.

The Myth of Oedipus

The basic story is very old. The *Iliad* mentions the funeral of Oedipus (23.679), but the earliest surviving reference to the story is in Book 11 of the *Odyssey*. Visiting the Underworld, Odysseus sees Epicaste, wife and mother of Oedipus, who had hanged herself while Oedipus, plagued by the Furies, continued to rule in Thebes. More details would have come down in epic poems, now lost, known as the *Thebaid* and the *Oedipodeia*, and in shorter poems by Stesichorus and Pindar. Aeschylus presented the story in a sequence of three plays, produced together, in 467, of which only the last survives (*Seven against Thebes*).

One version of the story, widely known in antiquity, made Oedipus the victim of a family curse inherited from his father, Laius, who had raped a young boy and inaugurated pederasty among humans. The boy's father, Pelops (for whom the Peloponnesus is named), had made the appropriate wish that Laius would either have no son or be destroyed by the son he had. Other versions involve the oracle and fate. In all cases, apparently, the episode with Oedipus is part of a larger saga leading to

the self-destruction of the royal family of Thebes, when Oedipus'
two sons kill each other in combat.

Myth is flexible, and Sophocles had the freedom to twist it into a
web that could carry a greater weight of emotion than earlier versions. Tracks left by earlier versions of the myth show that Sophocles made two startling changes.[10] First, he separated Oedipus'
tragedy from the larger story of Thebes' royal family. In Sophocles'
more focused version, Oedipus is the bearer of his own curse—not
the family curse—and the pain he takes on is his own. This personal focus is part of what gives the play its power. Democratic
Athenians would have had no tears for the demise of a royal family as such, but they could weep for Oedipus, the brilliant, deeply
suffering individual. Second, Sophocles cast Oedipus as the chief
investigator and witness in his own case. Homer says that the gods
brought the truth to light; Aeschylus probably delegates the task to
a messenger; but Sophocles puts the entire burden on Oedipus. He
alone squeezes the truth out of the frightened people who know its
parts, and he alone describes the scene of the murder.

Oedipus establishes his eminence by solving the riddle of the
Sphinx, but the riddle itself does not loom large in the play. Other
sources give us a text of the riddle (in Greek hexameters), and
this was probably so well known that Sophocles could have
assumed knowledge on the part of his audience, as Aeschylus
apparently did much earlier:

> It is two-legged on land and four-legged, not one shape,[11]
> And three-legged too. It changes its single nature when on earth.
> It moves crawling or in the air or on the sea.
> But when it goes bustling along on three legs,[12]
> Then the speed in its limbs becomes most feeble.[13]

---

10. On Sophocles' creative use of myth, see March (1987, pp. 119–54) and
Burkert (1991, esp. p. 10).

11. Or, in some sources, "having one voice."

12. Or, in all but one source, "on the most legs."

13. The text translated is that of Hugh Lloyd-Jones, derived from seven
sources. His reading of the text is influenced by his judgment of the pur-
pose to which Aeschylus put the riddle in Agamemnon (Appendix to
"Ten Notes on Aeschylus' Agamemnon," in *Dionysiaca: Nine Studies in
Greek Poetry,* R. D. Dawe et al., eds. Cambridge: Cambridge University
Press, 1978, pp. 60–1).

The myth of Oedipus has had a remarkable afterlife in psychoanalytic and anthropological literature in the 20th century, owing to the very different influences of Freud and Lévi-Strauss, whose theories treat the myth from which Sophocles worked as common human property.[14] Most classical scholars, by contrast, have tried to confine themselves to what is Greek in the myth and to the particular way in which it is used by Sophocles, but no thinker in our century can achieve complete immunity from such a colossal influence as that of Freud, though some have tried.[15]

Oracles and Divination

From a modern perspective, we cannot easily appreciate what oracles and divination meant to Greeks of Sophocles' period. Delphi was the most sacred spot in Greece, and its oracle was respected as an authority on both religious and constitutional matters.[16] "Greek religion had no other form of revelation, no sacred books, no founder, no organized priesthood, not theology, only oracles and seers. . . ." (Burkert 1991, pp. 23–4).

Still, Greeks were accustomed to taking the oracle's words with a grain of salt, and not as modern Christians take sacred writ. Homer's gods are not above deceiving the humans they wish to destroy, and his diviners are not above suspicion.[17] Even authentic

---

14. Freud's famous passage on the Oedipus myth is in his *Interpretation of Dreams* (1961 translation, pp. 261–7), on which see Mullahy 1948. Freudian readings of the play are still alive and well; see Jonathan Lear, *Open Minded: Working out the Logic of the Soul* (Cambridge, Mass.: Harvard University Press, 1998), pp. 33–55.

Lévi-Strauss's structuralist analysis of the myth is to be found in his *Structural Anthropology* (1963, pp. 213–8); Hawkes's discussion of this is helpful to the beginner (1977, pp. 44–8). On the universality of Oedipus-type myths, see Edmunds (1985) and Johnson and Price-Williams (1996).

15. For the case against Freudian interpretation, see Vernant 1967. Charles Segal's use of Freud's insights is especially valuable (1995, Chapter 7).

16. On the oracle, see Joseph Fontenrose, *The Delphic Oracle: Its Responses and Operations with a Catalogue of Responses* (Berkeley: University of California Press, 1978), and compare the critical review by Peter Green, "Delphic Responses," in his *Classical Bearings* (London: Thames and Hudson, 1989), pp. 91–111.

17. Priam follows instructions given to him directly by the goddess Iris; he would have rejected the same message had it come from human lips

messages from the gods may be ambiguous traps for the unwary, according to later literary tradition. Fifth-century Athenians believed that servants of the oracle were susceptible to political pressures, since the oracle had not supported Athens in either the Persian Wars or the Peloponnesian War. Early medical science in Sophocles' period sought to undermine the authority of diviners on questions of health, and Thucydides observed that the plague did not respond to any of the actions recommended by priests during the infestation of Athens in 430–29 B.C.E. (2.47 ff.).

Through all these events, most Athenians felt that they would be fools to disregard an oracle or a diviner; faith of this kind led to the destruction of their army and navy outside Syracuse in 413 and survived even the outburst of questioning that followed that disaster. Sophocles appears to have adhered consistently to the traditional view that the oracles are true. All religion depends on this, according to his chorus.[18] If Apollo is not vindicated, "everything divine departs" (line 910):

> No longer will I go in reverence
> To the sacred navel of the world—
> Not to Delphi, not to Abai,
> Or the temple at Olympia,
> If the oracles do not come true
> For all humanity to see. (Chorus, 897–902)

Time and Place

The scene is Thebes, and the time is even earlier than the Trojan War. Thebes is a city close to Athens geographically but worlds apart in terms of culture. The two cities had been on opposing sides for much of the Persian Wars, and they were in conflict again at the time Sophocles wrote the play. The geography of Sophocles' play conforms to the historical city, with its two centers, one on either side of a stream, and its double orientation toward crops (in the rich fields around the city) and cattle (in the foothills of the

---

(*Iliad*, 24.221–2). Jocasta's suspicions of merely human diviners at line 709 are consistent with the piety she shows to the gods in the next scene.

18. The chorus are not a reliable source for Sophocles' opinions, but in this passage they state what Walter Burkert, the eminent historian of Greek religion, takes to be the principal message of the play (1991).

wild mountains nearby). But Sophocles' Theban people, represented by the chorus, show some characteristics that his Athenian audience would have considered their own—their horror of excess, hubris, and tyranny, especially as expressed in the second stasimon ("Be with me always, Destiny," lines 863–910).

Athenian audiences seem to have been fascinated by the horrific myths attending Thebes' royal family, from its foundation by Cadmus to its bloody end, when Oedipus' two sons kill each other in combat, fulfilling their father's curse. Thebes is foreign enough to be a safe setting for such tales. Transfer them to Athens, and they would have been politically loaded.[19]

The play may have been animated, however, by one visitor from recent Athenian experience: the plague. In 430 a plague broke out in an Athens crowded with refugees of war; casualties over the next few years probably amounted to more than a quarter of the population and included Athens' powerful leader, Pericles. A second outbreak in 427–6 sent city leaders frantically in search of divine assistance, and this was the most likely occasion for Sophocles' writing of this play.

Plot

The brilliant design of the plot is apparent in its every divergence from the story as told before Sophocles wrote this play. The staged events of the play are tightly organized to exclude everything improbable—that is, leaving out everything that has been done or planned by the gods. Onstage we see only Oedipus at work on the riddle of his own identity, using the human tools available to him, and making the human choices that express his character. When we look beyond the world of the stage, we see improbabilities enough, but we will not look that way during the intense experience of a performance of the play. We do not wonder why Oedipus has never before asked about the death of his noble predecessor, or why one and the same herdsman carried the baby into the mountains and survived the killings at the crossroads.[20]

19. See Froma I. Zeitlin, "Staging Dionysus between Thebes and Athens," in Thomas H. Carpenter and Christopher A. Faraone (1993), pp. 147–82.

20. Aristotle first noticed that such improbabilities lie outside the staged action of this play (*Poetics* 54b8), and most scholars agree with him. But

Characters

The *Elder* speaks for the people of Thebes as they pray for help
from Oedipus. He addresses Oedipus almost as a god, though he
reverently marks the boundary between human and divine. The
Elder's supplication is a deeply felt ceremonial act, and it therefore conveys more information than Oedipus actually needs to
know, just as a prayer may be full of information for gods who
are all-knowing. Oedipus can see the effects of the plague for
himself, but the Elder treats him in this way like a god. At the
same time, his prayer to Oedipus gives us, the audience, an
understanding of the gravity of the situation in Thebes.

Creon is shallow but clever in his use of platitudes. He knows
how to turn a sophistic argument in his own defense, but he has
done nothing that requires defending. A cautious man, slow to
make decisions without authority from diviners, he has posed no
threat to the king, though as the queen's brother he is an obvious
candidate for the throne. The speech he makes in his own defense
is as unconvincing as any artifice of sophistic lawyers, and yet it
tells the truth: he is not ambitious for a tyrant's power. A tyrant is
a self-made ruler who must live in fear that others will follow his
example, a future tyrant climbing to power over the corpse of his
predecessor. But Creon prefers to sleep well at night. There is
nothing tragic about him as a character in this play: "in opposi-
tion to Oedipus there stands no more than the merely non-tragic"
(Reinhardt 1947/79, p. 133).

Jocasta is a more effective speaker than her brother. She
deploys her arguments clearly and without artifice to protect the
men to whom she is related as sister, wife, and mother. She is, we
must think, at the height of her powers, in her forties or early fif-
ties, and she will use those powers in any way she can to defend
her family. At one moment she scorns oracles from Apollo, at
another she decks herself with wreaths and entreats the same god
for help, for light out of darkness. Apollo hears her prayer, but as
it often is in human dealings with the gods of the Greeks, the
result is mixed: the light will come, but to Jocasta it brings the
darkness of death.

R. D. Dawe's analysis shows a substantial number of other difficulties in
the plot (1982, pp. 1–22), which are due to the concentration of events
that gives the play its emotional power.

The seer, *Tiresias*, is the ancient blind prophet who figures widely in myth and poetry from Homer through the tragedians, and who makes occasional appearances in modern poetry as well. In this play, though he sees with the eyes of the god Apollo, Tiresias is very much a human being. He is easily stung by anger into forgetting his resolve to keep silence. As a piece of theatre, his anger is a brilliant stroke; it prepares the audience to believe in the sincerity of the old prophet. They see that Tiresias does not speak in a spirit of clever competition as the chorus alleges[21] but also that he lets the story escape in the heat of anger. His words at this point are typical of prophets, vague and portentous; no wonder Oedipus does not grasp the full horror of what they convey. But a prophet's client usually knows his source; perhaps it is an oracle, a dream, or a reading of the flights of birds. Tiresias does not say how he knows what he knows, and Oedipus' response is the more pardonable for that.

The two old servants, the *Corinthian* and the *Herdsman*, are in sharp contrast to one another. They are aptly designed to figure in one of Sophocles' masterly three-way dialogues; both are very old, and therefore they are somewhat comical in the eyes of Sophocles' audience; yet both rise above comic expectations. Neither of them is exactly what he seems to be, and they repeat in miniature the play's theme of reality hiding within appearances.

The grasping Corinthian has come to Thebes in hope of profit; he expects to be rewarded for the news he brings, that Polybus is dead and the throne of Corinth is now open to Oedipus. But the Corinthian is not a mere opportunist; offstage, he has cared for a rejected baby and found for it a wealthy home, delivering the baby as a gift and not for profit. Now, onstage, he does what he can to quiet the fears of the ruler into whom the child has grown: "I came to do you good, after all," he says (line 1003).

The rustic Herdsman turns out to have adopted his rusticity as a defense, both against the pollution of the city where he was born and against the risk that his terrible knowledge will come to light. He is witness to two crimes, the murder of Laius and the attempted murder of the infant Oedipus, but he has kept silent in his distant refuge. Like Tiresias, he must be forced to speak, but unlike Tiresias he is a slave and subject to torture. Oedipus' threats to the Herdsman are not markedly cruel in their ancient

---

21. "... clever men compete; they put each other down" (line 503).

context (testimony of slaves was acceptable in court only if taken under torture); but even Sophocles' audience must have felt some horror at the brutality with which Oedipus' hunger for truth afflicts this loyal and venerable old man.

The two old servants must be better than they first appear in order to serve as truth bearers in the play. These men are pieces of a puzzle that fit together to show Oedipus who he really is. That, at least, is how most readers have interpreted their scene. A few scholars argue that Sophocles invites us to deny both the veracity of the old men and the wisdom of Oedipus in believing them.[22] But Sophocles has forestalled this misreading of the play by giving us reason to believe in the virtue of these witnesses, and if any suspicion remained in the minds of an Athenian audience, the smell of torture in the air would have removed it.

The two messenger speeches recall the origin of theatre in narrative poetry. Both are spellbinding. The first speech makes Oedipus a messenger and describes what will turn out to be the killing of Laius. Casting Oedipus as messenger is a bold stroke. Fragmentary evidence suggests that Aeschylus' play on the same theme employed an eyewitness (as is customary in Greek tragedy) to tell the tale. But here the investigator himself will find that he has been the witness, that he has already told in vivid detail how the king was killed. The second messenger speech is more conventional, but equally powerful: the *Messenger* from the house is not a character in the play, and yet he is not an omniscient narrator, either (as is the tragic messenger in Euripides' *Bacchae*, for example). He is a horrified servant of the house who tells what he saw as he saw it. And what he saw is not merely horrible; it is an intensely private horror. The scene is the bedroom of Oedipus' wife-mother. The action consists of private conversations with the dead, suicide, and self-blinding. Oedipus and the Messenger are where they should not be, and so are we,

---

22. Frederick Ahl argues that each such character becomes "another Sphinx whose riddle Oedipus fails to solve." The play, on this view, is "not about his final self-discovery but about his ultimate self-deception" (*Sophocles' Oedipus: Evidence and Self-Conviction*, Ithaca: Cornell University Press, 1991, pp. 264–5). But if Oedipus is not guilty, the gods have been false through their oracles and through Tiresias as well. Neither Sophocles nor his public would have countenanced this possibility. See Segal 1995, p. 256, n. 4.

almost, through the excited words that skirt the boundaries of what we may know of sex and death and inner torment.

The *Chorus* of Theban elders are protective toward Oedipus and his family, but they are also reverent to the gods and devoted to belief in oracles. They are reluctant to believe evil about anyone: they try to make peace between Oedipus and Creon, they resist Tiresias' charge against Oedipus, and they hope for the best when they hear that their king was a foundling child. Like Jocasta, they are divided between trust in the gods and doubt about the reliability of the gods' human instruments. Generally, they echo the views or prayers of the principal characters and have little to say that might affect the action of the play or our interpretation of it. But they sing one extraordinary ode. In the second stasimon ("Be with me always, Destiny," lines 863–910), they sing of reverence and its violation, which is called hubris, and they imply that Oedipus the Tyrannus has gone too far, that he is bringing on himself the anger of the gods. But what has Oedipus done wrong? How could he have done anything to deserve the fate that was foretold of him before his birth?[23]

The chorus do not speak directly for the playwright; they are characters who are easily swayed by events around them, and they are capable of great folly, as when, in the third stasimon, they forget their place in the scheme of things and make an amateur attempt at prophecy. They are, however, reverent men who live in awe of Zeus and the cosmic moral order that he represents.[24]

Oedipus, the ruler of Thebes, has a name resonant with strange meanings. "Swollen foot" may be pun or etymology, but it clearly brings to mind the sign that Oedipus bears with him of his strange past, the evidence of his wounded feet. Also, his name combines the two most prominent features of the human species: we are intelligent, and we walk on two feet. At the end of his name, we hear *dipous*, "two-footed," a word from the riddle, while the beginning of his name sounds the root of the word for eyewitness knowledge (*oid-*), a theme that echoes throughout the play.

---

23. On the second stasimon, see discussions in Carey (1986), Knox (1957/98), and, especially, Winnington-Ingram (1980).

24. Charles Segal, "The Gods and the Chorus: Zeus in *Oedipus Tyrannus*," in Segal (1995, pp. 180–98). On the moral order, see Lloyd-Jones (1971).

His suffering will be great, so great that it drives modern readers to a question that Sophocles seems to ignore: How could anyone deserve so much pain? The pain will come from knowledge,
knowledge that a man with lower aspirations could have
avoided. Oedipus could have chosen not to leave his first home
in Corinth; his leaving was the act of a brave and an impulsive
man bent on avoiding evil (which sounds good) but also on out-
running divine control and prophecy (which is not so good).
Again, he could have chosen to close the search for truth about
himself before forcing the Herdsman to bear witness. But he does
not do so. Fairly late in the play, Oedipus tells us how he sees
himself. It seems an attractive picture:

> That is my nature, and I will never play the part
> Of someone else, nor fail to learn what I was born to be. (1084–5)

This is a hero for modern readers to admire, a restless intellect,
devoted at all costs to self-knowledge. But Sophocles and his
audience would have been afraid for him and those near him, as
a famous chorus in *Antigone* attests for human learning, calling it
wonderful and terrible with one word, *deinon* (lines 332 ff.). We
need to remind ourselves that many Greeks of this period feared
nothing more than the hubris that crosses the line dividing gods
from humans, and that one marker for this line was knowledge of
the future. Gods had it. Humans did not.

Modern readers are attracted to Oedipus also because he is a
ruler devoted to the welfare of his people, whom he sees as his
children. He takes action for their own good without consulting
them, but he is not afraid to tell them what he is doing or to allow
them to hear messages brought to him. He also appears to be a
good family man, having done everything his brother-in-law has
asked him to do. In his rule over Thebes, he has been paternalistic, but not in any obvious way flawed. He is, nevertheless, a *tyrannos,* and many Athenians would link tyranny as closely to
hubris as fire to smoke. We cannot understand Oedipus without
probing the nature of his power. How well does he exemplify the
Athenian concept of *tyrannos*?

Tyrannos

Aristotle, who knew the play well, called it simply "Sophocles'
Oedipus," and we infer that the play was not christened *Oedipus*

Tyrannus until long after Sophocles wrote it. *Oedipus Tyrannus* is, nevertheless, a good title, and most modern scholars use it in referring to the play. (We follow them in using the Latin spelling *tyrannus* in place of the Greek *tyrannos* in the title and translation.) A good reading of the play must begin by recognizing that Oedipus is represented in it as a *tyrannos* (accent on the first syllable, second syllable long). A *tyrannos* is not a legitimate king (Greek *basileus*, Latin *rex*), but a ruler who has won power by his own efforts—roughly the position of Oedipus, who has been rewarded with power for saving Thebes from the Sphinx. Sophocles' text uses *tyrannos* for Oedipus many times and implicitly links him to the concept from the beginning, when the elderly priest addresses him as the one who has control of Thebes (line 14: *kratunôn*).[25]

Laius had been a king in the true sense,[26] and Oedipus might well have inherited the title if he had grown up in Thebes as the king's son. As it is, however, there is a taint of illegitimacy about his rule, which alone would explain the use of *tyrannos* for him. Scholars have noted that *tyrannos* is an easy word to use in the iambic meter of Attic tragedy, but this easiness by itself would not justify Sophocles' frequent use of this word and others from the same semantic cluster. No one calls Oedipus *basileus* until the chorus in the fourth stasimon (1202), who now begin to feel sympathy for him in disaster.

The association of *tyrannos* with its English derivative, "tyrant," is only partly misleading. Today we tend to think of a tyrant as an evil and a totalitarian ruler. Oedipus is certainly not evil. He loves and cares for the people of his city, and they apparently love and care for him in return. He will make any sacrifice to free them from the plague. But he satisfies some of the conditions for being a *tyrannos*.

In Greek thought at the time, a tyrant (for I will now use the English word) is subject to insatiable desires, which drive him to a career of wanton injustice. This is the one mark of the tyrant in Plato's *Republic*, written sixty or more years after *Oedipus Tyrannus*.

---

25. *Kratos* and its cognates are not for legitimate rule; it is personified at the opening of Aeschylus' *Prometheus Bound* as part of the power of the tyrannical Zeus of that play.

26. But Oedipus calls Laius *tyrannos* at 800 and 1043, perhaps to ease his conscience of regicide. See Knox 1957/98, p. 55.

Oedipus does not bear this mark. He has not enriched himself at the expense of his people, and his record in Thebes appears to have been entirely creditable. He has not thought it necessary to use spearmen, as some tyrants did, to hold onto his power (Knox 1957/98, Chapter 2).

But Plato has captured only part of the classic notion of the tyrant. Several tragic plays of Sophocles' period dwell on the tyrant as a model not so much of injustice, as Plato would have it, but of irreverent and unholy behavior—behavior that indicates a failure to recognize the limits separating human beings from gods, the principal limits being mortality and ignorance. Tyranny unaware of human limits is well illustrated by Creon in Sophocles' *Antigone* and by Pentheus in Euripides' *Bacchae*. These are both legitimate rulers by inheritance, but they act like tyrants when challenged. The most detailed account of tyranny from the period is in a work of history that followed the plot line of Athenian tragic plays—Thucydides' *History of the Peloponnesian War*. Here, Thucydides consistently uses the colors of stage tyrants for both the Athenian empire and the democratic faction within Athens.[27]

Oedipus shares three traits with stage tyrants and with the Athens of Thucydides' biased history: he is prone to fear of rebellion, he is liable to subvert the law when frightened, and he is a poor listener who flies into a rage when given advice that he does not want to hear. In other ways, he is unlike conventional tyrants. Tyrants may be slaves to their appetites for money and sex and power, but what drives Oedipus is a passionate desire for knowledge. And though he fears rebellion, as Creon points out, he has not feared it so much as to take preventive action, as most tyrants would, against the nearest contender for his position—that is, against Creon.

---

27. Knox cannot be right in suggesting (1957/98, pp. 67–77) that the tyrannical side of Sophocles' Oedipus is modeled on that of Athens in relation to the empire. A stage tyrant created in the early, successful years of the war would not have been designed around the image of Athens that formed in antidemocratic minds after Athens began to fail. But Knox may be right to suggest that Sophocles had Pericles in mind; after some thirty years of virtually uncontested power, in the year of the plague, many of his contemporaries may have thought Pericles guilty of tyrannical overreaching that brought on his own downfall.

Interpretations

Great critics have put their minds to this play. Their views are often subtle and do not lend themselves to summary. In this section I will point to the main lines of interpretation, leaving to adventurous readers the pleasure of delving further.

Tragedy of Character

Aristotle attributed Oedipus' downfall to *hamartia*, by which he probably meant a mistake concerning identity (his own—*Poetics* 13). But most readers, from the Renaissance to our own century, have thought he meant that Oedipus suffered from tragic flaws of character—"his vain curiosity in consulting the oracle about his birth, his pride in refusing to yield the way on his return from the oracle, and his fury and violence in attacking four men on the road."[28]

Readers who feel the need to justify Oedipus' suffering are drawn to this moral approach. If Oedipus has done no grievous wrong and if the gods are just, then how could he suffer so terribly? Opponents of this moral approach have attacked on both points: some claim that Oedipus is morally innocent,[29] others that Sophocles does not believe in the justice of the gods.[30] In *Oedipus at Colonus*, Oedipus argues for his own moral innocence on several occasions (at lines 265, 510, and 966), but even so he recognizes that he remains polluted, untouchable (line 1131). And in extreme old age, he is still prone to the outbursts of anger such as the one that killed his father and that will lead to the deaths of his sons (line 1198, see later, page lxvii).

---

28. Dennis, *The Impartial Critic* (1693), cited in D. W. Lucas, *Aristotle: Poetics* (Oxford: Oxford University Press, 1968), p. 304.

29. The innocence and virtue of Oedipus are argued with special eloquence by Knox: "He is a great man, a man of experience and swift courageous action, who yet acts only after careful deliberation, illuminated by an analytic and demanding intelligence. His action by its consistent success generates a great self-confidence, but it is always directed to the common good" (1957/98, p. 29).

30. So argues Dodds (1966). But see the more complex position of Lloyd-Jones: in Sophocles, "the pattern formed by successive crimes and punishments is often so complicated that the working of divine justice is not easy to perceive" (1971, p. 151).

The issue of character should not, however, be completely discounted. Sophocles will not let us forget that his hero is a tyrant, and he reminds us that tyranny is closely akin to failure of character. In the second stasimon, at line 873, the chorus say either that hubris grows from tyranny (as we interpret the text) or that hubris begets a tyrant (as many scholars would have it). Either way, the association between tyranny and moral failure through excess is clear, and we have seen that Oedipus does in some ways fit the paradigm of the tyrant and is therefore prone to some forms of hubris.[31] Ancient Greeks did not distinguish as sharply as we do between failures of character and failures of knowledge. They would see the confidence of Oedipus as a flaw when he cleaves to it in the face of his own ignorance, and they would feel that his tempestuous behavior early in the play calls for some punishment. This is an old theme: the violent quarrel between Agamemnon and Achilles at the opening of the *Iliad* promises suffering for both, and it concerns whether to believe a prophet. Oedipus' violent reaction to Tiresias alone would prepare an audience to expect his downfall—and even to relish it—until Sophocles' uncanny ability to express emotion brings viewers into empathy with the fallen hero.

The play shows to democratic Athenians ambitions that are forbidden to them on moral, religious, and political grounds. But the audience would be able to savor these ambitions in Oedipus nevertheless, because the play is set remotely in Thebes, and even Thebes will expel the tyrant.

Tragedy of Destiny

Apollo knew how Oedipus' life would turn out. How could he have known about it unless Oedipus' fate was predetermined? The only alternative to predetermination is causation running backward in time, from Oedipus' life to Apollo's prediction before birth. But this notion is absurd. Apollo's knowledge therefore implies that the main events of Oedipus' life have been determined before he lives them and that Oedipus has no choices

---

31. Some critics (e.g., Carey 1986, p. 176) have argued that this chorus cannot refer to Oedipus, because the chorus cannot reasonably hold him guilty of any act of hubris. And Knox has argued that Oedipus' only flaw is not a character flaw at all, but mere lack of knowledge (1957/98, p. 29).

that bear upon those events. But the play is all about choices that Oedipus is making: the investigation that brings him down is his own, and the curse under which he falls is a curse he has uttered with his own lips. None of this, in the context of the play, had to happen, and we do not know that Apollo foresaw the events of the play.[32] Indeed, if we saw Oedipus as an automaton without choice, we would not care to see the play through, and we would feel nothing but outrage at the denouement. Only choices could fascinate and move an audience as deeply as we are moved by this play.[33] The recent consensus, then, is that *Oedipus Tyrannus* is not a tragedy of destiny, and scholars have tried to show how Oedipus could choose to do what the all-knowing gods had long since determined he would do.[34] Such paradoxes are found in other religious systems and should not detain us here, save to point out that Greek literature from Homer through tragedy seems comfortable with the idea of dual causation. A hero's life is explained equally by his choices, his strength, or his wisdom, on the one hand, and by an intervention of the gods on the other.

Affirmation of Religion

Recent work by Richard Seaford has shown the way to reading Athenian tragedies as representing the foundation of cult (1994), and Burkert (1991) has taken the play as an affirmation of religion: "The horrible breakdown of Oedipus proves the veracity of divine prescience, proves the existence of an all-comprehending intelligence that envelopes this world of ours. . . . This proof is worth the sacrifice. . . ."[35]

Tragedy of Complexity

Human life is complex in that the success we admire often comes at the price of actions we must treat as abominations. The most intriguing and powerful readings of the play are built on a string of insights expressed by Nietzsche in *The Birth of Tragedy*

---

32. Much hangs on the interpretation of lines 376–7, on which see the note on page 211.

33. Dodds (1966), p. 41 (reference to Bloom's edition).

34. John Jones, "Action and Actors," passim, from his *On Aristotle and Greek Tragedy* (1962), reprinted in Bloom (1988, pp. 23–4).

35. Burkert 1991, p. 27.

(especially Section 9), and carried further in Reinhardt's brilliant book on Sophocles and in Knox's account of the play. Roughly in this family of interpretations belong the works of Jean-Pierre Vernant and Charles Segal. A student who wishes to go beyond a shallow reading of the text should read these authors at length, and I will not attempt to summarize them here. I will, however, close with a few brief quotations.

The Nietzschean core of these views is the very Greek idea that a human being who rises above the ordinary must pay a terrible price. Nietzsche holds that Oedipus has paid for his wisdom by means of incest, which carries its own price: "Wisdom . . . is an unnatural abomination; . . . He who by means of his knowledge plunges nature into an abyss of destruction must also suffer the dissolution of nature in his own person."[36]

Vernant takes up this theme in his discussion of the multiple ambiguities in the play. Ambiguities allow Oedipus to hear parts of the solution and not understand them as referring to himself, while solving the Sphinx's riddle has allowed him to occupy an ambiguous position, straddling the line between generations. "Here is the last tragic reversal: it is his victory over the Sphinx that turns Oedipus into, not the solution that he guessed, but the very question he posed. . . ." We find that Oedipus is "a man in the shape of a riddle—and this time a riddle to which there is no solution."[37]

Reinhardt steers us away from issues such as justice and freedom in a scene-by-scene discussion of the play: "What we have to consider is illusion and truth as the opposing forces between which man is bound, in which he is entangled, and in whose shackles, as he strives towards the highest he can hope for, he is worn down and destroyed."[38]

Segal's careful understanding of the episodes rivals that of Reinhardt and clearly exceeds it on the role of the chorus. He is the intellectual heir of both Freud and Nietzsche, and he has a deeper appreciation than most critics of the religious meaning of the play: "We understand ourselves in our mortal condition only when we have grasped our relation to the interconnected powers

---

36. Friedrich Nietzsche, *The Birth of Tragedy* (1872), Section 9 (p. 69 in the Kaufmann translation).

37. Vernant 1970, in Bloom (1988, p. 124).

38. Reinhardt (1947/79, p. 134).

of earth, death, and the gods. But this is tragic knowledge because we can reach and possess it only by suffering."[39]

Oedipus at Colonus

Oedipus will die a hero's death, endowed by the gods with powers to curse and bless. This will be an unexpected ending for a man whose life disgusted his fellow citizens. Somehow, nevertheless, he is not surprised. Once long ago he saw that his situation was loathsome, and so he put out his eyes. But the anguish soon cooled. Regret and responsibility and self-knowledge—all these he has put behind him in old age. Yet he will die a hero's death. Why? For modern readers, that is the most disturbing question about the play.

An old man in tatters, blind and crippled, is led onto the stage by a girl and takes his seat on sacred ground. They do not know *where* they are, and neither do we, but we do know *who* they are. The old man is Oedipus, the man who killed his father and married his mother. He has been a tyrant and a king, and he carries himself with magnificent dignity. He has taken his seat on a commanding site, and he will remain sitting, there or nearby, for the remainder of the play. The girl is his daughter and half-sister Antigone. They are homeless because he carries with him a frightful pollution, and he is untouchable. As strangers, they will depend utterly on the goodness of the people among whom they find themselves.

The local inhabitants turn out to be from Colonus, the close suburb of Athens where Sophocles was born. They are not welcoming, but Theseus, king of Athens, knows what is due a visitor, and Oedipus promises to bring a blessing to the land if he is buried there. In return, Theseus defends him against representatives of Thebes, Oedipus' militant home country. Later, one of Oedipus' two sons implores the dying man to help him make war against the other. But Oedipus is still capable of deadly anger. After cursing his sons to the fate of killing each other, he learns from thunderbolts that his time has come.

Now he knows exactly where he must go. Rising from his seat, he leads Theseus offstage. Soon we learn from a messenger that Oedipus is dead, but only Theseus saw what happened, and he is

---

39. Segal (1995, p. 212).

pledged to secrecy. As long as the secret is kept within the family
of Theseus, Oedipus' burial in Athenian soil will be a blessing,
and no army from Thebes will be victorious in Athens. The outcast has found a home; the beggar has used heroic powers to
destroy and defend; the curse he carries has become a blessing.

I used to dislike this play, though I was reluctant to admit it.
Along with many modern readers, I was distressed by the great
length of the piece and discouraged by the bizarre events that
push the miracle of Oedipus' death away from the promise of the
opening scene. We know that Oedipus will die at Colonus and
confer a blessing on Athens. Well, let him get on with it. And let
us see his miraculous death. Why all these intrusions of people
trying to take him to Thebes where he was king long ago? For
that matter, why all the fuss about where he sits in Colonus?

An old tale has it that Sophocles' sons accused him of neglect-
ing his business affairs while writing this play, and he defended
himself against accusations of senility by reciting from his work
in progress. The judge was convinced by this recitation that
Sophocles knew what he was doing, but not all modern scholars
have agreed.[40] Sophocles was well into his eighties, probably,
when he wrote the play, and perhaps he was beginning to fail. Or
perhaps he stuck scenes in after writing the play, without
smoothing over the seams.

Peter Meineck's translation changed my mind and brought me
to admire the play as a unique Sophoclean masterpiece. *Oedipus
at Colonus* is at every moment a stage play, and its power does not
survive a lame translation. *Antigone*, by contrast, is built on such
an engaging conflict that it can be read as a work of philosophy
or as great literature, on account of qualities that can survive the
most ham-fisted attempts at translation. Meineck's version of
Oedipus at Colonus, however, brings it to life not as literature or
philosophy but as a script for powerful performances. Every
scene is packed with action. Even the entry of the chorus is dramatic, though such entries are usually static in ancient theatre.
Here, it introduces conflict between the chorus and Oedipus,
resolves it, and turns rapidly to a new source of conflict. Every

---

40. The story comes from late sources and is almost too good to be true.
In this form it is told by Cicero in his essay on old age, *De Senectute* 7.22.
For modern criticism of the unity of the play, see most recently Tanner
(1966).

scene thereafter prickles with excitement, as one conflict gives way to another, and the sequence of events not only brings Oedipus into a towering rage but also restores him to a position from which he can take on the leadership of a sacred procession.

I had trouble with the play, I think, because of three false expectations, which I imagine I shared with many modern readers. First, I expected the play to revolve around Oedipus' death, and I was bored by the long scenes that deal with other matters. Second, I thought the play should have the structure of what I considered a typical tragic play, as I learned it from Aristotle and a few well-chosen examples. I was troubled by the failure of this play to fit the mold. Third, I missed one of the main underlying themes altogether—the transgression of what is sacred. I'll address these mistakes briefly before I take up an extended discussion of the play.

First, it is a mistake to think that the play is about Oedipus' extraordinary death. If you thought that, you would be astonished by the length of the play and puzzled by the ending, which does not even give us a report of the hero's final moments on earth. The play is not about death, which would have been a boring theme, because it is an event that—in itself—is outside the control of the person who is dying. No, this play is about life; it shows us the last day of Oedipus' life, and a very active life it is as he takes control of the circumstances in which he will die. At the outset of the play, he may seem resigned to his fate, as would become a homeless old man who is blind and crippled and apparently reduced to depending entirely on the good will of strangers. But as the action moves forward, we see him gathering his strength from where he sits and employing it more and more effectively. He will not be passive. He takes his seat and refuses to move until given good reasons; and when he does move, he does so by choice. When he is in danger, he displays a magnificent eloquence; he knows how to appeal to the pride that Athenians take in their reputation for virtue. Later we will see that he has the power to deliver fatal curses and lifesaving blessings. He knows his power, and he uses it to deadly effect. In all this he knows he is fulfilling oracles, but he is still conscious of his own active power to persuade and ultimately to lead.

Second, it is sheer ignorance to expect an ancient tragedy to fit a certain pattern. There was no single mold for tragedy in the great age in which this play was written. No one should be surprised to

find that the final drama in Oedipus' life defies common expectations of tragedy, both modern and ancient. We look in vain for this
play to show us what we have learned to expect toward the end of
ancient tragic drama—a scene in which the hero recognizes where
he has gone wrong and a scene in which the hero's actions lead to
a reversal of fortune. Our Oedipus does not know himself any better at the end of the play than at the beginning. On his last day, he
has only one regret—that he *did* have regrets immediately after
learning whom he had killed and whom he had married. Now, in
place of regrets, he has excuses.

He will experience a reversal, but it will not be due to anything
he has learned or done onstage. After three claps of thunder, the
blind cripple rises, throws down his walking stick, and leads others offstage. That action is the reversal. It is a great moment, but
we do not know how such a change came about. We are told to
attribute it to the gods, but we have not seen or heard them, and
we don't see clearly why they have taken Oedipus' side.

As for modern tragedy, Oedipus is the opposite of Shakespeare's King Lear. Lear loses control of events as his life draws to
its close, and he learns both to understand himself and to accept
his weakness as a "poor forked creature." Sophocles' Oedipus
moves the other way, from a sense of weakness to a sense of
power, from resignation to refusal, from the weakness of an outcast to the strength of a hero.[41] And he does not seem to deserve
that strength—not, at least, in any ethical sense.

My third error is more pardonable. I did not understand what
sacred space had to do with the play and why Sophocles drew a
veil over what I thought should be the most interesting part of
the story—the miracle by which Oedipus dies. Now I see that this
omission is exactly what we should expect. Sophocles belongs to
a culture which truly believes that certain places and people are
untouchable and that certain things are unsayable. We, who
touch everything and say anything, have a hard time understanding such beliefs. But the idea is at the center of this drama
from the moment we learn that Oedipus has taken his seat where
no one can follow him, on ground that may not be stepped upon.
That is, at least, a visual reminder of Oedipus' life story. He is
himself untouchable, because he has been where no man should
ever be, in bed with his mother, and now he sits on a mound

---

41. Knox 1982, p. 262.

sacred to goddesses of the earth who may not be named, the terrible Furies, to whom the Athenians refer delicately and hopefully by the name "Well-wishers," Eumenides.

Shakespeare's *Winter's Tale* ends with a scene that is not a real miracle, although we experience it as miraculous. A woman has been hiding from her angry husband for many years and is now restored to him, disguised as a statue. Odd, but not miraculous. Still, when the love and faith of the repentant husband bring the statue to life, we in the audience feel our spines tingle. We feel as if we are present at a miracle.

Sophocles' *Oedipus at Colonus* ends with a miracle, but we are not permitted to see it or hear about it. We are thrilled to see the blind man lead King Theseus out of our sight and onto sacred ground. But now we have missed the main event. Did the earth open for Oedipus? Did a god fly down from Mount Olympus to lead him underground? Or somewhere else? What did the god say to him at the last moment? We will never know. Sophocles actually believes in this miracle; he treats it with the awe and reverence he reserves for what is divine. For what is divine he maintains a religious silence; and so what he writes about belongs to what is human.

Background: Place, History, and Religion

Place

At one level this play explains the origin of a tradition about a place: the idea that Oedipus' unmarked grave at Colonus carries a protective blessing for Athens, for which Colonus was a kind of threshold (line 59). Sophocles' audience did believe that the graves of heroes could have protective powers. In some cases, heroic graves were the sites for religious observances. One of the few historical figures who was given the honor of a cult at his grave was Sophocles himself.[42] As Sophocles was writing this play, he probably had in mind the perils faced by Athens in the final years of the war against Sparta and Thebes and their allies. True, Theban forces were defeated in a skirmish not far from Colonus, but the war was going badly for Athens in Sophocles' later years. Soon after he died, the city would be defeated by its

---

42. For a useful introduction to the topic of heroic graves, see Knox 1982, pp. 256–8.

enemies, and it was saved from total destruction not by the Thebans (who hated Athens) but by the Spartan need to maintain a balance of power. The restoration of democracy in Athens a few years later must have seemed a miraculous rebirth, and Sophocles' audience, in seeing this play at that time, must have felt a thrill at the prescience of their poet. If any city seemed to have divine protectors, it was Athens.

History

Colonus is important in Athenian history not only as Sophocles' birthplace. It has special associations for the upper-middle class known as knights—citizens who could afford to keep horses and join the cavalry. In 411 B.C.E. (a few years before the probable date of composition for this play) Athens was taken by a conservative coup, which set up an oligarchical government of the "Four Hundred." In order to appeal to the knights against the lower classes, the oligarchs used Colonus as the site for the assembly that set aside the Athenian constitution in their favor. Whether this event has anything to do with Sophocles' choice of themes for the play, we do not know.[43] But there is nothing in the play to imply that Sophocles sided against the democracy in 411. The chorus is made up of old men of no particular class, and if there is a political bias in the play, it is against civil war.

Colonus had an altar to Poseidon, who is honored in the play for two great gifts to Athens—horses and ships (lines 710 ff.). Horses, of course, belong to the knights, but ships are the mainstay of Athens' military and commercial success, and ships give power to the common people. When Athens began to depend on shipping, the leaders of the city had to cultivate the lower classes that furnished the ships with crews. So Sophocles may have tried in the play to remind the warring factions in the city of their common heritage from Poseidon.[44]

Religion

Like most ancient Greek plays, this one is imbued with concerns for reverence and the sacred. Reverence forbids the violation

---

43. On Sophocles' use of space in this play and on his choice of Colonus, see Edmunds (1996) and Wilson (1997, pp. 92–106).

44. On Colonus, see Edmunds (1996), pp. 91–4, and especially 92.

of sacred places or people, and it enjoins even the most powerful human beings to treat suppliants and other visitors with respect.

Sacred space must not be trodden upon, because it belongs to the gods, and people who belong in sacred space take on a special status. They too belong to the gods. Priests, for example, are as untouchable as the altars they serve. When Tiresias feels threatened by Oedipus in *Oedipus Tyrannus*, he says, in effect, that his life and death belong to his god: "It is not you who will bring down my doom; / Apollo will be sufficient, and he has it all in hand" (lines 376–7, with our endnote). Suppliants, as we will see, belong to the god at whose altar they take refuge. And the dead belong to the gods of the Underworld. Threatening or violating people who belong to the gods seems to be a characteristic transgression of Theban tyrants. Creon threatens the suppliants Oedipus and his daughters in this play, and he tries to keep the dead Polynices away from the gods to whom he belongs in *Antigone*. Oedipus threatens the prophet Tiresias in *Oedipus Tyrannus* (line 355), and Euripides' Pentheus actually carries out a threat in the *Bacchae* to destroy Tiresias' place of prophecy.

Suppliants in ancient poetry are refugees seeking asylum; they claim the protection of the gods and supplicate the local rulers for protection against their enemies (who are usually in hot pursuit). Suppliants take on a kind of sacredness, usually by touching or occupying sacred space. They belong to a god. Whether or not Oedipus in this play has the status of a suppliant is debated by scholars. Certainly, if he is a suppliant, he is a most peculiar one. In the first play, he was the rightful king without knowing it; now, if he is a suppliant, he is a suppliant without knowing it. He does not know he is on sacred ground, he does not know that he is being pursued by his enemies, and he has made no explicit supplication to the city or its king. Still, he has taken his seat on holy ground, and he has asked for asylum.[45]

Suppliants and other lone visitors depend utterly on the goodness of those to whom they come; they have no other support. But the first local person whom Oedipus and Antigone meet is not friendly. Others come who are even less friendly, and one conflict after another enlivens the stage. Luckily for the old man,

---

45. Burian (1974) is the principal defender of the suppliant interpretation; Wilson argues for an alternative view, that Oedipus' status is that of a heroic guest-friend and ally-in-arms (1997, pp. 29–61).

the land where he has taken his seat is ruled by a man of exemplary human virtue—Theseus. All sorts of visitors give good people a chance to show how good they are; that's why gods are said to dress as beggars when they test the goodness of human beings. And that's why the homecoming of Odysseus is so dramatic—it brings out the viciousness of the suitors as nothing else would, when they insult the beggar in disguise.

Oedipus establishes a special relationship with Theseus by offering him the gift of his protective grave, and Theseus responds by offering him military protection against the pursuing Thebans. The ancient poets celebrated such relationships of guest and host under the concept of *xenia*, usually translated as "guest-friendship." Once established, guest-friendship is a very close tie.

Oedipus is more sacred than a suppliant, however, and more important than a typical guest-friend. He is literally untouchable, as he remembers when he checks his impulse to touch Theseus (line 1131). Everyone knows that he has lived a life no man should live, in bed with his mother, his hands polluted with his father's blood. Such a man cannot belong among other human beings. To whom does he belong, if not to the gods? The answer to this question becomes increasingly obvious as the play progresses. Not only is he untouchable, but like a god he carries both benign and malignant powers, and it is a deadly mistake to neglect him. So Creon will learn, and likewise the sons of Oedipus. If they had a vivid enough sense of the sacred, they would realize that Oedipus is marked for special status with the gods, and they would have attended to his needs long before he left Thebes.

Plot and Characters

Oedipus at Colonus is unusual in the complexity of its scenes, most of which seem to do double duty. Most troubling to some readers is the double aspect of the final scene, in which Oedipus delivers his deadly curse right into the face of his son and then prepares for his holy death. Some critics wonder how these events can belong in the same scene, and write of later interpolations by a faltering poet.[46] I prefer to ask how these events belong to the

---

46. On the issues, see the elegant defense of the unity of the play by Reinhardt (1947/79); on inconsistencies in the play, see Tanner (1966).

same character, as that is what is most disturbing to modern audiences. In what follows I will review the actions of the main characters in their order of appearance, except for Oedipus, who must be last. All the others are there for him, as contrasts or as occasions for his actions.

Oedipus' younger daughter, *Antigone*, is mainly onstage as the traditional guide and support that her father needs, but she emerges as a character in her own right in connection with her brother Polynices. It is she who persuades Oedipus to listen to her suppliant brother. Here she is the prototype of the spitfire we remember from Sophocles' first play about this family, the one who challenges a ruler's authority, and she does not hold back from lecturing her father, reminding him of the passion in which he took out his eyes:

You know very well how rage
Only serves to breed evil.
Your own blind eyes testify to that. (1198–1200)

We, on hearing this, must also be reminded of the tyrant's rage against Tiresias and Creon in *Oedipus Tyrannus*, as well as his younger road rage that killed Laius. Antigone loves Oedipus more than anyone, and yet she recognizes his principal failing, his uncontrollable anger, and brings it up in public.

Later, after Oedipus has cursed his son, Antigone tries again to change the course of events, but this time she fails. Polynices has raised his army and cannot face the shame of giving in. "Brother, will nothing change your mind?" she asks (1431). Nothing will; Polynices is as stubborn and as prone to wrath as his father. But her love for her brother is clear, and we have a foretaste of the passion that will lead to her great sacrifice. So too when her father dies, she wishes to cross the forbidden line and see his grave. Already like her father, she is a crosser of lines, and already she is fascinated by death and burial.

The *Local* has a name in the play that may mean a stranger who is either a visitor or host. His part is small: it is to let Oedipus— and us—know where he is and that the place is sacred. Like the chorus, the Local wishes Oedipus to leave but does not dare on his own to enter on the ground where Oedipus sits.

The *Chorus* of old men from Colonus have an unusually active role, especially at the opening of this play. They engage with

Oedipus, talk him into moving from the sacred space to its boundary (with a promise of safety), explore his past, and then break their promise when they threaten to drive him off their land altogether. Later, they teach Ismene the rites necessary to purify Oedipus for having stepped where he should not. When Creon arrives in force, they propose to oppose him with force (line 835). Unlike the chorus in *Antigone*, which is at least a consultative council for the ruler, this chorus has no political power. But also, unlike the *Antigone* chorus, this group have a mind of their own. Although the old men are flexible enough to change their minds about accepting Oedipus, they know where they stand.

The great choral odes of this play (stasima) show what the men of Colonus care about. First of all, they love Colonus; no surviving ancient poem glows so brightly with the love of place as does the first stasimon (668–719). And, second, their patriotism extends to battle. Once they have accepted Oedipus as belonging with them, they are willing to fight on his behalf (835, and the second stasimon, 1044–95). Most famous of the odes is the third stasimon (1211–48). Moved by the old man's pain at hearing of his son's arrival, they sing of the misery that comes to a long life:

> The best is never
> To have been born
> Or, once alive, die young
> And return to oblivion. (1225–8)

Do they speak here for Sophocles? As a boy he danced for the victory of Athens over the Persian invasion, but at the time of writing this play he has lived to see his beloved city fall steeply from greatness and then be torn by civil conflict. Perhaps also he has lived to see his sons turn against him and haul him to court, claiming for all to hear that he was losing his mind. But this is not Sophocles' last word, and it will not be the last word of the chorus. In the fourth and final stasimon (1556–78), they pray for an easy death for Oedipus:

> Let him pass away softly,
> A stranger slipping past
> On the shallow breath
> Of deep eternal sleep. (1575–8)

And later they will speak comfort to Antigone.

They are passionate and compassionate, these old men; they understand the tears of life, and they accept them, but they are not resigned to accept injustice without a battle. Rarely does a chorus in ancient tragedy do so much to win over the audience. They are the good Athenians.

Ismene has a minor role. She completes the picture of Oedipus with his two daughters, and she brings the news to Oedipus that elicits his deadly curse against his sons. As in *Antigone*, she provides a moderate foil for her passionate sister. More important, though, is her decision to step in and act when the men of the family fail. She takes it on herself to warn Oedipus of the plan to bring him back to Thebes. Her brothers should have done this, and would have, if they had recognized the ties that bind father and sons together. Her bold action underlines their failure, as Oedipus observes (line 335).

Theseus is absolute king of Athens, but he has none of the qualities of a tyrant. He is *basileus*, a legitimate king, and the son of a king. In his character, he serves as a foil for Oedipus, who was a *tyrannos* and continues to act like one when he has the opportunity. Oedipus, as we have seen, suffers from fits of anger in which he is unable to listen to other people and unable to control his tongue, unable to hold back from fierce actions he may later regret. But Theseus is a perfect exemplar of virtue.[47] He does everything right, without fanfare, since he hates to waste words (lines 1143–4), and he has perfect control of his feelings.

Theseus' chief action is to take Oedipus and his daughters under his wing, to offer them all the protection his city affords, and to allow Oedipus to seek his death and burial on Athenian ground. This is extraordinary: the Athenians in the chorus fear the curse that Oedipus carries with him, and the Thebans would not give him burial in Thebes at all, but only on the boundary. Theseus is unworried and feels a reverent duty to help Oedipus.

Why does Theseus take such risks for Oedipus? Scholars disagree. The majority now seem to hold that Theseus takes Oedipus in as a suppliant.[48] But there is little in the text to support this hypothesis. More prominent in the language of the play is the

---

47. Blundell (1989, p. 248–53).

48. In this they follow Burian (1974). For the case against taking Oedipus as a suppliant, see Wilson (1997, Chapter 2).

relationship of guest-friendship—*xenia* in Greek. *Xenia* (which could also be translated as "hospitality") has no exact counterpart in modern European cultures, but it was always a serious matter for the ancient Greeks. Theseus cites a particularly strong form of it when he calls Oedipus *doruxenos*—spear-friend (line 632). Spear-friends come to each other's defense, and that is exactly what will happen between these two. Theseus will defend Oedipus from Creon, and Oedipus (much later) will defend Theseus' descendants from Theban invasion. The spear-friendship in this case cannot have been formed before the play began,[49] because although the two men know of each other, they have not met. More likely, Theseus is here responding to Oedipus' offer of protection, as is clear from the remainder of the speech, and he is recognizing that this offer, once accepted, makes the two men spear-friends.

Of course, Theseus is such a good man that his good deeds are over-determined; they flow from all of his good qualities. But it is very clear where they start—in his recognition of common humanity, a recognition that is an essential component of ancient Greek reverence:[50]

> You should know that once I too
> Was an exile and had to struggle to survive,
> So how could I ever allow myself to ignore
> The pleas of one so lost in desperation?
> I know that I'm just a man and that tomorrow
> May hold nothing more for me than you. (563–8)

Theseus pays attention to Oedipus out of reverence, and because he pays attention, he learns about the benefit Oedipus will bring to Athens. And then, because Theseus' reverence extends to not refusing such a gift from a stranger, he accepts it ("Reverence forbids me to throw away this gift"—635). Add to this his sense

---

49. Reinhardt explains the lines in terms of the ancient friendship between Athens and Thebes (1947/79, p. 271, n. 14) and Wilson agrees (1997, p. 85). That is possible, but the relationship must be with Oedipus, not Thebes, since Theseus sides with the old man against Thebes.

50. See Woodruff (2001, pp. 81–101). The point is well made by Blundell (1989, p. 248 ff.) and wrongly denied by Wilson, who overemphasizes the hero status of Oedipus and Theseus (1997, p. 89 and passim). At this moment, there is nothing to lead Theseus to conceive of Oedipus as a hero.

of justice, and we see why he also accepts the obligations that are entailed by accepting such a gift. His goodness hangs together; it is a seamless whole.

This could have been a play about how good Theseus is, and how fine Athens is in consequence. But *Oedipus at Colonus* is not about Theseus, who is little more than a prop in this play, because nothing happens to challenge him and because he brings nothing to the stage that might surprise us.

Creon manages to be both a stage tyrant (because he rules from fear and depends on violence) and a politician (because he is a master of deceptive rhetoric). In stealing the women of the play, he would be like a villain in 19th-century melodrama, except that he believes he is doing this for everyone's own good. He is paternalistic in the extreme.[51] Like Theseus (and unlike himself in *Antigone*), he will not be given a chance to learn or to be changed. He is what he is; and, as he is, he will be defeated. Offstage, the defeat will be military and to Theseus' credit, but onstage the defeat is an unmasking, and the credit goes to Oedipus, who reveals the truth about Creon—what one critic calls "the primeval threat to humanity: cold utility in the guise of justice and sincerity," a threat frequently encountered in modern political life.[52] The scenes Creon galvanizes onstage are full of high drama. They give the chorus an opportunity to show patriotism, and they give Oedipus a chance to show his clarity of vision. He sees right through Creon; he knows that Creon has never been his friend, and he will not be taken in by him.

Oedipus knows what the oracle has said of his future—the burial at Colonus, the gift to Athens. In his youth, before the action of the first Oedipus play, Oedipus attempted to thwart an oracle, without success. Now he is being tempted, first on behalf of his city, and soon on behalf of his family, to make such an attempt a second time. He resists both temptations, but not because of the oracle. As so often in Sophocles, the causes of human action are all before us, in the actions of the human beings themselves.[53] How could Oedipus be moved to save his city,

---

51. Blundell (1989, p. 235).

52. Reinhardt (1947/79, p. 210).

53. So Reinhardt: "Just as in the *Electra* and the *Philoctetes*, so too in the second *Oedipus* the causes of suffering are entirely human. And more and more, as the human takes the place of the divine in the causation of

when he knows that he has no city? He has never truly had a city at all; he left Corinth before becoming an adult citizen there, and he arrived at Thebes as a hero, never having been properly initiated into either place. And now the Thebans will not allow him inside their borders; they fear too greatly the pollution he carries. All they want is the protection he might offer *at* their border. It is no mystery that the old man sees through Creon.

Polynices brings Oedipus his most serious challenge, his most real temptation. The young man is both attractive and repulsive. He is a prodigal son begging to be taken back into his father's arms and, and the same time, a monstrous abuser of family ties. If Oedipus could be tempted to try once again to thwart an oracle, it would be to save a member of his family. Oedipus may not have a city, but he certainly has a family; he was married and he had children. He cares more about family love than anything else, as we learn from his last speech to his daughters:

There is one small word that can soothe—
And that is 'love.' I loved you more than
Anyone else could ever love. . . . (1616–8)

And at the end of the first Oedipus play, we see him consumed with love for all of his children. He ought to be moved by Polynices, as Antigone points out, and from this observation arises the psychological truth behind his reluctance to meet with him: it will be painful for Oedipus to face down his son.

Family has meant nothing to Polynices, however. The boy neglected his father, and he neglected his sisters when he let Antigone and then Ismene take on the roles he should have played as eldest son. Now he has neglected his ties to his younger brother by declaring a war that must end in fratricide, literally in brother-killing.

Few ancient Greeks could have rejected the call of family, but Oedipus rises above it. And in doing so, he rises above Polynices' call for what we have rendered "mercy," along with most other translators (line 1268). The word is a complicated one, *aidos*, one

suffering, so the divine becomes something which stoops down from above, at the last moment, to guide and to reconcile" (1947/79, p. 207). And Wilson: Sophocles "very nearly eliminates supernatural elements from the play" (1997, p. 153).

of many that introduce aspects of reverence. Here it implies the forgiveness that should arise from the respect that is due between family members.[54] Forgiveness is not necessarily a good thing in ancient Greek ethical thought, but it does seem attractive here. Why not try to save your son, save both sons while you are about it, and try to heal your shattered family?

Oedipus' refusal of this family temptation is the climax of the play. At first Oedipus will not hear the young man, and when he does consent to listen, he will not reply, but holds the ominous silence of a god who is about to turn away from the prayers of his worshipers. Polynices makes as good a case as he can for forgiveness, but it is not good enough to calm the rage of Oedipus.

Perhaps we should admire Oedipus for resisting Polynices. But "resist" is too weak a word for what Oedipus does. First he refuses to hear a suppliant, then by a curse he condemns his two sons to terrible deaths. This is the same rage we have seen before, in the earlier play, and this is the rage we heard about, that led to Oedipus' killing an old man at the crossroads. For some readers, the scene reveals Oedipus' human limitations.[55] Others are delighted by the spirit of the dying man, who is actually capable of what young Dylan Thomas can only pray for from his father:

> And you my father, there on the sad height,
> Curse, bless, me now with your fierce tears, I pray.
> Do not go gentle into that good night.
> Rage, rage, against the dying of the light.[56]

But from Oedipus to his sons there is only a curse and no blessing. Something is wrong with the old man. But what is wrong with him is not in the normal run of human error. This anger is demonic. Once, it led him blindly to kill his own father, and now, after many years, it is so far from cooling down that it leads to the deaths of his own sons. In this, Oedipus is like a bad storm or an earthquake or a god. He is not like the common humanity of the chorus or the kingly humanity of Theseus. The chorus members are capable of passions, but they are moderate

---

54. Blundell (1989, p. 242)

55. Reinhardt (1947/79, p. 216).

56. Dylan Thomas, "Do Not Go Gentle Into That Good Night," the final four lines of the villanelle.

men. Theseus, as a man of reason, would never fly into such rages at all and has no passions requiring moderation.

Plato must have hated this scene. Plato thought that heroes should be good, and the gods should be good, in any story presented to the public (*Republic*, Book 2). And goodness (he believed) entails rationality, or at least moderation. Plato feared that tragic plays like this one were hopelessly damaged both by the poetic tradition from which they came (which did not share Plato's moral standards) and by the conditions of mimetic performance (which tended to elicit emotional excesses from actors and audience alike). We have to ask why Sophocles thinks that the gods love Oedipus, when he is capable of such a blistering scene with his son. None of us would want such a man for a neighbor, much less a father.

Certainly, the gods love Oedipus. The *Messenger* makes this clear. He is a standard-issue tragic messenger, with a gift for narrative and no special engagement in the action of the play. On one point he is unusual: he is not allowed to see the main event on which he reports. I used to find his ignorance frustrating, but now I realize that this is Sophocles' way of making vivid the gravity of this event. It is not to be spoken about. Any attempt to put it in words would diminish its dramatic effect, and, in any case, such a revelation would violate reverence.

We know that the gods love Oedipus because they tell him where to go. At first, when he is onstage, they speak to him in the language of thunderclaps, which only he is given to understand. But later, when he is offstage, the call comes in language even the messenger can understand, but we are not allowed to hear. Always, Sophocles keeps us at one remove from the divine:

Oedipus—Oedipus,
It has been too long,
Now is our time. (1627–8)[57]

Oedipus goes to his blessed death leaving a memory of demonic rage in the minds of the audience, and this is no accident, no

---

57. Literally, the question is "Why are we waiting?" Reinhardt writes of this "we" that it "implies the joint nature of what is happening . . . with its terrifying yet tender kind of intimacy, partly involving Oedipus yet somehow at the same time mysteriously outside him. . . ." (1947/79, p. 223).

failure on the part of the poet. Jebb speaks of the "malign sublimity" of the hero's anger: "The total impression made by the play as a work of art depends essentially on the manner in which the scene of sacred peace at Colonus is brought into relief against the dark fortunes of Polynices and Eteocles."[58]

What is the source of this anger, and how does it reflect on the character of Oedipus? Oedipus in old age is no better than he ever was, and he still does not know himself for what he is. He appears to have only one regret—the anguish of self-reproach that led to his blinding himself and to his accepting, briefly, his status as an outcast from Thebes.[59] No repentance, no reform, no moral salvation. The play reminds us again and again that we are seeing the same Oedipus. The moment he walks onstage, limping and leaning on the heavy stick that killed his father, we are reminded of who he is and what he has done. And he gives us a visual echo of what he did to his mother as well, when he takes his seat on a sacred prominence that no man should touch. We see that he is still liable to unwitting transgression—to touching what should never be touched. Like his younger self, who tumbled into his mother's bed without realizing it, this old man has stumbled onto ground where no human being should set foot. It makes no difference, either time, that he comes from far away and does not know any better; he has crossed a line he should not cross and entered a place he should not be, and doing so is an outrage for which there is no excuse—only a kind of ritual purification.

Oedipus is full of excuses:[60] ignorance and self-defense in the case of his father; and, in the case of his mother, the improbable plea that the city of Thebes forced the marriage upon him. But, as we have seen in the case of stepping on sacred ground, there is no excuse for transgression. He has been polluted by what he did, and he knows it very well (1131). His string of excuses is a kind of bad faith. They allow him to avoid facing up to his failings, his savage angers, his careless feet, his jumping to conclusions, his passion for controlling any situation in which he finds himself.

You may think that he has learned one thing from his younger life: not to try to frustrate an oracle. Certainly he is aware of what

---

58. Jebb (1899/1962, Introduction, pp. xxiii–xxiv).

59. Jebb (1899/1962, p. xxii).

60. Lines 265 ff. and 510 ff. to the chorus; lines 960 ff. to Creon and Theseus.

the oracle has predicted for him, and he does take actions that lead to the predicted result. But the same could be said of the younger Oedipus—he did exactly what he needed to do in order to fulfill the oracle. And now the old Oedipus is no better informed. He does not know that he has arrived at the place that was ordained; he came there blindly. And he does not resist Creon or Polynices on account of the oracle. His reasons for resisting them are very clear: they insulted him with neglect, and now they are trying to make use of him. It is as if Oedipus stumbled backward, in his anger at the Thebans, into fulfilling the oracle.

The curse against his sons, then, is the sort of thing we should expect from Oedipus. In his defense, however, I must insist that this curse was not the cause of the conflict between the two young men (as earlier poets had it), but the other way around.[61] Part of the reason Oedipus curses them is that they fight each other instead of looking after him. As Jebb argues, the quarrel between the sons was "inspired by the evil genius of their race and their own sinful thoughts."[62] This is an innovation in the story typical of Sophocles—to overlook a magical or divine explanation emphasized by earlier poets in order to present in its place a purely human explanation, illustrated onstage. The quarrel of sons over inheritance is natural enough, and it is natural enough also that it would provoke a curse from the father.

Why, then, do the gods love this intractable old man? For that matter, ask yourself why we in the audience care so much about him. It is not that we like him, but that we find him awe-inspiring. To be so full of himself and his destiny when he is homeless and dying—how could he not fill us with a kind of shuddering admiration? He never gives in. He sees through hypocrisy and sycophancy, he stands up for his daughters, whom he loves with an outsized love, and he refuses to see himself as the sinner that others see in him. Yes, he does what human beings do not do, again and again, making the boundaries of human decency flare up in our consciousness by crossing them again and again. We see in him not what we are, but rather a gigantic image of what we secretly want to be, because he has gone where our passions would lead us if we had no boundaries. We would not do these

61. See the endnote on lines 1375–6, later, p. 212.
62. Jebb (1899/1962, p. xxv). See lines 369 and 1300, where the curse mentioned is the one that has followed the family all along.

things outside our dreams: he has loved his mother as his wife, he has gone against his father and against his sons, fighting for himself against the generations before and after his own. This is an enormous, breathtaking life of self-affirmation.

Oedipus is revealed in this last play as heroic, not in his moral character, but in his powers for good or evil. That is to say, he is becoming like the gods—not the sanitized gods of Plato's moral universe, but the dark-and-light powers that inspire reverence among the old Greeks. And this reverence is due the gods not as moral examples (they are often horrible) but as powers that are not constrained by human limitations.

Why do the gods care about Oedipus? Is it because he is so much like them? Or is it simply because, after crossing so many times into their territory, he has simply come to belong to them?

PAUL WOODRUFF

Suggestions for Further Reading

(Full citations of these works are to be found in the Selected Bibliography on page 217.)

1. Sophocles and His Art

Karl Reinhardt's book on Sophocles (1947/79) is unmatched for its sensitive reading of the plays as literary texts. Charles Segal was the finest Sophocles scholar of our time; his two books (1981) and (1995) are essential reading. For a general introduction to Sophocles scholarship, Buxton (1984) is invaluable. Blundell (1989) provides an illuminating account of one main strand in the ethical viewpoint presupposed by Sophocles.

For the study of ancient tragedy in general, consult the essays in Easterling (1997) as well as those in Vernant and Vidal-Naquet (1972 and 1981) and those in Winkler and Zeitlin (1990) and Silk (1996). Seaford (1994) has changed the way we read ancient tragedy.

Among general commentaries, the elegant classic by Jebb (1897–1900/1962) is still indispensable, and Campbell (1879) is well worth a visit. There are good recent commentaries on *Antigone* and *Oedipus Tyrannus*, but the second Oedipus play requires more attention from scholars.

Grene's admirable translation (1991) stays very close to the original, and Lloyd-Jones's Loeb edition of 1994, with Greek and English on facing pages, is helpful on many points. Fagles's translation (1982) has been an inspiration to both of us, and the accompanying introductions by Bernard Knox are superb—a good starting place for novices and scholars.

2. *Antigone*

Antigone has appealed to literary critics and philosophers alike; at the same time, the play has kept a great many classical scholars busy on historical and textual issues. No careful reader should be confined to an exclusive approach, whether literary, philosophical, or historical; indeed, all of the works discussed here take heed of the full range of what is known and thought about the play. Nevertheless, I have separated the three approaches for the purpose of this note. Full bibliographical details are to be found in the Selected Bibliography.

Among literary treatments, the best are those by Reinhardt (1947), Goheen (1951), and Segal (1981 and 1995). The first two do not bear the mark of recent critical theories, but both show depth and sensitivity that are immune to the ravages of time and the cycles of fashion. Charles Segal's work also must be read by anyone with a literary interest in the play. *Antigone* is the source of a wide stream of influence on modern literature, which is thoroughly discussed in Steiner (1984).

As for philosophy, Hegel used *Antigone* both to undergird his phenomenology and to illustrate his theory of tragedy; most modern studies of the play begin with his work, which concerns the conflict of the two main characters on ethical points (Paolucci 1962). Recently, two philosophers, Nussbaum (1986) and Blundell (1989), have studied the ethical meaning of the play in depth. Both carry the discussion beyond Hegelian theory. A valuable article by Foley (1996) brings up the gender-related issues involved in moral reasoning.

Classical scholars, especially in recent years, have studied the play in its historical context; for this they discuss ancient attitudes toward politics, law, gender, and religion. Although most of this work is published in scholarly journals, some of it deserves to be read by general readers. Griffith's superb introduction (1999) covers the entire gamut of scholarship and interpretation; Foley (1995) reviews two recent accounts of the play that are based on history.

Among translations, those of Blundell (1998) and Lloyd-Jones (1994) closely follow the Greek and reflect recent scholarly opinion; of the two, I prefer Blundell, who accepts more conservative, and more likely, readings of the text. Readers with a little Greek should consult the new commentary by Griffith (1999).

3. *Oedipus Tyrannus*

Few works of literature have been discussed by as many thinkers as has *Oedipus Tyrannus*. The most famous writers about the play are Aristotle (in his *Poetics*, Chapters 11–5) and Freud (in *The*

Interpretation of Dreams, 1961). In recent years, scholars have sought to explain the play through its context in ancient Greece; most notable of these is Bernard Knox (1957; new edition, augmented, 1998). Charles Segal provides a balanced study in *Sophocles' Tragic World* (1995), which is now essential reading. The most influential study of Sophocles as a playwright is by Karl Reinhardt (1947; translated 1979). Beginners interested in the interpretation of the play should read Harold Bloom's collection of essays by leading scholars and thinkers (1988), with special attention to the famous essay by E. R. Dodds (1966).

In translating the text, we have for the most part followed the text and commentary of Dawe (1982), though on some points we have used the new Oxford text of Lloyd-Jones and Wilson (1990a). We have consulted Jebb's classic edition (2nd ed., 1887/1962) on everything and considered also Kamerbeek's commentary (1967) and the studies in Lloyd-Jones and Wilson (1990b).

4. *Oedipus at Colonus*

Authors who have written about Sophocles usually allow a chapter for this play, but little has been written for general readers. The introduction by Knox in Fagles (1982) and the chapter in Reinhardt (1947) are two good introductions for beginners. There is also a fine chapter in Bowra (1994). Charles Segal is less helpful on this play than on the other two, (1981, 1995). Blundell's work on the ethical background of Sophocles' plays (1989) fits especially well with *Oedipus at Colonus*. Wilson's recent study of the play (1997) is accessible to general readers, although written for a scholarly audience. It reviews much of the recent scholarship and provides eloquent correctives on many points. We also recommend Vidal-Naquet's "Oedipus between Two Cities" (in Vernant and Vidal-Naquet 1990).

Scholars should tussle with Tanner's essay (1966), which is interestingly wrongheaded, and they will enjoy the recent books on the play by Edmunds (1996) and Travis (1999). Edmunds's book is especially valuable for students of literary theory. Burian's essay has had a very wide influence and should be on every scholar's reading list (1974).

Note on the Translations

Sophocles' text is a script for production, and so are our translations. Students encountering these plays should be able to read them as plays and not as word-for-word renderings of ancient manuscripts. We have tried to be especially faithful to the emotional power and directness of Sophocles; accordingly, our version is simple and concise. We have sacrificed some nuances but kept true to the broad meaning of every line and every image. Where the manuscript text is especially hard to understand, we have followed those editors whose corrections make good sense to modern readers; where the alternatives give significantly different meanings, we have supplied endnotes. Footnotes should tell readers what they need to know in order to understand the basic meaning of the text. Line numbers refer to the Greek text as numbered in Lloyd-Jones and Wilson (1990a).

The translations are the work of both of us. *Oedipus Tyrannus* was a joint project, *Antigone* was the work of Paul Woodruff, and *Oedipus at Colonus* was the work of Peter Meineck.

Peter Meineck supplied or approved the stage directions, which of course are absent from the Greek text. His experience with stage productions of ancient plays has affected every aspect of our work on these plays. Paul Woodruff wrote the Introduction, aside from the section on performance, which was contributed by Peter Meineck.

Acknowledgments

Working on a new translation of the Theban plays has been an extraordinary experience. It has been a rare pleasure collaborating with Paul Woodruff. Our two voices and opinions here have, I believe, led to a much stronger volume of translations. Paul's excellent scholarship, knowledge of Greek, philosophical insights, and sheer love for Sophocles have kept me going when it seemed sometimes as if this enormous project would never be completed. I am especially grateful for his superb *Antigone*.

My work on *Oedipus Tyrannus* (with Paul) and *Oedipus at Colonus* would not have been possible without the ability to test these translations in production. I believe that this is an essential element in presenting any new work of drama, either on the printed page or onstage. The Aquila Theatre Company staged a reading of *Oedipus Tyrannus* at New York University and then developed this translation into a production, which toured the United States in the spring of 2000. I would like to thank the cast of that production which was staged in masks—particularly Kenn Sabberton, Lisa Carter, and Louis Butelli—Anthony Cochrane for his evocative music, and the director, Robert Richmond, for his creativity in bringing the text to vivid life. Films for the Humanities taped portions of this show, and I am grateful that they are making it widely available.

One of the most moving productions of a Greek play I have ever seen was Lee Breuer's *Gospel at Colonus*. That production showed me that *Oedipus at Colonus* is primarily a spiritual play, deeply moving and incredibly powerful. From then on I fell in love with this story. I feel honored to have been able to render a new translation, which I hope captures some of the visceral power of the Greek. I would like to thank Arthur Bartow, Artistic Director of the Tisch School of the Arts at New York University, and Una Chaudhuri, departmental chair, for allowing the students and faculty of NYU to present my translation of *Oedipus at Colonus* as part of their main stage season in the fall of 2000. Brian Parsons directed a beautiful play with great care and attention, and I learned a great deal from him and his young cast.

Matthew Santirocco, Dean of the College of Arts and Science at New York University, has provided both the Aquila Theatre Company and myself with constant support and valuable resources. Peter Sederberg, Dean of the Honors College at the University of South Carolina, was a great help in facilitating the beginnings of this project. The Humanities Council of Princeton University granted me a fellowship that enabled me to complete work on this project in serene and supportive surroundings. Jay Hullett, Brian Rak, and Meera Dash at Hackett Publishing Company were incredibly patient and supportive of this project every step of the way.

PETER MEINECK

I wish to acknowledge the assistance of James Collins on the Introduction to *Antigone*, and the advice of Erwin Cook, Lowell Edmunds, Michael Gagarin, and Thomas Palaima on the Introduction to *Oedipus Tyrannus*. Peter Meineck's knowledge of stagecraft and gift for clear, dramatic expression in translation have been instructive and inspiring throughout my work on these three plays. Brian Rak's editorial suggestions have been most helpful, and his selection of cover materials has been brilliant.

PAUL WOODRUFF

Theban Royal Family Tree

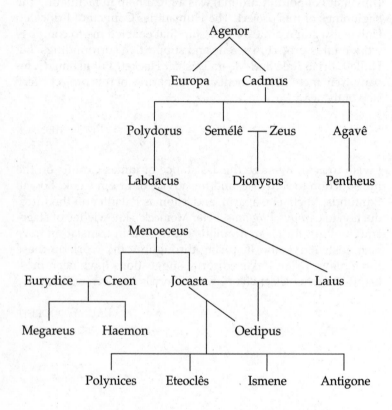

Antigone

Antigone: Cast of Characters

ANTIGONE	daughter and half-sister of Oedipus
ISMENE	Antigone's sister
CHORUS	the council of elders in Thebes
CHORUS LEADER	has lines in conversations
CREON	Antigone's uncle on her mother's side
WATCHMAN	one of those set to guard the corpse
TIRESIAS	prophet of Apollo
HAEMON	Creon's son, Antigone's fiancé
MESSENGER	a servant of Creon's
EURYDICE	Creon's wife, Haemon's mother

Nonspeaking Roles

ATTENDANTS	to Creon
ATTENDANTS	to Antigone (when under arrest)
SERVANTS	to Eurydice
BOY	who guides Tiresias

Antigone

SCENE: *The royal house at Thebes, fronting onto a raised plat-*
         form stage. Wing entrances right and left allow for char-
         acters to be seen by the audience and the chorus long
         before they are seen by the main characters. The great
         doors of the house stand upstage center.

         (Enter Antigone leading Ismene through the great
         doors that lead from the palace.)

ANTIGONE:
  Ismene, dear heart, my true sister:
  You and I are left alive to pay
  The final penalty to Zeus for Oedipus.
  I've never seen such misery and madness—
  It's monstrous! Such deep shame and dishonor—   5
  As this, which falls upon the pair of us.
  And now, a public announcement!
  They say the general has plastered it around the city.
  Have you heard this terrible news or not?
  Our enemies are on the march to hurt our friends.   10

ISMENE:
  No, Antigone, I have had no news of friends,
  Nothing sweet or painful, since the day
  We lost our brothers, both of us, on one day,
  Both brothers dead by their two hands.
  Last night the army that came from Argos   15

10: By "friends" Antigone means her brother Polynices, who is her
friend, come what may, because he is part of her immediate family. But
who are her enemies? As I understand her, Antigone is revealing that she
has already identified Creon as the enemy. See endnote for alternative
readings.

14–15: The two brothers, Eteoclês and Polynices, had planned to take
turns ruling Thebes; but Eteoclês refused to give Polynices his time on
the throne. An army came from Argos in support of Polynices' claim and

Disappeared, and after that I don't know
Anything that could bring me happiness—or despair.

ANTIGONE:

I knew it! That's the whole reason
I brought you outside—to hear the news alone.

ISMENE:

20   Tell me. You're as clear as a fog at sea.

ANTIGONE:

It's the burial of our two brothers. Creon
Promotes one of them and shames the other.
Eteoclês—I heard Creon covered him beneath
The earth with proper rites, as law ordains,
25   So he has honor down among the dead.
But Polynices' miserable corpse—
They say Creon has proclaimed to everyone:
"No Burial of any kind. No wailing, no public tears.
Give him to the vultures, unwept, unburied,
30   To be a sweet treasure for their sharp eyes and beaks."
That's what they say the good Creon has proclaimed
To you. And me. He forbids me, too.
And now he's strutting here to make it plain
To those who haven't heard—he takes
35   This seriously—that if anyone does what he forbids
He'll have him publicly stoned to death.
There's your news. Now, show your colors:
Are you true to your birth? Or a coward?

ISMENE:

You take things hard. If we are in this noose,
40   What could I do to loosen or pull tight the knot?

ANTIGONE:

If you share the work and trouble . . .

---

was defeated at the seven gates of the city. The two brothers killed each
other. Argos, in the northeast corner of Peloponnesus, was seen as an
enemy of Thebes.

21: "Creon"—In her breathless haste, Antigone frequently starts a
thought just before the end of a line.

25: See Introduction, pp. xix–xx on burial rites.

ISMENE:
  In what dangerous adventure?

ANTIGONE:
  If you help this hand raise the corpse . . . *(Indicating her own hand)*

ISMENE:
  Do you mean to bury him? Against the city's ordinance?

ANTIGONE:
  But he is mine. And yours. Like it or not, he's our brother.   45
  They'll never catch me betraying him.

ISMENE:
  How horrible! When Creon forbids it?

ANTIGONE:
  He has no right to keep me from my own.

ISMENE:
  Oh no! Think carefully, my sister.
  Our father died in hatred and disgrace   50
  After gouging out his own two eyes
  For sins he'd seen in his own self.
  Next, his mother and wife—she was both—
  Destroyed herself in a knotted rope.
  And, third, our two brothers on one day   55
  Killed each other in a terrible calamity,
  Which they had created for each other.
  Now think about the two of us. We are alone.
  How horrible it will be to die outside the law,
  If we violate a dictator's decree!   60
  No. We have to keep this fact in mind:
  We are women and we do not fight with men.
  We're subject to them because they're stronger,
  And we must obey this order, even if it hurts us more.
  As for me, I will say to those beneath the earth   65
  This prayer: "Forgive me, I am held back by force."
  And I'll obey the men in charge. My mind
  Will never aim too high, too far.

ANTIGONE:
  I won't press you any further. I wouldn't even let
  You help me if you had a change of heart.   70

Go on and *be* the way you choose to be. I
Will bury him. I will have a noble death
And lie with him, a dear sister with a dear brother.
Call it a crime of reverence, but I must be good to those
75 Who are below. I will be there longer than with you.
That's where I will lie. You, keep to your choice:
Go on insulting what the gods hold dear.

ISMENE:
I am not insulting anyone. By my very nature
I cannot possibly take arms against the city.

ANTIGONE:
80 Go on, make excuses. I am on my way.
I'll heap the earth upon my dearest brother's grave.

ISMENE:
Oh no! This is horrible for you. I am so worried!

ANTIGONE:
Don't worry about me. Put your own life straight.

ISMENE:
Please don't tell a soul what you are doing.
85 Keep it hidden. I'll do the same.

ANTIGONE:
For god's sake, speak out. You'll be more enemy to me
If you are silent. Proclaim it to the world!

ISMENE:
Your heart's so hot to do this chilling thing!

ANTIGONE:
But it pleases those who matter most.

ISMENE:
90 Yes, if you had the power. But you love the impossible.

ANTIGONE:
So? When my strength is gone, I'll stop.

89: "Those who matter most"—the dead, or the gods of the dead.
90: "You love the impossible"—more accurately, perhaps, "You long for
the impossible." But the verb is the same as the one used for sexual love.
On Antigone's love, see Introduction, pp. xxvii–xxviii.

ISMENE:
  But it's the highest wrong to chase after what's impossible.

ANTIGONE:
  When you say this, you set yourself against me.
  Your brother will take you to him—as his enemy.
  So you just let me and my 'bad judgment'   95
  Go to hell. Nothing could happen to me
  So bad that it would cloud my noble death.

        *(Exit Antigone toward the plain, through the stage
        left wing.)*

ISMENE:
  Then follow your judgment, go. You've lost your mind,
  But you are holding to the love of your loved ones.

        *(Exit Ismene through the great doors into the palace,
        as the chorus enter from the city, stage right wing.)*

CHORUS:

Parodos (Entry-song)

[Strophe *a*]

  Let us praise the Sun: 100
  These brilliant beams
  Shine glory never seen before in Thebes,
  Our City of Seven Gates.
  O bright eye of golden day!
  You came striding over River Dirkê,   105
  And the White Shield of Argos ran away.
  He has fled,
  Man and weapon racing from your light,
  On sharpened spur.

  He was roused against our land   110

100: "Let us praise the Sun"—See Introduction, p. xxxii on this choral
passage.
105: Dirkê is one of the rivers of Thebes.
106: "White Shield of Argos"—the army of Argos.

For a fight that Polynices, haggling, picked.
And, like a screaming eagle,
He dropped on our land:
The shadow of his white-snow wing—
115   A multitude of armored men,
Helmets crested with horsehair.

[Antistrophe *a*]

He stooped over our homes,
Mouth gaping wide for the kill,
He engulfed our Seven Gates with spears of death;
120   But he has gone,
Gone before plunging his beak in our blood,
Gone before torching our crown of towers
With the flames of Hephaestus.
For behind his back there arose too loud
125   The clamor of war;
His dragon-foe was too strong for him.

Zeus hates an arrogant boast,
With towering hatred.
He saw the river of men attack,
130   Their golden armor clashing in contempt,
And so he struck the man down with a missile of fire
As he swooped toward his highest goal,
Eager to shout "Victory!"

[Strophe *b*]

He crashed to the ground
135   Like a weight slung down in an arc of fire,
This man who had swooped like a dancer in ecstasy,
Breathing hurricanes of hatred.

111: Polynices—The chorus pun on the meaning of the young man's name, "much-quarreling."

126: "Dragon-foe"—The people of Thebes believed that they were descended from men who grew from the teeth of a dragon slain by Cadmus.

131–40: These lines refer to the attacker who boasts too much; according to the legend, this was an Argive named Capaneus.

But his threats came to nothing:
The mighty war god, fighting beside us,
Swept them aside.   140

Seven captains at seven gates,
Matched with seven defenders,
All left trophies for Zeus the protector
(They took off their armor and ran).
Except for a savage pair, full brothers: 145
Their two spears stand upright, conquering,
Each in the other's dead breast.

[Antistrophe *b*]

Now Victory is ours,
Great be her name! Now Thebes rejoices.
Therefore let us forget our pain.   150
The war is over: let us dance all night,
Fill all the sacred precincts with joy:
We must now be ruled by Bacchus,
Dance-master of Thebes.

(Enter Creon through the great doors.)

CHORUS:
Here is the king of our land   155
Creon, the son of Menoeceus,
Our new ruler given us by chance and the gods.
What plan has he been churning over on his way?
Why has he summoned us—
The council of elders—   160
By public announcement?

CREON:
Gentlemen, the city is safe again, we may thank the gods:
After a great upheaval, they have rescued Thebes.
You are here because I chose you from the whole crowd

156: "Creon, the son of Menoeceus"—See Theban Royal Family Tree.

157: "Our new ruler"—Creon is not altogether new, since he was the
regent for Oedipus' sons. See line 289 with note.

165   And summoned you by escort. You always showed
             respect
        For Laius' power when he held the throne,
        And the same again for Oedipus, when he rescued Thebes.
        After he died I know you stood by their sons;
        You were always there with good advice.
170   Now they are dead, both on one day;
        Each stabbed the other and was stabbed.
        Brother struck brother, and the blows were cursed.

        So now the throne and all the power in Thebes are mine,
        Because I am closest kin to those who died.

175   No man has a mind that can be fully known,
        In character or judgment, till he rules and makes law;
        Only then can he be tested in the public eye.
        I believe that if anyone tries to run a city
        On the basis of bad policies and holds his tongue
180   Because he's afraid to say what is right,
        That man is terrible. So I have always thought.
        But it's even worse when he plays favorites,
        Puts family or friends ahead of fatherland.
        As for me—I call to witness all-seeing Zeus—
185   I will never hold my tongue about what I see
        When ruin is afoot or the city is not safe.
        I will never call a man my friend
        If he is hostile to this land. I know this well:
        The city is our lifeboat: we have no friends at all
190   Unless we keep her sailing right side up.
        Such are my laws. By them I'll raise this city high.

        And I have just announced a twin sister of those laws,
        To all the citizens, concerning Oedipus' sons:

165: "You always showed respect"—The same word covers "reverence"
and is used with that broader sense elsewhere in the play. See lines 744–5
with note.

168: "You stood by their sons"—The plural "their" in the Greek is startling. We do not know whether it refers to Oedipus and Laius or to Oedipus and Jocasta. See endnote.

175–6: Cf. Aristotle, *Nicomachean Ethics* 5.1, "Ruling shows what a man is."

Eteoclês fought for the city, and for it he died,
After every feat of heroism with his spear.   195
He shall be sanctified by every burial rite
That is given to the most heroic dead below.

As for his blood brother, Polynices by name,
He broke his exile, he came back hungry for our blood,
He wanted to burn his fatherland and family gods   200
Down from the top. He wanted to lead his people—
Into slavery. This man will have no grave:
It is forbidden to offer any funeral rites;
No one in Thebes may bury him or mourn for him.
He must be left unburied. May birds and dogs   205
Feed on his limbs, a spectacle of utter shame.

Such is the character of my mind: Never, while I rule,
Will a criminal be honored higher than a man of justice.
But give me a true friend of this city
And I will pay him full honor, in death or life.   210

CHORUS:
That is your decision, son of Menoeceus,
As to the one who meant our city well
And the one who meant it ill. It's up to you:
Make any law you want—for the dead, or for us who live.

CREON:
Now, look after my commands. I insist.   215

CHORUS:
Ask someone younger to take up the task.

CREON:
No, no. I have men already watching the corpse.

CHORUS:
Then what's left for us to do? What are your orders?

CREON:
That you do not side with anyone who disobeys.

215–6: Creon meant "see that my commands are obeyed," but the chorus
understood "watch over the corpse."

CHORUS:

220   No one is foolish enough to ask for death.

CREON:

Right. That would be their reward. But hope—
And bribery—often have led men to destruction.

(Enter Watchman from the stage left wing.)

WATCHMAN:

Sir, I am here. I can't say I am out of breath.
I have not exactly been "running on light feet."
225   I halted many times along the road so I could think,
And I almost turned around and marched right back.
My mind kept talking to me. It said, "You poor guy,
Why are you going there? You'll just get your ass kicked."
Then it said, "Are you stopping again, you damn fool?
230   If Creon hears this from another man, he'll give you hell."
Well, I turned this idea up and down like that,
And I hurried along, real slow. Made a short trip long.
What got me here in the end was this: My report.
It doesn't amount to much, but I might as well give it,
235   Because I won't let go this handful of hope
That things won't be any worse than they have to be.

CREON:

What is it, man—where's your courage?

WATCHMAN:

First, I want to tell you where I stand:
I didn't do this thing, and I don't know who did,
240   And it wouldn't be fair if I got hurt.

CREON:

All right, your defense perimeter is up.
Now, let's have your report.

WATCHMAN:

It's terrible news. I can't come right out with that.

224: "Running on light feet"—An audience would normally expect a
messenger to arrive gasping and out of breath. This one consciously
flouts convention. The passage corroborates Haemon's claim, line 690
and following, that people are afraid to tell the truth to Creon.

CREON:
  Speak up! And then get lost.

WATCHMAN:
  OK, here it is. The body out there—someone buried it   245
  Just now and went away. They spread thirsty dust
  All over the skin and did the ceremony in full.

CREON:
  What? No man would dare! Who did it?

WATCHMAN:
  I don't know. The ground was so hard and dry.
  It showed no marks. No spade scratches,   250
  No pickaxe holes, not even chariot ruts.
  The perpetrator had not left a single clue.
  When the first day-watchman showed it to us,
  We were all amazed. It was incredible:
  The guy had vanished. There was no tomb,   255
  Only fine dust lying over the body, enough to take
  The curse away. No sign of wild animals,
  No dogs sniffing or tugging at the corpse.

  We burst out shouting at each other;
  Everyone was hurling accusations.   260
  We kept coming to blows, no one to stop us.
  Any one of us could have done the thing.
  No one caught red-handed, everyone pled ignorance.
  We were about to test each other with red-hot iron
  Or run our hands through fire and swear by all the gods: 265
  "I didn't do it, and I had no part in any plot
  To do it, not with anyone else, not by hand or word."
  Well, we weren't getting anywhere, and in the end
  Someone told us to do a thing we couldn't see how
  To refuse *or* accept. So we dropped heads, stared at the
      ground   270
  In fear. There was no way it would turn out good for us.
  We simply had to bring word to you,
  Because we could not hide a thing like this.

255: "The guy had vanished"—The subject of this sentence probably is
the corpse of Polynices.

We voted to do it, and I am so damned unlucky
275   I won the lottery to have this lovely job.
I didn't want to come. And you sure didn't want to see me:
No one loves the man who brings bad news.

CHORUS: *(To Creon.)*
You know, sir, as soon as I heard, it came to me:
Somehow the gods are behind this piece of work.

CREON: *(To the chorus leader.)*
280   Stop right there, before I'm gorged with rage!
You want to prove that you're as stupid as you are old?
It's totally unacceptable, what you said about the gods—
That they could have a caring thought for this man's corpse.
You think they buried him for his good deeds?
285   To give him highest honor? They know he came with fire
To burn down their fine-columned shrines, their land,
Their store of treasure—and to blow their laws away.
Have you ever seen a criminal honored by the *gods*?
Not possible.

                    But some *men* here have always champed,
290   Like surf, against my orders, and obeyed me, if at all,
Without cheer. They shake their heads when I'm not
      looking,
Pull out of the yoke of justice, and are not content with me.
They are the ones, I'm absolutely sure, who used bribes
To lead our watchmen astray, into this crime.

295   Money is the nastiest weed ever to sprout
In human soil. Money will ravage a city,
Tear men from their homes and send them into exile.
Money teaches good minds to go bad;
It is the source of every shameful human deed.
300   Money points the way to wickedness,

289: "Some *men* here have always champed"—The line suggests that
Creon has been ruling for a long time. See line 157, with notes, and Introduction, p. xxviii.

292: "The yoke of justice"—With this powerful and undemocratic image,
Creon speaks of holding his citizens to justice as he would of breaking
animals to the yoke.

Lets people know the full range of irreverence.
But those who committed this crime for hire
Have set themselves a penalty, which, in time, they'll pay.

   (To the Watchman.)

Now listen here. So long as I am reverent to Zeus
I am under oath, and you can be absolutely sure   305
That if you don't find the hand behind this burial
And bring him so I can see him with my own eyes,
Death alone will not be good enough for you—
Not till I've stretched you with ropes and you confess
To this outrageous crime. That will teach you   310
Where to look to make a profit. And you will learn:
Never accept money from just anyone who comes along.
Those who take from a source that is wicked, you'll see,
Are ruined far more often than saved.

WATCHMAN:
Permission to speak, sir? Or about face and go?   315

CREON:
Don't you see how badly your report annoyed me?

WATCHMAN:
So where's it biting you? On your ears or in your mind?

CREON:
What's it to you? Why should you analyze my pain?

WATCHMAN:
If it hurts your mind, blame the perpetrator.
If it's only your ears, blame me.

CREON:
Damn it, man, will you never stop babbling?   320

WATCHMAN:
Well, at least I never did the thing.

CREON:
Yes, you did. And for money! You gave up your life!

WATCHMAN:
Oh no, no, no.
It's terrible when false judgment guides the judge.

CREON:

> All right, play with the word 'judgment.' But you'd better
>   catch
325 The man who did this thing or I'll have proof:
> You men ruined your miserable lives to make a profit!

> *(Creon turns and exits through the great doors to
> the palace.)*

WATCHMAN:

> We'll find him. You'd better believe it.
> But if we don't—you know, if he gets lucky—
> No way you'll ever see me coming back to you.
330 As it is, this has gone better than I expected—
> I'm still alive, thanks be to the gods.

> *(Exit Watchman toward the plain, through the stage
> left wing.)*

First Stasimon

CHORUS:

[Strophe *a*]

> Many wonders, many terrors,
> But none more wonderful than the human race
>   Or more dangerous.
335 This creature travels on a winter gale
> Across the silver sea,
> Shadowed by high-surging waves,
> While on Earth, grandest of the gods,
> He grinds the deathless, tireless land away,

332–75: First Stasimon—See Introduction, p. xxxii.

332: "Many wonders, many terrors" (*polla ta deina*)—A word-for-word translation would be "Many things are wonderful-terrible, but none is more so than a human being." The word *deinon* is used of things that are awe-inspiring in both good and bad ways. I have rendered this double meaning by using "wonder," "terror," and "dangerous" in the opening lines.

339: "Grinds the . . . land away"—The Greek verb implies that he does this for his benefit.

Turning and turning the plow   340
From year to year, behind driven horses.

[Antistrophe *a*]

Light-headed birds he catches
And takes them away in legions. Wild beasts
    Also fall prey to him.
And all that is born to live beneath the sea   345
Is thrashing in his woven nets.
For he is Man, and he is cunning.
He has invented ways to take control
Of beasts that range mountain meadows:
Taken down the shaggy-necked horses,   350
The tireless mountain bulls,
And put them under the yoke.

[Strophe *b*]

Language and a mind swift as the wind
    For making plans—   355
These he has taught himself—
And the character to live in cities under law.
He's learned to take cover from a frost
And escape sharp arrows of sleet.
He has the means to handle every need,   360
Never steps toward the future without the means.

347: "Man"—The ode begins at line 333 with the generic "human," but here the male of the species is plainly indicated. The quarrel between a man and a woman that lies at the heart of the play is in the background; Greek men of this period frequently used images of taming and controlling animals for the relation between the sexes.

348: "Ways to take control"—The Greek word is used for conquest or the illegitimate rule of a tyrant.

352: "Yoke"—This word too is politically charged. See line 292 with note.

357: "The character to live in cities"—Literally, the untranslated phrase indicates the emotions that give order to cities. Probably the line refers to such virtues as reverence, justice, and a sense of shame, all of which civic life was widely thought to depend upon. See Plato's *Protagoras* 322c–d. But the word translated "character" can also mean "anger," as at line 875.

Except for Death: He's got himself no relief from that,
Though he puts every mind to seeking cures
For plagues that are hopeless.

[Antistrophe *b*]

365   He has cunning contrivance,
               Skill surpassing hope,
        And so he slithers into wickedness sometimes,
        Other times into doing good.
        If he honors the law of the land
370   And the oath-bound justice of the gods,
        Then his city shall stand high.
        But no city for him if he turns shameless out of daring.
        He will be no guest of mine,
        He will never share my thoughts,
375   If he goes wrong.

        (Enter Watchman leading Antigone through the stage
        left wing.)

CHORUS:
        Monstrous! What does this mean?
        Are gods behind it? I don't know what to think:
        Isn't this Antigone? I can't deny it.
        You miserable child of misery,
380   Daughter of Oedipus,
        What have you done?
        Is it you they arrested?
        Are you so foolish?
        So disloyal to the laws of kings?

WATCHMAN:
        Yes, she's the one that did the burial.
385   We caught her in the act. Hey, where's Creon?

        (Enter Creon through the great doors.)

CHORUS:
        Here he is. Coming back from the palace.

376: "Monstrous"—The word refers to anything so foreign to common
experience that it may be taken as a special omen from the gods.

CREON:
  What's all this? Lucky I turned up now.

WATCHMAN:
  Sir, there's no point swearing oaths if you're a mortal.
  Second thoughts make any plan look bad.
  I swore I'd never come to you again   390
  Because those threats of yours gave me the shakes.
  But you know: "Joy beyond hope
  Surpasses every other pleasure."
  I've come, though I swore on oath I wouldn't.
  And I've brought this girl, arrested her at the grave   395
  When she was tidying it up. No lottery this time.
  The windfall's mine and no one else's.
  Now it's up to you. Take her, question her,
  Make your judgment. As for me,
  The right thing is to let me off scot-free.   400

CREON:
  Circumstances under which you arrested her? Location?

WATCHMAN:
  She was burying that man. Now you know it all.

CREON:
  Do you honestly know what you are saying?

WATCHMAN:
  Well, I saw this girl burying the dead body.
  The one you put off-limits. Clear enough for you?   405

CREON:
  How did you see this? Caught her in the act?

WATCHMAN:
  It was like this. We went back to the body
  After all your terrible threats,
  And we brushed off the dust that covered it,
  So as to make the rotting corpse properly naked.   410
  Then we settled down on the hill,
  Upwind, so the stink wouldn't hit us.
  We kept awake by yelling insults
  At each other when a slacker nodded off.
  That went on for a long time, till the sun   415

Stood bright in the center of the sky.
And we were really getting cooked. Then,
Suddenly, a tornado struck. It raised dust
All over the plain, grief to high heaven.
420 It thrashed the low-lying woods with terror
And filled the whole wide sky. We shut our eyes
And held out against this plague from the gods.

After a long while it lifted, and then we saw the girl.
She gave a shrill cry like a bird when she sees her nest
425 Empty, and the bed deserted where her nestlings had lain.
That was how she was when she saw the corpse uncovered.
She cried out in mourning, and she called down
Curses on whoever had done this thing.
Right away she spread thirsty dust with her hands,
430 Then poured the three libations from a vessel of fine bronze.
And so she crowned the corpse with honor.

As soon as we spotted her, we started to run.
She showed no fear; it was easy to catch her.
Then we questioned her about her past and present actions.
435 She did not deny a single thing.
For me, that was sweet, and agonizing, too.
It's a great joy to be out of trouble,
But bringing trouble on your friends is agony.
Still I don't mind that so much. It's nature's way
440 For me to put my own survival first.

CREON:
You there! With your head bowed to the ground—
Are you guilty? Or do you deny that you did this thing?

ANTIGONE:
Of course not. I did it. I won't deny anything.

CREON: *(To the Watchman.)*
You're dismissed. Take yourself where you please;
445 You're a free man, no serious charge against you.

419: "Grief to high heaven"—The phrase may mean "high as the sky."
430: The libations, pouring wine from a ceremonial vessel, form an essential part of ancient Greek burial ritual.

(To Antigone.)

As for you, tell me—in brief, not at length—
Did you know that this had been forbidden?

ANTIGONE:
I knew. I couldn't help knowing. It was everywhere.

CREON:
And yet you dared to violate these laws?

ANTIGONE:
What laws? I never heard it was Zeus   450
Who made that announcement.
And it wasn't justice, either. The gods below
Didn't lay down this law for human use.
And I never thought your announcements
Could give you—a mere human being—   455
Power to trample the gods' unfailing,
Unwritten laws. These laws weren't made now
Or yesterday. They live for all time,
And no one knows when they came into the light.
No man could frighten me into taking on
The gods' penalty for breaking such a law.   460
I'll die in any case, of course I will,
Whether you announce my execution or not.
But if I die young, all the better:
People who live in misery like mine
Are better dead. So if that's the way   465
My life will end, the pain is nothing.
But if I let the corpse—my mother's son—
Lie dead, unburied, that would be agony.
This way, no agony for me. But you! You think
I've been a fool? It takes a fool to think that.   470

CHORUS:
Now we see the girl's as wild by birth as her father.
She has no idea how to bow her head to trouble.

CREON: *(To the chorus.)*
Don't forget: The mind that is most rigid

473: Creon apparently does not think it worth his while to answer Antigone; instead, he responds to the chorus in a speech that consists mainly

Stumbles soonest; the hardest iron—
475 Tempered in fire till it is super-strong—
Shatters easily and clatters into shards.
And you can surely break the wildest horse
With a tiny bridle. When the master's watching,
Pride has no place in the life of a slave.
480 This girl was a complete expert in arrogance
Already, when she broke established law.
And now, arrogantly, she adds insult to injury:
She's boasting and sneering about what she's done!
Listen, if she's not punished for taking the upper hand,
485 Then I am not a man. *She* would be a man!
I don't care if she is my sister's child—
Or closer yet at my household shrine for Zeus—
She and her sister must pay the full price
And die for their crime.

> (*The chorus indicate their surprise that both
> must die.*)

Yes, I say they have equal guilt,
490 Conniving, one with the other, for this burial.

Bring her out. I saw her in there a minute ago;
She was raving mad, totally out of her mind.
Often it's the feelings of a thief that give him away
Before the crimes he did in darkness come to light.

> (*Turning to Antigone.*)

495 But how I hate it when she's caught in the act,
And the criminal still glories in her crime.

ANTIGONE:
You've caught me, you can kill me. What more do you want?

---

of a ringing list of clichés about the risks attending arrogance and inflexible judgment—risks he is unconsciously taking himself. His opening image of hard, fragile iron prefigures Haemon's mention of stiff trees breaking in a flood, lines 712–4.

480–2: "Arrogance . . . injury"—The Greek word hubris includes the meanings of arrogance, insolence, outrage, and crime. Typically violating justice and reverence, hubris is practiced by the strong against the weak.

CREON:
  For me, that's everything. I want no more than that.

ANTIGONE:
  Then what are you waiting for? More talk?
  Your words disgust me, I hope they always will.   500
  And I'm sure you are disgusted by what I say.
  But yet, speaking of glory, what could be more
  Glorious than giving my true brother his burial?
  All these men would tell you they're rejoicing
  Over that, if you hadn't locked their tongues   505
  With fear. But a tyrant says and does
  What he pleases. That's his great joy.

CREON:
  You are the only one, in all Thebes, who thinks that way.

ANTIGONE:
  No. They all see it the same. You've silenced them.

CREON:
  Aren't you ashamed to have a mind apart from theirs?   510

ANTIGONE:
  There's no shame in having respect for a brother.

CREON:
  Wasn't he your brother, too, the one who died on the
      other side?

ANTIGONE:
  Yes, my blood brother—same mother, same father.

CREON:
  When you honor the one, you disgrace the other. Why do it?

ANTIGONE:
  The dead will never testify against a burial.   515

CREON:
  Yes, if they were equal. But one of them deserves disgrace.

500: "Your words disgust me"—Although the literal translation is closer
to "are not pleasing to me," ancient Greek understatements often imply
powerful sentiments.

ANTIGONE:
He wasn't any kind of slave. He was his brother, who died.

CREON:
He was killing and plundering. The other one defended
our land.

ANTIGONE:
Even so, Hades longs to have these laws obeyed.

CREON:
520   But surely not equal treatment for good and bad?

ANTIGONE:
Who knows? Down below that might be blesséd.

CREON:
An enemy is always an enemy, even in death.

ANTIGONE:
I cannot side with hatred. My nature sides with love.

CREON:
Go to Hades, then, and if you have to love, love someone
dead.
525   As long as I live, I will not be ruled by a woman.

(Enter Ismene under guard, through the great doors.)

CHORUS:
Now Ismene stands before the doors
And sheds tears of sister-love.

519: Hades is the god of death; his name is also used for the Underworld,
to which the dead belong. See Introduction, p. xx.

523: "I cannot side with hatred. My nature sides with love"—Antigone
coins new words here for her extraordinary feelings. She means that
even if her brothers hate each other, it is her nature not to join them in
hatred, but in the family love (philia) they have for her. Note also that
family love is natural, i.e., by birth, unlike any sort of enmity: "I have
friends by birth, not enemies" (Lloyd-Jones 1994). See Introduction, pp.
xxvii–xxviii on Antigone's love.

527–30: Because the actor is wearing a mask, Ismene's expression must
be described. What shows on her face is important because Creon takes
it as a sign of guilt.

From her brows, a blood-dark cloud
Casts a foul shadow
And stains her lovely face.   530

CREON:
Now you. Hiding in my house like a snake,
A coiled bloodsucker in the dark! And I never realized
I was raising a pair of deadly, crazed revolutionaries!
Come, tell me: How do you plead? Guilty of this burial
As an accomplice? Or do you swear you knew nothing?   535

ISMENE:
I did it, I confess. That is, if we are partners, anyway.
I am an accomplice, and I bear responsibility with her.

ANTIGONE:
I will not permit this penalty to fall on you.
No. I never wanted to give you a share.

ISMENE:
But these are your troubles! I'm not ashamed;   540
I'll be your shipmate in suffering.

ANTIGONE:
I have witnesses: the gods below saw who did the work.
I won't accept a friend who's only friends in words.

ISMENE:
No, please! You're my sister: Don't despise me!
Let me die with you and sanctify our dead.   545

ANTIGONE:
No, you may not die along with me. Don't say you did it!
You wouldn't even touch it. Now leave my death alone!

ISMENE:
Why would I care to live when you are gone?

ANTIGONE:
Creon's the one to ask. He's the one you care for.

ISMENE:
Why are you scolding me? It won't help you.   550

538–9: Cf. lines 69–70.

ANTIGONE:
Of course not. It hurts me when my mockery strikes you.

ISMENE:
But I still want to help you. What can I do?

ANTIGONE:
Escape! Save yourself! I don't begrudge you that.

ISMENE:
O misery! Why am I cut off from your fate?

ANTIGONE:
555   Because you chose life, and I chose death.

ISMENE:
But I gave you reasons not to make that choice.

ANTIGONE: *(Pointing to Creon and the chorus.)*
Oh yes, you are sensible; these men agree.

> *(Pointing to the ground, speaking of the dead or the
> gods below.)*

But *they* agree with me.

ISMENE:
Yes, I know. And now the sin is mine as much as yours.

ANTIGONE:
Be brave. You are alive. Already my soul is dead.
560   It has gone to help those who died before me.

CREON:
What a pair of children! One of you lost her mind
Moments ago; the other was born without hers.

ISMENE:
That is right, sir. Whenever we commit a crime,
Our minds, which grew by nature, leave us.

CREON:
565   Yours did, when you deliberately joined a criminal in crime.

ISMENE:
Without her, why should I live? I'd be alone.

555: Cf. lines 71–81.

CREON:
Her? Don't speak of her. She is no more.

ISMENE:
But will you really kill the bride of your son?

CREON:
There's other ground for him to plow, you know.

ISMENE:
But no one is suited to him as well as she is. 570

CREON:
I loathe bad women. She's not for my son.

ANTIGONE *(or possibly Ismene, or possibly Chorus):*
O Haemon, dearest, what a disgrace your father does to you!

CREON:
Shut up! What a pain you are, you and your marriage!

CHORUS *(or Ismene, or Antigone):*
Will you really take away your son's bride?

CREON:
Not me. Death will put a stop to this marriage. 575

CHORUS *(or Ismene):*
So she will die. Has it really been decided?

CREON:
Yes. By you and me. Now, no more delays.

572: The old manuscripts do not reliably tell us which character speaks which lines. In this case, modern editors are divided. Some think that Ismene speaks throughout the scene; others assign this line to Antigone. Sophocles does not elsewhere change speakers in mid-conversation; but in 573, Creon is more likely to be responding to Antigone than to Ismene, and in 577 he cannot be replying to Ismene. So the conversation is broken in any event. Besides, if any tragic character would break into a conversation, it would be Antigone.

The line does not imply sentimental love for Haemon so much as family-feeling; he is after all the sisters' cousin. On Antigone's love, see Introduction, pp. xxvii–xxviii.

574, 576: Some editors assign these lines to Ismene, some to the chorus, and some to Antigone.

577: "By you and me"—Who has joined Creon in condemning Antigone

Servants! Take them inside. They are women,
And they must not be free to roam about.
580   Even a brave man flees from Death
When he sees his life in immediate danger.

(Servants take Ismene and Antigone through the
great doors.)

Second Stasimon

CHORUS:

[Strophe *a*]

Happy are they that never taste of crime,
But once a house is shaken by the gods,
Then madness stalks the family without fail,
585   Disaster for many generations.
It is like a great salt wave
Kicked up by foul winds from Thrace,
It surges over the hellish depths of the sea,
Roils the bottom,
590   Churns up black sand,
And makes the screaming headlands howl
Against the gale.

---

to death? Not Ismene. The chorus support the decree at 211–4, and Antigone seems to accept her fate at 461–6; in a sense she has condemned herself by her actions. But only the elders of the chorus have the standing to ratify the ruler's decision.

582–625: Second Stasimon—See endnote. Creon, who is present throughout the ode, must assume that the chorus are singing about the ruin of Antigone and, consequently, of the house of Oedipus; but the chorus may have the entire royal family in mind, including Creon's branch of it. See Introduction, p. xxxiii, and Else (1976) on the charge of madness against Antigone.

582: "Happy are they that never taste of crime"—The word translated as "crime" could mean simply "trouble," but line 622 shows that the chorus are thinking of serious wrongdoing.

584–5: "Madness . . . disaster"—*atê.* The ode revolves around the double meaning of this one word—blindness or madness on the one hand, ruin or destruction on the other. In lines 614 and 625, I have rendered it "disaster."

[Antistrophe *a*]

I see grief falling from old days on Labdacus' family:
New grief heaped on the grief of those who died.
And nothing redeems the generation that is to come: 595
Some god is battering them without relief.
Now I see a saving light
Rising from the sole remaining roots
Of the house of Oedipus. But this, too, falls
In a bloody harvest,   600
Claimed by the dust
Of the Underworld gods, doomed by foolish words
And frenzied wits.

[Strophe *b*]

O Zeus! Who could ever curtail thy power?
Not a man, never—   605
No matter how far he oversteps his bounds—
Not sleep, that weakens everyone,
Not the untiring months of gods.
No, Zeus, you do not grow weak with time,
You who hold power in the luminous glow of Olympus.   610
And this will be the law,
Now and for time to come, as it was before:
Madness stalks mortals who are great,
Leaves no escape from disaster.

[Antistrophe *b*]

Beware of hope! Far-reaching, beguiling, a pleasure—   615
For a lot of men.
But a lot are fooled by a light-headed love,
And deception stalks those who know nothing
Until they set their feet in fire and burn.
Wisdom lies in the famous proverb: 620
"Those who judge that crime is good,

601: See endnote.

605: "Man"—The Greek word *anêr* picks out the male of the species more often than not; to mean "human being" Greek uses *anthrôpos* or one of several words for "mortal." Because of the importance of gender issues in the play, I have observed the distinction throughout this translation.

Are in the hands of a driving god
Who is leading them to madness."
Time is very short for them,
625   Leaves no escape from disaster.

(Enter Haemon through the stage right wing.)

CHORUS:
Now, here is Haemon, the last of your children.
Is he goaded here by anguish for Antigone,
Who should have been his bride?
Does he feel injured beyond measure?
630   Cheated out of marriage?

CREON:
We'll know the answer right away, better than prophets:
Tell me, son, did you hear the final verdict?
Against your fiancée? Did you come in anger at your father?
Or are we still friends, no matter what I do?

HAEMON:
635   I am yours, Father. You set me straight,
Give me good advice, and I will follow it.
No marriage will weigh more with me,
Than your good opinion.

CREON:
Splendid, my boy! Keep that always in your heart,
640   And stand behind fatherly advice on all counts.
Why does a man pray that he'll conceive a child,
Keep him at home, and have him listen to what he's told?
It's so the boy will punish his father's enemies
And reward his friends—as his father would.
645   But some men beget utterly useless offspring:
They have planted nothing but trouble for themselves,
And they're nothing but a joke to their enemies.

624–5: See endnote.

626: Haemon would have been played either by the actor who represented Antigone or by the one who represented Ismene.

635: "I am yours"—your what? friend, child, enemy? Haemon is ambiguous here as elsewhere in this scene, careful not to criticize his father directly until he has been goaded out of decency.

Now then, my boy, don't let pleasure cloud your mind,
Not because of a woman. You know very well:
You'll have a frigid squeeze between the sheets   650
If you shack up with a hostile woman. I'd rather have
A bleeding wound than a criminal in the family.
So spit her out. And because the girl's against us,
Send her down to marry somebody in Hades.
You know I caught her in the sight of all,   655
Alone of all our people, in open revolt.
And I will make my word good in Thebes—
By killing her. Who cares if she sings "Zeus!"
And calls him her protector? I must keep my kin in line.
Otherwise, folks outside the family will run wild.   660
The public knows that a man is just
Only if he is straight with his relatives.

So, if someone goes too far and breaks the law,
Or tries to tell his masters what to do,
He will have nothing but contempt from me.   665
But when the city takes a leader, you must obey,
Whether his commands are trivial, or right, or wrong.
And I have no doubt that such a man will rule well,
And, later, he will cheerfully be ruled by someone else.
In hard times he will stand firm with his spear   670
Waiting for orders, a good, law-abiding soldier.

But reject one man ruling another, and that's the worst.
Anarchy tears up a city, divides a home,
Defeats an alliance of spears.
But when people stay in line and obey,   675
Their lives and everything else are safe.
For this reason, order must be maintained,
And there must be no surrender to a woman.
No! If we fall, better a man should take us down.
Never say that a woman bested us!   680

663–71: See endnote.

669: "And, later, he will cheerfully be ruled by someone else"—Creon
had been appointed regent when the sons of Oedipus were young, but in
the recent battle he served under Eteoclês. See endnote to lines 663–71
for an alternative meaning.

CHORUS:
Unless old age has stolen my wits away,
Your speech was very wise. That's my belief.

HAEMON:
Father, the gods give good sense to every human being,
And that is absolutely the best thing we have.
685   But if what you said is not correct,
I have no idea how I could make the point.
Still, maybe someone else could work it out.

My natural duty's to look out for you, spot any risk
That someone might find fault with what you say or do.
690   The common man, you see, lives in terror of your frown;
690a   He'll never dare to speak up in broad daylight
And say anything you would hate to learn.
But I'm the one who hears what's said at night—
How the entire city is grieving over this girl.
No woman has ever had a fate that's so unfair
695   (They say), when what she did deserves honor and fame.
She saved her very own brother after he died,
Murderously, from being devoured by flesh-eating dogs
And pecked apart by vultures as he lay unburied.
For this, hasn't she earned glory bright as gold?
700   This sort of talk moves against you, quietly, at night.

And for me, Father, your continued good fortune
Is the best reward that I could ever have.
No child could win a greater prize than his father's fame,
No father could want more than abundant success—

---

683 ff.: Haemon's speech is carefully worded; he guards himself, by means of a series of ambiguities, from openly criticizing his father's judgment.

687: Although Haemon modestly implies that he is not capable of refuting his father, he also suggests that his father might be refutable. See endnote on this and on the next two lines for alternative readings.

690a: A line has apparently dropped out of the manuscripts; I have supplied this one to suit the context, against the advice of Lloyd-Jones and Wilson (LJW).

693: "The entire city is grieving"—If so, Antigone has not heard about it (see lines 847, 881–2). Haemon may be too far gone in love to be a credible witness, but his claim that common people are afraid to speak to Creon is corroborated by the Watchman's scenes.

From his son.

　　　　And now, don't always cling to the same anger,　705
Don't keep saying that this, and nothing else, is right.
If a man believes that he alone has a sound mind,
And no one else can speak or think as well as he does,
Then, when people study him, they'll find an empty book.
But a wise man can learn a lot and never be ashamed;　710
He knows he does not have to be rigid and close-hauled.
You've seen trees tossed by a torrent in a flash flood:
If they bend, they're saved, and every twig survives,
But if they stiffen up, they're washed out from the roots.
It's the same in a boat: if a sailor keeps the footline taut,　715
If he doesn't give an inch, he'll capsize, and then—
He'll be sailing home with his benches down and his hull
　　to the sky.
So ease off, relax, stop being angry, make a change.
I know I'm younger, but I may still have good ideas;
And I say that the oldest idea, and the best,　720
Is for one man to be born complete, knowing everything.
Otherwise—and it usually does turn out otherwise—
It's good to learn from anyone who speaks well.

CHORUS:
Sir, you should learn from him, if he is on the mark. And you,
Haemon, learn from your father. Both sides spoke well.　725

CREON: *(To the chorus.)*
Do you really think, at our age,
We should be taught by a boy like him?

HAEMON:
No. Not if I am in the wrong. I admit I'm young;

715: A footline is the rope that runs from the foot of the sail, equivalent to what today's sailors call a sheet. Easing the sheet can save a boat from capsizing in a sudden gust of wind.

720–1: "The oldest idea" —The Greek word suggests precedence in rank in a way that would appeal to a conservative like Creon. Contrast this with Haemon's earlier and more democratic idea that every human being is endowed by nature with good sense (683), where "human beings" contrasts with "the man" at 721 and "good sense" (*phrenes*, intelligence) contrasts with "knowing everything." See endnote for an alternative reading.

That's why you should look at what I do, not my age.

CREON:
730 So "what you do" is show respect for breaking ranks?

HAEMON:
I'd never urge you to show respect for a criminal.

CREON:
So you don't think this girl has been infected with crime?

HAEMON:
No. The people of Thebes deny it, all of them.

CREON:
So you think the people should tell me what orders to give?

HAEMON:
735 Now who's talking like he's wet behind the ears?

CREON:
So I should rule this country for someone other than myself?

HAEMON:
A place for one man alone is not a city.

CREON:
A city belongs to its master. Isn't that the rule?

HAEMON:
Then go be ruler of a desert, all alone. You'd do it well.

CREON: *(To the chorus.)*
740 It turns out this boy is fighting for the woman's cause.

HAEMON:
Only if *you* are a woman. All I care about is you!

CREON:
This is intolerable! You are accusing your own father.

HAEMON:
Because I see you going wrong. Because justice matters!

CREON:
Is that wrong, showing respect for my job as leader?

744–5: Haemon holds that the respect Creon demands as leader cannot be separated from the wider virtue of reverence. By "the rights (or honors)

HAEMON:

You have no respect at all if you trample on the rights of gods!   745

CREON:

What a sick mind you have: You submit to a woman!

HAEMON:

No. You'll never catch me giving in to what's shameful.

CREON:

But everything you say, at least, is on her side.

HAEMON:

And on your side! And mine! And the gods' below!

CREON:

There is no way you'll marry her, not while she's still alive.   750

HAEMON:

Then she'll die, and her death will destroy Someone Else.

CREON:

Is that a threat? Are you brash enough to attack me?

HAEMON:

What threat? All I'm saying is, you haven't thought this through.

CREON:

I'll make you wish you'd never had a thought in your empty head!

HAEMON:

If you weren't my father I'd say you were out of your mind.   755

CREON:

Don't beat around the bush. You're a woman's toy, a slave.

HAEMON:

Talk, talk, talk! Why don't you ever want to listen?

CREON:

Really? Listen, you are not going on like this. By all the gods,
One more insult from you, and the fun is over.

---

of the gods," Haemon means that Creon wants to deprive Hades of the dead man who belongs to them.

753: See endnote for an alternative reading.

(To attendants.)

760   Bring out that hated thing. I want her to die right here,
       Right now, so her bridegroom can watch the whole thing.

HAEMON:
       Not me. Never. No matter what you think.
       She is not going to die while I am near her.
       And you will never, ever see my face again. Go on,
765   Be crazy! Perhaps some of your friends will stay by you.

       (Exit Haemon through the stage left wing.)

CHORUS:
       Sir, the man has gone. He is swift to anger;
       Pain lies heavily on a youthful mind.

CREON:
       Let him go, him and his lofty ambitions! Good riddance!
       But those two girls shall not escape their fate.

CHORUS:
770   Are you really planning to kill *both* of them?

CREON:
       Not the one who never touched the crime. You're right.

CHORUS:
       By what means will you have the other one killed?

CREON:
       I'll take her off the beaten track, where no one's around,
       And I'll bury her alive underground, in a grave of stone.
775   I'll leave her only as much food as religious law prescribes,
       So that the city will not be cursed for homicide.

       Let her pray to Hades down there; he's the only god
       That she respects. Maybe she'll arrange for him to save her life;
       Maybe she'll learn, at last, that she's wasting her time
780   Showing respect for whatever's in Hades.

       (Exit Creon through the great doors.)

780: What does Creon do during the choral passage that follows? Probably
he goes offstage to give detailed orders for Antigone's execution. Some
editors, however, would have him remain backstage or in the wings.

Third Stasimon

CHORUS:

[Strophe]

In battle the victory goes to Love;
Prizes and properties fall to Love.
Love dallies the night
On a girl's soft cheeks,
Ranges across the sea,   785
Lodges in wild meadows.
O Love, no one can hide from you:
You take gods who live forever,
You take humans who die in a day,
And they take you and go mad.   790

[Antistrophe]

Destroyer Love, you seize a good mind,
And pervert it to wickedness:
This fight is your doing,
This uproar in the family.
And the winner will be desire,   795
Shining in the eyes of a bride,
An invitation to bed,
A power to sweep across the bounds of what is Right.
For we are only toys in your hands,
Divine, unbeatable Aphrodite!   800

Kommos

*(Enter Antigone under guard through the great
doors.)*

CHORUS:
Now I, too, am swept away,
Out of bounds, when I see this.
I cannot contain the surge of tears:

798: See endnote for an alternative reading.

801: "I, too"—The chorus find themselves carried away by forbidden
feelings, as they say happened earlier to Haemon.

For now I see Antigone, soon to gain
805   The marriage bed where everyone must sleep.

ANTIGONE:
See how I walk the last road,
You who belong to my city,
How I fill my eyes with the last
Shining of the sun.
810   There's no return: I follow death, alive,
To the brink of Acheron,
Where He gives rest to all.
No marriage hymns for me.
No one sounds
815   A wedding march:
I will be the bride of Acheron.

CHORUS:
But won't you have hymns of praise?
So much glory attends you
As you pass into the deep place of the dead.
820   For you are not wasted by disease, not maimed by a
          sword.
But true to your own laws, you are the only one,
Of mortals, who'll go down to Hades while still alive.

ANTIGONE:
No. I hear Niobe was lost in utmost misery—
Daughter of Tantalus, visitor in Thebes,
825   Wasted on a Phrygian mountain.

816: Acheron—a river in the Underworld.

821: "But true to your own laws"—The Greek is *autonomos*, rendered by some scholars as "of your own will"; but the word means more than that in ancient Greek, and the root word "law" (*nomos*) is clearly heard. See Introduction, p. xxvii on Antigone's law.

822: "While still alive"—The chorus mean that she will be entombed while still alive.

823–38: Niobe—Antigone misunderstands the chorus to be saying that she will live forever underground and cites the case of Niobe, who was entombed alive and then turned to stone. Niobe had many children and boasted of them by comparison with Leto, who had only two children, Artemis and Apollo. For this she was punished by seeing her children die of disease.

Rock sprouted up around her, firm,
Erect as shoots of ivy,
And it subdued her. So men say.
Rain and snow pelted her
Without a break, and she melted away,
Dripping from her mournful brows,   830
Tears streaming down her flanks.
It's the same for me, exactly:
Something divine lays me to sleep.

CHORUS:
Really! Niobe was a god; she had a god for a father.
We are mortal, and our fathers pass away.   835
But you—when you die, you will be great,
You will be equal in memory to the gods,
By the glory of your life and death.

ANTIGONE:
You're laughing at me.
For the gods' sake, why now?   840
You could have waited till I'm gone.
But now you make insults to my face,
You grasping, rich old men! What a city you have!
I call on the rising of rivers in Thebes
And on the great chariot-reaches of the plain.   845
The rivers and the plain are on my side, at least.
They'll testify that no friends wept for me,
That the laws of Thebes sent me to prison
In a rock-hollowed tomb.
They see how unusual and cruel this is.   850
But I have no place with human beings,
Living or dead. No city is home to me.

CHORUS:
You've gone too far! You are extreme, impetuous.
My child, you caught your foot and fell
When you tried to climb against high justice.   855
This is your father's legacy—pain and punishment.

ANTIGONE:
Now you raise the agony that hurts my mind the most:
Grief for my father,
Like raw earth plowed three times,

860   Grief for the whole huge disaster of *us*,
        Our brilliant family,
        Labdacus' descendants.
        I weep for the ruin in my mother's bed,
        The sexual intercourse and the incest
865   My father had with our mother.
        Ill-fated parents make a miserable child.
        I am going to them now,
        Unholy and unmarried, to lodge with them.
        Oh, my brother, you were married once,
870   But what a disaster it was:
        Your death snuffed out my life.

CHORUS:
        You have one kind of reverence.
        But a man whose job it is to rule
        Will never let you trample on his power.
875   You chose anger, and anger destroyed you.

ANTIGONE:
        No tears for me, no friends, no wedding hymns.
        They are taking me away
        In misery by the road before me,
        Now and forever forbidden to see
880   This blessed eye of light.
        No friends cry for me,
        No one is mourning.

            (*Enter Creon with his attendants through the
            great doors.*)

CREON:
        Singing and wailing? They would never end
        Before death, if they made any difference.
885   Take her away immediately. And when she's locked up,
        In the embrace of her covered tomb—exactly as I said—
        Leave her alone, deserted. Let her die if she wants,
        Or else live there in her grave, if she feels at home there.
        We wash our hands of this girl. But either way,
890   Her permit to reside above the earth is canceled.

869: "You were married once"—Polynices married the daughter of the
king of Argos, and Argos provided the army that attacked Thebes.

ANTIGONE:
My tomb, my marriage, my hollow, scraped in dirt,
I'm coming home forever, to be held in
With my own people, most of them dead now,
And gone where Persephone welcomes them.
I am the last of them that will go under, and my death—   895
It is the worst by far—so much before my time.
As I leave, even so, I feed this one strong hope:
That I will have a loving welcome from my father,
More love from you, my mother, and then, love
From you, dear heart, my brother. When you died,   900
I took you up, all three, and laid you out,
And poured libations at your graves.
And, Polynices, look: This is my reward
For taking care of you. I was right, but wisdom knows
I would not do it for a child, were I a mother,   905
Not for a husband either. Let them lie, putrefied, dead;
I would not defy the city at such cost for their sake.

What law can I claim on my side for this choice?
I may have another husband if the first should die
And get another child from a new man if I'm a widow.   910
But my mother and my father lie in the land of death,
And there is no ground to grow a brother for me now.
That is the law I followed when I made you first in honor,
Even though Creon thought I did a terrible thing,
A rash and sinful crime, dear heart, my brother.   915
Now he has taken me by force, he is driving me down
Unmarried. I've had no man, no wedding celebration,
Shared nothing with a husband, never raised a child.
My friends and family have abandoned me in misery,
And I am going—alive—to the scraped hollow of the dead.   920
What have I ever done against divine justice?
How can I expect a god to help me in my misery?
To whom should I pray now? Do you see?
They are counting all my reverence to be
Irreverence. If the gods really agree with this,   925
Then suffering should teach me to repent my sin.

904–20: See endnote.

But if the sin belongs to those who condemned me,
I hope they suffer every bit as I do now.

CHORUS:
Still she is tossed by gusts of wind;
930   They tear through her soul as strongly as before.

CREON:
Listen, it's the guards who will weep
If they don't get a move on now.

ANTIGONE (or CHORUS): *(With a cry of pain.)*
That word—
It's almost death itself!

CREON:
935   I have no hope to give.
The death sentence stands.

ANTIGONE:
City of my fathers, Thebes!
Gods of my people!
They are taking me against my will.
940   Look at me, O you lords of Thebes:
I am the last remnant of kings.
Look what these wretched men are doing to me,
For my pure reverence!

Fourth Stasimon

CHORUS: *(To Antigone.)*

[Strophe *a*]

Courage! Danaë, too, endured
945   The exchange of heavenly light
For a bronze-bolted prison.
And there she was kept down
Secretly in a bedroom tomb.

944–50: Danaë's father locked her away from men because of an oracle warning him against any son she might bear. But Zeus visited her in a shower of gold, and they conceived a child, Perseus.

947: "Kept down"—yoke motif, cf. line 955.

She was of noble birth, too, my daughter, O my daughter,
And Zeus trusted her to mind his golden-rainfall child.   950
    Fate has a terrible power
    That nothing escapes, not wealth,
    Not warfare, not a fortress tower,
    Not even black ships beating against the sea.

[Antistrophe *a*]

Another case: Lycurgus was kept down,   955
And he was a king in Thrace.
But because of his angry jeering,
Dionysus had him jailed in a cell of rock,
And there the terrible flood-force
Of his madness trickled away, drop by drop, until he learned,   960
At last, that it was a god he had stung in his madness
    With those jeering insults.
    For he tried to quench the holy fire,
    Reined in the god-filled women,
    And drove flute-loving Muses into a rage.   965

[Strophe *b*]

At the Black Waters,
    Where a thrust of land divides the Bosporus from the Sea,

---

955–65: Lycurgus had tried to suppress the worship of Dionysus, which involved ecstatic rituals. In some versions of the story, he went mad and killed his son before being imprisoned.

958: Dionysus was believed by the ancient Greeks to have brought his worship to Greece from Asia, along with the practice of making wine. See Euripides' play, the *Bacchae*.

964: "God-filled women"—These women, variously called Maenads, Bacchae, and bacchants, are women who worship Dionysus through ecstatic dance and song in the mountains, away from their homes. "God-filled" means "inspired."

965: "Flute-loving Muses"—The *aulos*, usually translated "flute," was a reed instrument; its music was considered to be the most exciting in ancient Greece.

966–87: Phineus, a king in Thrace (northern Greece), had two sons by his first wife, Cleopatra (no relation to the famous queen of Egypt). This Cleopatra was the daughter of an Athenian princess who had been stolen by Boreas, the North Wind, to be his bride. Cleopatra's sons were

Lies a city of Thrace known as Salmydéssus.
War god Ares was hard by and saw the curséd blows
970 When Phineus' two sons were blinded by the beast
   He called a wife. Darkness came
   Over the disks that had been eyes,
   That would have looked for vengeance
   To gashing hands, stained in blood,
975   Shuttles torn from the loom
   And used as knives.

[Antistrophe *b*]

The boys melted away
In misery, mourning their own sad fate
And their mother's, for her marriage was hateful
980 Although she was born to be a queen of the ancient line,
Royal in Athens, and she was raised in distant caves
   Where her father's tempests blew.
   For he was North Wind, Boreas,
   And she was a child of gods,
985   Swift as horses on a rocky slope.
   But the eternal Fates kept after her,
   Her too, O my daughter.

(As the chorus bring their ode to an end, the attendants lead Antigone out through the stage left wing. Enter Tiresias, led by a boy, through the stage right wing.)

TIRESIAS: *(To the chorus, indicating the boy who guides him.)*
  Gentlemen of Thebes, we two have come by the same path;

---

blinded by their stepmother after Phineus had imprisoned their mother and taken a new wife. The audience, probably knowing about the imprisonment of the mother, would have seen the analogy with the fate of Antigone.

966: "Black Waters"—The manuscripts are unclear. The phrase may refer to the Black Sea or the two Dark Islands at the mouth of the Bosporus.

973: "Vengeance"—Had the boys not been blinded, they would have avenged the crime against their mother.

980: "Born to be a queen"—Here we follow the text as corrected by LJW.

988: Tiresias announces his own arrival. Unlike the previous entrances, this one is unexpected by both Creon and the chorus. During the fourth

He alone has eyesight, and we both see by this:
A blind man takes the way his guide directs.   990

CREON:
Why, old Tiresias! What brings you here?

TIRESIAS:
I will speak: I am the soothsayer, and you will learn.

CREON:
Well, I never have rejected your advice.

TIRESIAS:
That is how you've been steering the city straight.

CREON:
Yes, I know firsthand how helpful you are, and I can testify.   995

TIRESIAS:
Then know this: Once again, your fate stands on a knife-edge.

CREON:
What is it? Your voice puts my hair on end!

TIRESIAS:
                                        You'll see.
Listen to what I have read from the signs of my art.
I took my seat, the ancient seat for seeing omens—
Where all the birds that tell the future come to rest—   1000
And I heard a voice I've never known from a bird:
Wild screeching, enraged, utterly meaningless.
But the thrashing of their wings told me the truth:
They were clawing each other to death with their talons.
I was frightened. Immediately, I tried burnt sacrifice.   1005
The altar had been blazing high, but not one spark
Caught fire in my offerings. The embers went out.
Juice was oozing and dripping from thighbones,

---

stasimon, Creon has evidently remained on stage, but without paying close attention to the chorus.

999: "I took my seat"—Tiresias read the omens of the birds from a seat in a sacred spot.

1005: "Burnt sacrifice"—Ancient Greeks offered thighbones wrapped in fat to the gods, along with other inedible parts of a cow or sheep, by burning these parts on an altar.

Spitting and sputtering in clouds of smoke.
1010 Bladders were bursting open, spraying bile into the sky;
Wrappings of fat fell away from soggy bones.

And so the ritual failed; I had no omens to read.
I learned this from the boy who is my guide,
As I am the guide for others. Now, it was *your* idea
1015 That brought this plague down on our city.
Every single altar, every hearth we have,
Is glutted with dead meat from Oedipus' child,
Who died so badly. Birds and dogs gnawed him to bits
That is why the gods no longer hear our prayers,
1020 Reject our sacrifice of flaming thighbones. And that is why
The birds keep back their shrill message-bearing cries:
Because they have fed on a dead man's glistening blood.

Take thought, my son, on all these things:
It's common knowledge, any human being can go wrong.
1025 But even when he does, a man may still succeed:
He may have his share of luck and good advice
But only if he's willing to bend and find a cure
For the trouble he's caused. It's only being stubborn
Proves you're a fool.

So, now, surrender to the dead man.
1030 Stop stabbing away at his corpse. Will it prove your strength
If you kill him again? Listen, my advice is for your benefit.
Learning from good words is sweet when they bring you
gain.

CREON:
I hear you, old man: You people keep shooting arrows at me
Like marksmen at a target. Do you think I don't know?
1035 I have a lot of experience with soothsayers. Your whole tribe
Has made market of me from the start. "Benefit"? "Gain"?
If you want to turn a profit, speculate in gold from India
Or go trade with Sardis for electrum and traffic in that.

1019–23: See lines 1042–4, with note.

1038: Electrum is an alloy of gold and silver made in Sardis, the city
where Croesus, famous for his wealth, had ruled in the sixth century.

You'll never put that man down in a grave,
Not even if eagles snatched morsels of his dead flesh   1040
And carried them up to the very throne of Zeus.
I won't shrink from that. And don't you call it "pollution"
Or tell me I have to bury him to fend off miasma—
Surely no human power could pollute a god.

You're terribly clever, old man, but listen to me: 1045
Clever people tend to stumble into shameful traps
When they make a wicked speech sound good
For their personal gain.

TIRESIAS:
                        This is very sad:
Does any human being know, or even question . . .

CREON: *(Interrupting.)*
What's this? More of your great "common knowledge"?

TIRESIAS:
How powerful good judgment is, compared to wealth.   1050

CREON:
Exactly. And no harm compares with heedlessness.

TIRESIAS:
Which runs through you like the plague.

CREON:
I have no desire to trade insults with a soothsayer.

TIRESIAS:
But you're doing it. You implied that I make false prophecies.

CREON:
Prophecies? All your tribe wants to make is money.   1055

TIRESIAS:
And what about tyrants? Filthy lucre is all you want!

1042–4: Pollution, miasma—Either an unburied corpse or an unavenged murder was thought to infect the land with *miasma*, pollution. Creon dismisses this on rational grounds.

1045: "Terribly clever"—The Greek word *deinos* carries both positive and negative meanings. See line 332, with note.

CREON:
Remember, you are speaking about your commander-in-chief.

TIRESIAS:
I haven't forgotten. It was by my powers that you saved
the city.

CREON:
Cunning soothsayer! Yes, but you'd rather do what's wrong.

TIRESIAS:
1060 You are provoking me. I have a secret we have not touched.

CREON:
Well, touch it then. But do not speak as you've been paid
to do.

TIRESIAS:
Do you really think that's why I've spoken out?

CREON:
You'll never collect your fee; I'm not changing *my* mind.

TIRESIAS:
So be it. But you must know this and know it well:
1065 You'll hardly see the sun race around its course
Before you'll make a trade with your own boy's corpse—
Your only child, born from your guts, traded for corpses.

You took one who dwells above and tossed her below,
You rejected a living soul and peopled a tomb with her.
1070 And you took one who belongs down there and kept him
here,
Untouched by gods, unburied, unholy, a corpse exposed.
The dead are no business of yours; not even the gods above
Own any part of them. You've committed violence against
them.
For this, an ambush awaits you—slow, crippling avengers,
1075 Furies sent by Hades and the gods above.
You will be tangled in the net of your own crimes.

1067: See line 626. Haemon is Creon's last surviving child.
1075: Furies—avenging spirits.

Now look carefully: Have I been paid to speak out?
No. The passage of a little time will prove the point;
Men and women will be wailing over death in your family.
And all the cities of our enemies are in a rage   1080
For their dead, whose funeral rites were held by dogs
Or wild beasts or vultures, and for the stench of bodies
Carried by birds to defile their hearths at home.

These are my arrows. You stung me, and I let fly,
In my anger, like a marksman aiming for your heart.   1085
And I never miss. You can't outrun the pain.

    (To his guide.)

Take us home, boy.
Let him vent his anger on younger men;
May he learn to cultivate a gentler tongue
And a mind more cogent than he has shown today.   1090

    *(Exit Tiresias led by the boy through the stage
    right wing.)*

CHORUS:
The man is gone, sir. His prophecies were amazing,
Terrible. Ever since my hair turned white
I'm quite certain he has never sung a prophecy,
Not once, that turned out to be false for the city.

CREON:
I know that, too. My mind is shaken.   1095
Giving in would be terrible.
But standing firm invites disaster!

CHORUS:
Good judgment is essential, Creon. Take advice.

CREON:
What should I do? Show me. I'll do what you say.

1080–3: These lines refer to the tradition, not otherwise mentioned in this
play, that Creon left not just Polynices but all the enemy troops unburied.
See Introduction, p. xix. (Some editors reject these lines as spurious in
order to maintain the consistency of the play.)

1091–2: "His prophecies were amazing, terrible"—same double-edged
word (*deinos*) as in line 1045, here translated as "amazing, terrible."

CHORUS:

1100   Let the girl go. Free her from underground.
       And build a tomb for the boy who lies exposed.

CREON:

       Really? You think I should give in?

CHORUS:

       As quickly as you can, sir, before you're cut off.
       The gods send Harm racing after wicked fools.

CREON:

1105   It's so painful to pull back; it goes against my heart.
       But I cannot fight against necessity.

CHORUS:

       Go and do this *now*. Don't send others in your place.

CREON:

       I'll go immediately. Come on, come on, everyone,
       Wherever you are, grab a pick and shovel,
1110   Hurry up! Get over to the place you see.
       It's up to me, now my mind has changed.
       I put her away, I must be there to release her.
       I'm afraid it is best to obey the laws,
       Just as tradition has them, all one's life.

          (Exit Creon, with his attendants, through the stage left wing.)

CHORUS:

Fifth Stasimon

[Strophe *a*]

1115   God of many names,
       Glorious child of Thebes,
       Whose mother was bride

1115: "God of many names"—Dionysus is known by a number of names, including the ones the chorus use here, "Bacchus" and "Iacchus."

1117: The line refers to the mother of Bacchus. Semélê was a princess of Thebes who became pregnant with Dionysus, after being visited by Zeus, and gave birth to the infant god when Zeus struck her with thunder.

To Zeus' deep thunder!
It is you who guard the fame of Italy,
You who look after the embrace, at Eleusis,   1120
Of Demeter, all-welcoming goddess.
O Bacchus, your home is Thebes,
Thebes, the mother of Maenads,
Where River Ismenus gently flows,
And the fierce dragon-teeth were planted.   1125

[Antistrophe *a*]

Torches flash through smoke,
Catch sight of you at Delphi
High above the twin-peaked crag.
The Castalian Stream has seen you
By nymphs of the cave who dance for Bacchus.   1130
The Nysaean Mountains know you, too,
The ivy-covered shores, the coasts,
The green tangles of grapevines.
They are sending you to Thebes: Watch over us,
Hear our sacred hymns that sound for you.   1135

[Strophe *b*]

You hold Thebes in honor
Above all cities;
Your mother, too,
Thunderstruck woman.

1119: Italy—Dionysus was evidently honored in the Greek cities of southern Italy.

1123: "Maenads"—See the note on line 964.

1124–5: The Ismenus flows through Thebes. According to legend, Cadmus founded Thebes by killing a dragon and planting its teeth as seeds; where he planted them, the warriors of Thebes sprouted from the earth.

1127: Delphi—Though sacred mainly to Apollo, Delphi was also a principal site for the worship of Dionysus.

1129: The Castalian Stream flows from a sacred spring at Delphi.

1130: Nymphs were minor divinities believed to inhabit caves and other special places.

1131: Nysaean Mountains—probably refers to mountains on the long island of Euboea, separated from Attica by a narrow strait.

1140   And now we pray: Watch over us:
        The violence of plague
        Strikes all our people.
        Come, your presence is healing.
        Soar above Parnassus
1145   Or cross the howling straits of the sea.

                    [Antistrophe *b*]

        O Leader in the dance of stars,
        That circle across the night,
        Breathing fire,
        O shepherd of dark voices,
1150   Child of Zeus, let us see you now.
        Come, O Lord, with your throng of Maenads
        Iacchus, steward of joy,
        Grant them ecstasy
        To dance all night for you.

        (*Enter Messenger through the stage left wing.*)

MESSENGER:
1155   Listen, all you neighbors of Cadmus' family:
        The course of our lives never stops; it runs past good
        Or ill. I'll never declare success or failure for anyone.
        It's only chance that keeps your boat upright,
        And chance that sinks you—good luck or bad is all you have.
1160   Soothsayers give no guarantees for human lives.
        This Creon—you know, I used to envy him.
        He saved the land of Cadmus from its enemies
        And took command as the only ruler of this ground.
        He set us straight, and he set his house abloom
1165   With well-born sons. Now all of that is gone.
        When every source of joy deserts a man,
        I don't call him alive: he's an animated corpse.
        For my money, you can get as rich as you want,
        You can wear the face of a tyrant,

1143: "Come, your presence is healing"—A more literal version would
be "Come on cleansing foot." The chorus mean that Dionysus' presence
would purify Thebes and so save its people from the plague.
1144: Parnassus is the high mountain dividing Thebes from Delphi.

But if you have no joy in this,   1170
Your life's not worth the shadow of a puff of smoke.

CHORUS:
What's this new grief that weighs on the king's family?

MESSENGER:
Death. And the living are to blame for it.

CHORUS:
Who's the killer? Who's the victim? Speak up!

MESSENGER:
Haemon is dead, killed by his own flesh and blood.   1175

CHORUS:
What! His father? Some other relative?

MESSENGER:
He killed himself, in a rage with his father, for her death.

CHORUS:
That soothsayer! He had it right.

MESSENGER:
Those are the facts; the judgment is up to you.

(Enter Eurydice through the great doors.)

CHORUS:
Wait, I see her coming, Creon's wife.   1180
Poor Eurydice, has she heard about her son?
Or did she leave her home by chance?

EURYDICE:
Tell me, men of the city—I caught what you said
As I was about to leave the house
To pray for help to the goddess Athena.   1185
I was just sliding the bolt to unlock the door
When word of disaster in the family struck my ears.
I fell back into my servants' arms,
Terrified out of my mind.
Please tell me again. What happened?   1190
Speak freely. I am quite used to hearing bad news.

MESSENGER:
I will, beloved queen. I was *there*,

And I'll tell you everything, the whole truth.
No point taking off the rough edges;
1195   You'd soon find out I was lying. Truth's right,
Always.
                    Well, I went with your husband as his guide
To the upper field where the body was lying,
What was left of Polynices—cruel!—torn by dogs.
First we prayed to the goddess of passageways,
1200   Pluto also, and we begged that their good will attend us.
Then we performed the sacred cleansing of the corpse,
Gathered up the pieces we could find,
Burned them over fresh-cut boughs,
And heaped up the earth into a tomb,
A high-crested home for him.
1205   Then we went for the girl,
Toward her deadly marriage bed, blanketed with rocks.
There was a voice—you could hear it from far off—
It sliced through you, wailing around that unsanctified
        tomb.
One of us got Creon to listen. He crept forward; cries
        of misery
1210   Welled up around him, wordless, without meaning.
Suddenly he let out a groan of utter despair—
"Oh no! Now *I* am reading signs: Could this be the path?
The one that leads me to the worst disaster of my life?
My son! My son's voice! Neighbors, be quick, please help.
1215   On the tomb, look, that gap in the mound—
Stones ripped out—can you slip in through those jaws?
Tell me if I am right, that it *is* Haemon,
Unless the gods have robbed me of my mind."

That was the order our master gave, his courage gone.
1220   We looked. In the last depth of the tomb,
She was there, we saw her hanging by the neck
On a noose she'd twisted from her own fine clothes.

_____

1199–1200: Hecate, goddess of passageways (including the one to the Underworld), was honored along roads, especially at intersections. Pluto, also called Hades, is god of the Underworld.

1212: "Now *I* am reading signs"—Creon has taken on the role of Tiresias by finding meanings in inarticulate cries.

He was there, too, tumbled around her, hugging her waist,
Grieving for his marriage lost, gone under—
His father's doing—as he, in misery, kissed his bride.   1225
When Creon saw them, he gave a horrible cry
And came up to them. He was in tears, sobbing:
"Poor soul," he said, "how could you do this?
What were you thinking? Had you lost your mind?
O my child, come out, please, I beg you on my knees."   1230
The boy did not answer. His eyes were fierce.
He fixed them on his father, then spat in his face
And drew his two-edged sword. The father darted back,
Dodged the blow. Thwarted, the angry boy
Turned against himself. He took his blade   1235
And leaned on it, drove it half through his lungs.
Then, still conscious, he pulled the girl into the curve
Of his sagging embrace. He gasped and panted,
Spattered blood on her white cheek, a spurt of scarlet.
Then he was dead. His body lay with hers;   1240
They'd brought their marriage off at last in the house
    of Death—
Which proves the point: In a human life,
It's deadly for bad judgment to embrace a man.

(Exit Eurydice through the great doors.)

CHORUS:
What could it mean? The woman's gone inside.
She did not stay for a word, good or bad.   1245

MESSENGER:
I'm astonished, like you. But I feed on hope. Probably,
When she heard her son was dead, she chose to mourn
    indoors,
Rather than make a public display of grief.
She'll have her servants join in the lament.
She's always planned ahead, to avoid mistakes.   1250

1227: "And came up to them"—The manuscripts read "came up to him."
Some editors prefer "came up to her" so that Creon's first two lines can
be understood as spoken to Antigone's corpse. But Creon may well be
using those lines to address Haemon for his desperate breaking into the
tomb. I have chosen "them" in order to preserve the ambiguity. Let the
reader choose.

CHORUS:
  I don't know. If you ask me, a silence so extreme
  Is as dangerous as a flood of silly tears.

MESSENGER:
  We'll know soon enough if she's holding something in,
  And hiding it secretly in a seething heart.
1255 I'm going into the house. You may be right:
  Silence, when extreme, is dangerous.

  *(Exit Messenger through the great doors. Creon
  enters through the stage left wing; assisted by his
  attendants, he is carrying the body of Haemon.)*

CHORUS:
  Now here is the king himself. He carries in his arms
  A Reminder (I hope I'm right to be blunt)
  Pointing clearly to the madness that destroys,
1260 And it's no one else's but his own. The sin was his.

[Strophe *a*]

CREON:
  Oh, howl for the sins of a stubborn mind,
  Evil-minded, death-dealing! O you who are witnesses,
  You saw those who killed and those who died,
  All in one family,
1265 Cry out against the sacrilege that I called strategy!
  Oh, howl, my son, my young son, for your young death.
  Ah! Ah!
  You were expelled from life
  By my bad judgment, never yours.

CHORUS:
1270 Yes, it is late, but you have seen where justice lies.

[Strophe *b*]

CREON:
  Oh yes:
  I have learned, and it is misery.
  Some god leapt full force onto my head

1259: "Madness that destroys"—*atê*. See note on lines 584–5.

And steered me onto a wild path, shaking my reins,
And I have trampled joy with sharp hooves.   1275
Oh weep, weep for the pain of human pain!

(Enter Messenger through the great doors.)

MESSENGER:
You have so many troubles, master, troubles in hand—
You carry them yourself. And troubles at home—
You'll see them for yourself, soon enough, when you arrive.   1280

CREON:
What, after this, could be worse?

MESSENGER:
Your wife is dead, poor woman.
Fresh-killed, a mother to match this dead boy.

[Antistrophe a]

CREON:
Howl, howl! O Death, refuge that cannot be appeased,
Why me? Why me, Destroyer?

(To the Messenger.)

And you,   1285
What is this noise you're making? Your horrible message?
It is only grief.
I was a man in ruins, and you crushed me again.
Speak to me, my son, tell me, is there more killing?
Ah! Ah!   1290
Is it a woman's sacrifice,
Her death piled on yours?

(The great doors open, and Eurydice's body is brought
out or revealed.)

CHORUS (or MESSENGER):
Look, she is here, brought out from the inner rooms.

[Antistrophe b]

CREON:
Oh yes:
Here's the second disaster for my misery to see.   1295

What could be worse? Does fate have more for me?
A moment ago, I took my dead son in my arms.
Now I see her face to face—my wife. And she is dead.
Oh weep, weep for the mother in torment, weep for the child.

MESSENGER:
1300 She died at the altar.
A sharp sword-thrust brought darkness to her eyes,
But first she grieved over Megareus, dead before his
  wedding,
And then over Haemon.
Last of all she called out to you,
1305 "These are your crimes, Childkiller!"

[Strophe *c*]

CREON:
Ah! Ah!
I am on wings of fear.
Take a sharp sword, someone.
Why don't you kill me now?
1310 My misery is so huge,
I am dissolved in misery.

MESSENGER:
Yes, she brought this charge against you as she died:
"You're to blame for his death, and the other boy's, too."

CREON:
Tell me, how was she killed?

MESSENGER:
1315 Stabbed in the guts by her own hand,
As soon as she heard what horrors came over her boy.

[Strophe *d*]

CREON:
The grief is mine, all mine.
I'll never pin the blame on anyone else that's human.

1302: Megareus—Haemon's only brother, son of Creon and Eurydice.
The audience probably knew that Megareus had been sacrificed earlier
to ensure victory over Argos.

I was the one, I killed you, poor child.
I did it. It is all true. 1320
Now, my neighbors,
Please take me away,
Take me quickly.
I must not be underfoot;
I am worth less than a nobody. 1325

CHORUS:
A worthy request—if there's any value in suffering.
Shortest way is strongest way when trouble's afoot.

[Antistrophe *c*]

CREON:
Let it come! Let it come!
I look for the light
Of my last day. 1330
My ultimate fate
Oh, let it come
I never want to face another day!

CHORUS:
That lies in the future. Our duty is for the present.
Leave your death to the Ones whose concern it is. 1335

CREON:
But that's what I long for. I prayed for that.

CHORUS:
Then don't pray at all.
A mortal has no escape from fate.

[Antistrophe *d*]

CREON: *(Praying.)*
Please take this useless man,
Put him out of your way. He killed you, my child, 1340
Though that is not what he wished.
And you, too, my wife.

What a miserable wretch I am!
Never to see them again!
On whom can I lean? 1345

Everything I touch turns against me,
My head bows to the fate that has leapt on it.

CHORUS:
Wisdom is supreme for a blesséd life,
And reverence for the gods
1350   Must never cease.
Great words, sprung from arrogance,
Are punished by great blows.
So it is one learns, in old age, to be wise.

–END–

1348: "Wisdom is supreme for a blesséd life"—*Phronein* (wisdom, good sense) is essential for *eudaimonia* (flourishing, happiness in a broad sense).

Oedipus Tyrannus

Oedipus Tyrannus: Cast of Characters

OEDIPUS

ELDER	a Theban priest
CHORUS	of Theban elders
CREON	brother-in-law of Oedipus
TIRESIAS	the blind prophet
JOCASTA	wife of Oedipus
HERDSMAN	a Theban, formerly of the house of Laius
CORINTHIAN	formerly a herdsman
MESSENGER	from the house of Oedipus

Nonspeaking Roles

A GROUP OF SUPPLIANTS	
ATTENDANTS	to Oedipus
BOY	servant of Tiresias
ATTENDANT	to Jocasta
ATTENDANTS	to Creon
ISMENE *and* ANTIGONE	daughters of Oedipus

Peter Meineck and Paul Woodruff's translation of Sophocles' *Oedipus Tyrannus* was first performed at the Clark Theatre, Lincoln Center, New York in January 2000: directed by Robert Richmond; music by Anthony Cochrane; design by Peter Meineck and Robert Richmond; masks by Peter Meineck and Nate Terracio; lighting by Peter Meineck. Original cast (in order of appearance): *Oedipus,* Kenn Sabberton; *Elder,* Mark Cameron Pow; *Chorus of Thebans,* Tracey Mitchell, Shana Cooper, Mark Cameron Pow, Lisa Carter, Louis Butelli; *Creon,* Louis Butelli; *Tiresias,* Louis Butelli; *Jocasta,* Lisa Carter; *Corinthian,* Louis Butelli; *Herdsman,* Lisa Carter; *Messenger,* Lisa Carter.

Oedipus Tyrannus

SCENE: *Before the royal house of Thebes. The great doors of the*
house stand upstage center. There are two wing
entrances, one onstage left and one onstage right. There
is a holy altar center stage. A throng of citizens have
gathered there as suppliants.

(Enter Oedipus through the great doors.)

OEDIPUS:
  My children, new nurtured by old Thebes,
  Why have you come here pleading,
  Wearing wreaths and clutching boughs?
  The city burns with pungent spice.
  Healing hymns echo the sounds of suffering.   5
  To have heard such news from others
  Would not have been right.
  My children, I am here, famous Oedipus.

(Oedipus addresses an elderly priest.)

  Old man, it is your duty to speak for all.
  Why are you kneeling in supplication—   10
  What do you fear, what do you want?
  I will help. Only a heartless man could bear
  To see such sorrow and not feel pity.

ELDER:
  Oedipus, master of my country, look.
  Every age gathers at your altar: fledglings   15
  Not yet fit to fly, elders bending beneath time,
  Ministers of Zeus, as I, and the flower of our youth.
  Your people cram the city's squares

3: The olive branch and wool wreaths were carried by suppliants, mortals who sought protection from the gods.

18: The city of Thebes was split into two areas by the river Strophia; therefore, it had two marketplaces, and there may have been two shrines

Crowding Athena's two temples,
20 The river god's sacred shrine
And the blood-charred altar of the prophet.

Look, see for yourself: the city is plunged
Headlong into the depths of disaster,
Engulfed by a murderous seething tide.
25 Desolation wastes away the harvest,
Destroys our herds grazing in the fields,
Blights the women and makes them barren.
Some furious god hurls pestilence and plague,
Draining the house of Cadmus,
30 As Hades bloats on dirges of death.

We know that you are not a god;
These children came to your hearth to plead
To the man who knows best the trials of life,
For you understand divine power.
35 You came to Thebes, saved us from the Sphinx,
And without any help, delivered us from despair.
We could do nothing; we knew nothing.
It is said that once you were helped by a god;
We believed it, and you saved all our lives.

40 Now, Oedipus, our master and greatest power,
We are all in your care, and we beg of you:
Come to our aid.
Have you heard from a god, a man,
Is there something that you know?
45 You understand what to do at such times,
That is clear; all of us trust your judgment.
Come, noblest of men, save the city.
Come, be true to your fame.

---

to Athena, the protector of the city. The river god was Ismenos, son of
Apollo, and his shrine (Ismenian Apollo) was an important oracular
sanctuary.

29: Cadmus was the legendary founder of Thebes.

35: A Sphinx was a winged creature with the body of a lioness and the
head of a woman. Thebes was beset by a Sphinx that plagued the city
until Oedipus arrived and solved her riddle (see Introduction, p. xxxviii).

Our country calls you its savior;
You earned the title. Let it never be remembered   50
That you once raised us up, only to let us fall.

You brought us lucky signs and good days;
Now you need do the same for us again.
If you want to rule as master of this land,
You need men to master, not walls and ships.   55
A nation of no one can only be nothing.

OEDIPUS:
My poor children, I understand the hope
That brings you here—how could I not?
I know you are all in pain; every one of you
Feels it, but at least that pain is only yours.   60
None of you can know the anguish that I feel.
Sick to my soul, I grieve not only for myself
But for the whole city, for everyone, for you.
You have not disturbed me; I could not sleep.   65
These nights have seen me weep a flood of tears.
My mind has wandered so many trails of thought
Until at last my search sought out the one and only cure.
I have already sent Creon, my own wife's brother,
To the Pythian oracle, Apollo's shrine at Delphi.   70
There he will learn the will of the gods
And what I must say or do that I might save the city.
But he should have returned by now;
Too much time has passed since he left.
I fear what might have happened—where can he be?   75
When he does come, I would be worthless if I failed
To do what is made apparent by the word of a god.

ELDER:
Well said and timely too.
These men say they have seen Creon.

OEDIPUS:
Bless us, Lord Apollo! Let it be deliverance.   80
Let good news shine bright in his eyes.

70: Delphi was the site of the shrine of Apollo, god of both healing and
prophecy. It was named Pythian after the great serpent Pytho that once
inhabited the area. On oracles, see Introduction, pp. xxxix–xl.

ELDER:
Good news, yes. Can you see him?
He's wearing a thick, fresh laurel wreath . . . good news!

OEDIPUS:
Soon he will hear us; then we'll know for sure.

(Enter Creon from the stage left wing.)

85   Creon, royal brother, son of Thebes,
What word have you brought from the god?

CREON:
Good words. If fortune smiles,
It will set these troubles straight.

OEDIPUS:
Yes, certainly, but what of the oracle?
90   Is there any hope? Have we anything to fear? Tell me!

CREON:
Here? With all these people around us? If you wish,
I'm ready to talk. Or we can go inside.

OEDIPUS:
Let everyone hear. I grieve for them
Far more than I do for myself.

CREON:
95   Then hear the words I heard from the god.
Lord Apollo has made his will clear:
Drive out defilement nurtured in your land.
Cherish it no longer; it must be purged.

OEDIPUS:
How should we purge this curse? What is the cause?

CREON:
100   The purge is banishment, or else death for death.
The cause is murder, and blood guilt storms over our city.

OEDIPUS:
Who is this man whose fate has been revealed?

CREON:
We had a leader here whose name was Laius,
Before you came to steer our city straight.

OEDIPUS:

I know. I've heard of him, though I never saw the man myself. 105

CREON:

He's dead, and the command is clear:
Punish the killers by force.

OEDIPUS:

And where on this earth are they? Where can the faint
Track of this old blood-crime be found?

CREON:

On Theban soil, the god proclaims. 110
Search leads to capture; what is ignored escapes.

OEDIPUS:

But where was Laius murdered? In the palace?
Out in the country? Or did it happen abroad?

CREON:

He'd been abroad, seeking an oracle, they said,
And he never came home from his journey. 115

OEDIPUS:

Did anyone see it happen? Someone on the same journey,
A messenger? A clue to solve this crime?

CREON:

No, they all died, except one who fled in fear.
But he said he saw only one thing for certain.

OEDIPUS:

What was that? One thing could reveal much more. 120
Hope can spring from such a small beginning.

CREON:

A pack of thieves killed him in ambush;
Not one man alone, but many.

OEDIPUS:

How would a thief dare to do such a thing
Unless he had been paid off by someone here? 125

124: "A thief"—Oedipus is drawn back to the singular form (perhaps
by subconscious knowledge), though Creon has plainly said "thieves."
See also the plurals at lines 292 ("travelers") and 308 (literally, "the

CREON:
　　There were suspicions. But Laius was dead,
　　And we had no one to help in our crisis.

OEDIPUS:
　　Your ruler had been murdered! What crisis
　　Could have kept you from a complete investigation?

CREON:
130　The Sphinx. Her riddles made us set aside
　　That mystery; we had to deal with the trouble at hand.

OEDIPUS:
　　Then I will start again. I will see it exposed.
　　You are right, Apollo is fully justified
　　To remind us of our obligations to the dead.
135　Watch, as I join the fight for this land
　　As the god's true instrument of vengeance.
　　I do not do this for some far-off cousin.
　　I have my own reasons for driving out this infection;
　　The killer, whoever it may be, could kill again
140　And lay those deadly hands on me.
　　As I serve this cause, so I serve myself.
　　Now quickly, my children, up off the steps,
　　Take your boughs of supplication and go.
　　Call the people of Thebes to assemble here,
145　And I will do everything. Apollo be with us,
　　He will reveal our fortune—or our fall.

ELDER:
　　Up, children; he has given his word
　　That he will do all that we asked,
　　And we have all heard the oracle from Apollo.
150　Come to our aid, Apollo, save us from the sickness!

　　　　(Exit Oedipus through the great doors; exit Creon
　　　　stage right. Exit the suppliants through the stage
　　　　right wing. Enter the chorus of Theban citizens from
　　　　the stage right wing.)

---

killers"). The passage at lines 842–7 shows how important the plural is.
Contrast the singulars at lines 229, 246, 278, and 293 (literally, "no one
saw the man who did it").

Choral Entry-song (Parodos)

CHORUS:

[Strophe *a*]

Be good to us, O Word of Zeus! What is your meaning?
Rich in gold, the prophet speaks to shining Thebes.
But I am strung between fear and hope. Panic beats at
   my mind.
Blessed Healer to whom we cry,
I await your answer with awe and dread: 155
Will it be a new demand?
Or will the passing years fulfill an ancient curse?
Tell me, Child of Hope, golden immortal word.

[Antistrophe *a*]

Daughter of Zeus, I first call on you,
Immortal Athena—
And on the earth-holder, your sister   160
Artemis, who is seated on her rounded throne,
Glorious in the center of Thebes—
And on Apollo, who strikes from afar. Come,
O you three protectors, let me see you now.
If ever you have saved us, when disaster raged over the city,   165
If ever you sent the flames of misery far away,
Come, save us now.

[Strophe *b*]

Pain, misery beyond reckoning:
My people, all my people, sick with plague.
I search my mind for some defense,   170

154: "Blessed Healer"—Apollo, the son of Zeus.

158–63: Here, three gods are invoked to provide protection and a cure
from the plague—Athena in her role as a protector of the city, Apollo as
the god of healing, and Artemis, who was said to preside over childbirth.
The "rounded throne" may be a reference to the *agora* (marketplace) of
Thebes; it also could be an allusion to the circular orchestra of the theatre, where the chorus are gathering. The early Theatre of Dionysus orig-
inated in the Athenian agora before it was relocated to the southeast
slope of the Acropolis.

But there is none.
No crops will grow, none from our fabled earth.
No children crown the birth pangs of our women.
But they cry out, and, one by one,
175   You see them take bird wings and rise
Like flame on flame, unassailable in flight,
To the dark shore of the western god.

[Antistrophe *b*]

Death, beyond the city's reckoning:
180   Beyond pity, children lie on the ground unmourned,
Bearing death to the living,
While wives and gray-haired mothers
Stream to the bank of altars,
Exhausted by their sadness,
185   Moaning, begging for relief.
Hymns flash out to the healing god
With cries of lamentation.
Over us, we pray, golden daughter of Zeus,
Raise the bright face of your shield.

[Strophe *c*]

190   Blazing Ares, god of war, comes against me now.
With no bronze sword or shield.
He scorches me, and the shouts rise about him.
Turn him back, put him to flight out of our land.
Give him a fair wind
195   Either back to the broad lap of the Atlantic
Or back to the cruel surf of the Thracian sea.
For now the horror left undone
By night is finished in the day.

177: "Dark shore of the western god"—the realm of Hades, lord over the dead, which was said to lie at the western end of the earth where the sun sets.

188–9: The daughter of Zeus who carries a shield is Athena.

195–6: "Of the Atlantic"—The Greek has "of Amphitrite," the name of a sea goddess who is, according to Hesiod, the wife of Poseidon. Thrace was the region to the north of Greece, and "Thracian Sea" is probably a reference to the Black Sea.

Smite the war god, Father Zeus, 200
For yours is the power of ultimate fire:
Smash him with your thunderbolt.

[Antistrophe *c*]

Lord of light, Apollo, lift your bow, I pray.
Loose from its gold-spun string
A shower of arrows, irresistible. 205
And send down also the radiant beams
Of Artemis, who sets the mountain peaks
Of Lycia shining in the night.
And I call upon you, god of the golden crown,
You who share your name with our land, 210
Bacchus, glowing with wine and happy cries of
    Maenads:
Bring your torches of blazing pine
And strike the god whom the gods detest.

(Enter Oedipus through the great doors.)

OEDIPUS:

You plead for help. Let me provide the answer: 216
If you listen to me and do as the disease demands,
You will rise again and find relief from this curse.
I tell you these things as a stranger,
A stranger to all that happened here,
But I cannot go far on this trail alone 220
Unless I have some sort of sign.
Therefore, as I have since become a citizen,
I will make this decree to all of Thebes:
If any man knows who killed Laius, son of Labdacus,
I command him to disclose everything to me. 225
Do not fear that you will condemn yourself.

207–8: Lycia—a mountainous region in southwest Asia Minor (modern-day Turkey). Artemis is goddess of the moon.

211: Bacchus (or Dionysus) was god of wine and revelry and patron deity of the theatre. His mother, Semélê, was a daughter of Cadmus, the founder of Thebes (see Theban Royal Family Tree).

221: "Some sort of sign"—The word translated as "sign" can also mean "proof of identity," such as may be found with an abandoned child.

I offer amnesty and will drop all charges—
Only exile, and you will leave this land unharmed.
Should anyone know that the murderer is a foreigner,
230   Let him not keep silent any longer;
I will pay a rich reward and give my grateful thanks.
But if you should keep silent out of fear,
To protect yourself or shield a friend,
Then hear what I will do,
235   Should my ruling be ignored:
I forbid any inhabitant of the land
Where I hold the seat of power
To speak with or shelter this man,
To share the sacred or hold sacrifice,
240   Or to sprinkle the water of holy rites.
Banish him, shun him from your homes.
This is the man who has plagued us
With the curse the oracle revealed to me.

So I stand, side by side with the god,
245   Fighting for the rights of the murdered man.
I damn the killer, whoever he may be,
An unknown man, or one of many.
May he suffer and die, pain beyond pain.
I damn myself, if I should come to know
250   That he shares my hearth and home—
Then I call this curse to fall on me.

I command you, see this to its end,
For my sake, for the gods, and for your country,
Decaying into a godforsaken wasteland.
255   Even if Apollo had not sent his decree,
It was not right that the crime went unpurged.
Your king, the best of men, was cruelly killed,
But you sought no answers. Now I rule,
I have the authority that once was his,
I own his bed and make his wife mine.
260   My children, planted in the same mother as his,
Could have forged a bond of blood between us,

243: "To me"—Creon had received the oracle on behalf of Oedipus.

If fate had not fallen and he had not died childless.
His cause is mine, and I will fight for him,
As if he were my very own father,
And I will stop at nothing to find   265
The one who has this man's blood on his hands,
For the sake of ancient Agenor, Cadmus, Polydorus,
And Labdacus, and for Laius, the last of his line.

Those who disobey me be damned by the gods:
Your barren land will know no harvest,   270
Nurture no children. This curse or something
Far, far worse will doom you to destruction.
Those faithful Thebans who accept my words
Can claim that Justice stands at their side.
May the good grace of the gods be with you forever.   275

CHORUS:
As you request, sir, I will speak on oath:
I did not kill him, and I cannot name
The man who did. Apollo set us to this search;
Apollo should reveal the man who did this.

OEDIPUS:
You are right, but there is not a man alive   280
Who can force the will of the gods.

CHORUS:
May I tell you what I think is second best?

OEDIPUS:
Tell me, and the third best; I'll hear it all.

CHORUS:
There is one I know who has the gift of sight,
Clear as Apollo—Tiresias. Inquire of him,   285
If you wish to learn precisely what took place.

267–8: Agenor was the legendary king of Phoenicia and the father of
Europa. One of his three sons was Cadmus, who founded the city of
Thebes after searching in vain for Europa, who had been abducted by
Zeus. Polydorus, the son of Cadmus and Harmonia, was the second king
of Thebes. Laius, the son of Labdacus, was the ruler of Thebes prior to
Oedipus' arrival. See Theban Royal Family Tree.

OEDIPUS:
I have seen to that already. On Creon's advice
I sent a herald to fetch him. Twice now. Where is he?
I can't believe he has not yet arrived.

CHORUS:
290   Without him, all we have are meaningless old rumors . . .

OEDIPUS:
Rumors? I must look everywhere; tell me every word.

CHORUS:
He was killed, they say, by travelers on the road.

OEDIPUS:
I know, but nobody saw anything.

CHORUS:
Even so, this curse of yours will make him flee,
295   If he can still feel any shred of fear.

OEDIPUS:
A man who acts without fear will not flee from words.

(Enter Tiresias, the blind prophet, led by a boy from
the stage left wing.)

CHORUS:
Here is the one who will put him to the test,
The godlike prophet they are leading in,
The only man who was born to know the truth.

OEDIPUS:
300   Tiresias, great visionary, mystic teacher,
Medium to other worlds, above and below,
Though you are blind, I know you sense
The sickness that has infected the city.
You can deliver us, you can keep us safe.
305   We questioned Apollo—did the heralds
Tell you?—the god has sent his answer;
We must discover who murdered Laius
And sentence them to banishment or death.
Only then will this sickness be purged.
310   Please help us now, interpret the signs,
Use every part of your prophet's craft.

Save yourself, your city, save me,
Save everything that this death has defiled.
We are all in your care, and the finest gift
To give is to use your powers for greater good.   315

TIRESIAS:
Oh, oh. It is a hateful thing to know, when nothing
Can be gained from knowledge. I saw it clearly
But forced it from my thoughts! How else could I be
    here?

OEDIPUS:
What is it? Why this despair?

TIRESIAS:
Please let me go home. It's for the best.   320
You bear your load; let me bear mine.

OEDIPUS:
But this hostility is unlawful! This city raised you.
You cannot cheat us of this prophecy!

TIRESIAS:
I see your words, dangerous words.
In such precarious times it's best that I say nothing.   325

OEDIPUS:
By all the gods! Don't turn your back on us.
We're all on our knees, begging you.

TIRESIAS:
You all know nothing and I will never speak of it!
You'll not hear of these horrors from me.

OEDIPUS:
What? So you do know but refuse to speak?   330
Traitor! You condemn your city to destruction.

TIRESIAS:
I'll not cause this pain, not yours, not mine.
Stop your investigation. I've nothing more to say.

---

316 ff.: The word translated as "knowledge" can mean "good sense" or
"intelligence."

328: "You all know nothing" could also mean "you all lack good sense."

OEDIPUS:
335 Nothing? Damn you! You could make the coldest stone
Burn with rage. Is there anything that moves you?
Will you never speak? You could end this now!

TIRESIAS:
You condemn my temper yet fail to see
Where your own dwells. Instead, you blame me.

OEDIPUS:
Could anyone not be angry after hearing
340 How you hold our city in such contempt?

TIRESIAS:
I've kept my secret, but what will be will be.

OEDIPUS:
What will be? If you know what's coming, you must tell me.

TIRESIAS:
I have nothing more to say. Go on, rage against me
If you want, vent your savagery, do what you will.

OEDIPUS:
345 If it's anger you want, then I'll spare you none
And speak what's on my mind. I see it now:
You had a hand in this, you were part of the plot.
It was you, and if you'd had eyes in your head,
You would have murdered the man yourself!

TIRESIAS:
350 What? Then hear me speak. Obey the edict
That you yourself proclaimed: No one here
Shall ever speak with you again.
You are this land's defiler, you are the curse!

OEDIPUS:
Insolence! How dare you stir up such a story?
355 Do you think you'll escape the consequences?

TIRESIAS:
Yes, I do. Truth protects me.

336: "You could end this now"—Text and meaning have been questioned by scholars. Another possible reading yields, "You are not put off by entreaties."

OEDIPUS:
This is not prophecy! Who put you up to this?

TIRESIAS:
You did; you forced me to tell you.

OEDIPUS:
Tell me what? Say it again so there will be no misunderstanding.

TIRESIAS:
How could you not understand? Do you dare me to speak
of this? 360

OEDIPUS:
Again! Let there be no doubt.

TIRESIAS:
I say that the murderer you seek is you.

OEDIPUS:
You'll be sorry you said that vile thing twice.

TIRESIAS:
Rage on and I'll tell you even more!

OEDIPUS:
Say what you will; your lies mean nothing. 365

TIRESIAS:
I say you can't comprehend it, living in abomination,
Intimate with nearest and dearest, failing to see the evil.

OEDIPUS:
Do you believe you can say these things with impunity?

TIRESIAS:
I do, if there is power in truth.

OEDIPUS:
Indeed there is, but not for you; you have no power— 370
Your ears and your mind are as blind as your eyes.

TIRESIAS:
You poor fool, the same abuse you hurl at me
They'll soon enough be hurling back at you.

OEDIPUS:
Never-ending night shrouds you in darkness.
You're harmless to those of us who see the light. 375

TIRESIAS:
It is not I who will bring down your doom.
Apollo will be sufficient, and he has it all in hand.

OEDIPUS:
Did you plot all of this, or could it be Creon?

TIRESIAS:
Creon doesn't plague you, you plague yourself!

OEDIPUS:
380   Prosperity, power, skill surpassing skill—
These should be admired, not envied.
What jealous craving eats away at you people?
Is it because of my tyranny? I never asked for it;
It was handed to me by the city.
385   For this, my dear old friend, loyal Creon,
Longs to cast me out, stalking in secret,
Ambushing me with this conniving trickster.
You cheating old beggar! All you can see
Is personal profit. To the future you're blind!
390   Tell me, when have your prophecies been proved?
When the Sphinx sounded her deadly song
Did you speak to save our people then?
The riddle could not be solved by just any man.
It needed the skills of a seer, but where were you?
395   You saw no omens, you made no revelations,
There was no divine inspiration, you knew nothing.
Then I came, ignorant Oedipus. I silenced her
By using my mind, not signs from the sky!

Did you really think you could just cast me out
400   And align yourself with the throne of Creon?
Conspirators! You will pay dearly for trying
To put the blame on me. If you weren't so old
I would have taught you your lesson already.

CHORUS:
Our judgment is that this man spoke

376–7: "It is not I who will bring down your doom"—We translate a corrected text. See endnote.

398: Diviners, such as Tiresias, read omens from the flights of birds.

In anger, and so did you, Oedipus.   405
But we have no need of angry words, only this:
Explain the oracle, the word of the god.

TIRESIAS:
Yes, you hold the power, but I am still your equal
In at least having the right to reply.
I am not one of your minions; I answer to Apollo.   410
Nor do I stand with Creon; he is not my patron.
You ridicule me and call me blind,
But your eyes cannot see your own corruption
Or where you live and just who you live with.
Do you even know your parents? You, an oblivious   415
Enemy to all your kith and kin, both living and dead.
The double-edged curse of your mother and father,
Treading the terror, will hound you out of this land,
And then your keen eyes will see only darkness.
What place will not harbor your cries   420
Echoing from the slopes of Mount Cithaeron
When you come to understand the marriage you made?
You thought that fortune had sailed you to a safe haven,
But you cannot perceive the deluge of disasters
That will be the measure of you and your children.   425
So sling your mud at Creon and soil
My words with your foul insults—
No man will ever suffer as much as you.

OEDIPUS:
Must I tolerate this, from him?
Damn you! Scurry back where you came from,   430
Get away from my house! Get away!

TIRESIAS:
I would not have come if you had not summoned me.

408: "You hold the power"—"you are Tyrannus."

411: "My patron"—In fifth-century Athens a resident alien (metic) was
required to be registered by a citizen sponsor who acted as a legal
patron. Here, Tiresias asserts his right as a full citizen. A very democratic
notion in the face of a tyrant.

421: Cithaeron—a mountain to the south of Thebes that borders Attica
and Boeotia.

OEDIPUS:
> And I never would have sent for you
> If I had known you were a babbling fool!

TIRESIAS:
435   I am what I am; a fool, if that is what you think,
> But those that bore you thought me wise enough.

OEDIPUS:
> Wait! What did you say? Who gave birth to me?

TIRESIAS:
> This day bears your birth and brings your devastation.

OEDIPUS:
> Is everything you say shrouded in dark riddles?

TIRESIAS:
440   Are you not the greatest solver of riddles?

OEDIPUS:
> Insult me there and you'll discover just how great I am.

TIRESIAS:
> Yet your blessing proves to be your curse.

OEDIPUS:
> I couldn't care less what you say; I saved this city.

TIRESIAS:
> Then I will leave you to it. Come, boy, lead me away.

OEDIPUS:
445   Then take him away! He'll just impede us here.
> He'll cause me no more trouble once he's gone.

TIRESIAS:
> I'll go, when I've said why I came. I'm not frightened
> By your angry glare; you could never hurt me.
> I tell you, the murderer of Laius, the object
450   Of your self-proclaimed manhunt,
> The one you've sought for so long—he is here.
> He seems at first to be a newcomer from abroad,
> Yet soon he'll be seen as a born Theban. But no joy
> For him in that. Hopeless, a blind man who once could see,
455   A beggar who before was rich, led by a stick,

Picking his way across lands unknown.
All will be seen; both brother and father
To the children he holds so dear, husband
And son to the woman who bore him. He bred
In his father's bed and his father's blood he shed!   460
Now go in and think on that; when you prove me false,
Then you can say that the seer has no sight!

*(Exit Tiresias and the boy through the stage left wing.
Exit Oedipus through the great doors.)*

Second Chorus (First Stasimon)

CHORUS:

[Strophe *a*]

Who is the man? The holy oracle
From Delphi sings from the rock
Unspeakable, unspeakable crimes: 465
Who is it stained his hands in blood?
Now, even horses of the wind
Are too slow for his escape.
The son of Zeus leaps after him
With blazing thunderbolts,   470
And the horrible death-goddesses
Cannot be shaken off his trail.

[Antistrophe *a*]

The shining word flashes from Parnassus:
"Dog his tracks, everyone,
Whoever he may be."   475
Through wild forests, in caves,
On rocky crags, the fugitive roams,
Alone, like a bull in pain,
His foot in pain,

469: "The son of Zeus"—here, Apollo, using his father's weapons.

471: "Death-goddesses"—the Furies, terrifying creatures who pursue those who have committed crimes against family.

473: Parnassus—the mountain that overlooks Delphi, the shrine of Apollo in central Greece. The crossroads where Oedipus met Laius lie on the slopes of Parnassus between Delphi and Daulis.

480   Putting behind him the prophecies
From center earth; but they rise up,
Always, they live and flutter around him.

[Strophe *b*]

And now I'm amazed! Worried. Frightened.
That clever soothsayer—
485   I can't believe him, I can't deny him,
I don't know what to say.
I'm floating on hope,
Blind here and now, blind to the future.
Was there a feud between the families
490   Of Laius and Polybus?
No evidence.
I never heard of a feud,
Now or before.
So how can I take sides?
495   How can I join the cause of Laius
Against Oedipus, with all his popularity?
This murder is not yet solved.

[Antistrophe *b*]

Zeus and Apollo are wise;
They know what mortals do.
500   But a human prophet?
There's no true way to tell that he knows more than I.
Tiresias is clever.
Well, clever men compete; they put each other down.
No. I will not add my voice to the accuser's
505   Until I see the charge made good.
We saw him plainly—Oedipus—

481: "Center earth"—Zeus declared Delphi to be the center of the earth. A stone marked the exact spot. It was inscribed with the word "earth's," and known as the *omphalos* (navel) of the earth.

490: "Laius and Polybus"—The chorus wonder whether a feud between families could have caused Oedipus to attack Laius. Oedipus was believed to be the son of Polybus, king of Corinth.

506: "We saw him plainly"—Ancient Greeks held that eyewitnesses give compelling testimony.

When the winged Sphinx attacked.
And we saw that he was clever.
That was proof. The city loved him.
I can't convict him in my mind, 510
Not yet, not of any crime.

(Enter Creon from the stage right wing.)

CREON:
Fellow citizens, this is terrible, what I hear.
This accusation against me, by our ruler Oedipus,
It's outrageous. Amid all this trouble, 515
If he now thinks I have done him any harm,
In word or deed, any harm whatever,
I'd rather die and not prolong my life
Than carry such a reputation. The damages
Are enormous from a charge like that: 520
I'd be called a traitor to my city,
A traitor to you and even to my family.

CHORUS:
But it was driven by anger, not thought.
I don't think he meant to blame you.

CREON:
But did the word come out in the full light of day: 525
That I planted lies for the prophet to tell?

CHORUS:
Yes, but I know he didn't mean it.

CREON:
Did his eyes shift when he accused me?
Was he in his right mind?

CHORUS:
I don't know. I never see what rulers do. 530
He's on his way from the palace now.

(Enter Oedipus through the great doors.)

OEDIPUS:
You? You dare to come here, to my house?
What bare-faced audacity!
Here's the murderer in plain sight.

535   Clearly, he meant to steal my power
        Gods! What was it that you saw in me—
        Weakness, stupidity? Did you really think
        That I'd never see through your scheme
        And take steps against your creeping conspiracy?
540   What a fool, to think you could even try
        To pursue power with no allies, no following.
        Without men and means, there can be no conquest.

CREON:
        Do you know what you should do? You had your say;
        Now it is your turn to listen to me. Learn first, then judge.

OEDIPUS:
545   There's nothing more to learn from your malicious words.
        I know that you are my most deadly enemy.

CREON:
        The very point on which I wish to speak . . .

OEDIPUS:
        The very point is that you are plainly guilty.

CREON:
        Do you really take pride in being so stubborn
550   And thoughtless? You've lost your mind!

OEDIPUS:
        And you're out of your mind! Do you really think
        You can harm your own family with impunity?

CREON:
        In principle I agree, but no one
        Has done you wrong. You must have proof.

OEDIPUS:
555   Did you, or did you not, persuade me
        To send for that self-righteous soothsayer?

CREON:
        I did. And I'd still give the same advice.

OEDIPUS:
        How long has it been since Laius . . .

CREON:
        Since he what? I've no idea.

OEDIPUS:
Since he vanished, violently.   560

CREON:
You'd have to go back a long, long time.

OEDIPUS:
And this old prophet, was he in business back then?

CREON:
Yes, as expert then as now and highly revered.

OEDIPUS:
And at that time did he ever mention me?

CREON:
No. Not that I know of.   565

OEDIPUS:
Was there no murder investigation?

CREON:
We tried. We never heard . . .

OEDIPUS:
And what of your expert? Why did he not speak then?

CREON:
I don't know—and so I have the sense to keep quiet.

OEDIPUS:
You know; and if you had any sense, you'd tell.   570

CREON:
What do you mean? If I knew something I wouldn't
    deny it.

OEDIPUS:
Without your support, he never would have dared
To name me as the killer of Laius.

CREON:
Is that what he said? Then you're the one who knows,
And I have just as much right to question you.   575

OEDIPUS:
Ask your questions. I'll never be found a murderer.

CREON:
So you say. You are married to my sister, aren't you?

OEDIPUS:
There's no denying that.

CREON:
And you have equal power with her, as ruler of this land?

OEDIPUS:
580   Whatever she desires, I provide.

CREON:
And is it not true that I am equal to you both, that we
    three are equal?

OEDIPUS:
Exactly! The evil in our family is revealed.

CREON:
No! Look at yourself from my point of view,
And ask this question first: Do you think anyone
585   Would choose to rule in constant fear
When he could sleep without trembling,
And have exactly the same power? Not me.
Why should I want to be Tyrannus?
I'd be insane! I already do as I please.
590   I have everything from you, and nothing to fear.
As ruler, I'd have to do things against my will,
But the power I have now is exactly to my taste.
Why would I find tyranny more attractive?
I'm not a fool, I'm not enthralled,
595   I do not hunger for more than what is fair—
And profitable. As it is, I'm friends
With everyone! People fawn on me
Whenever they want anything from you,
Because I am their best hope of success.
600   So how could I give that up and be a traitor?
Look, I hate the very idea of such a plot,

588: "Why should I want to be Tyrannus"—Such arguments as the one
that follows were frequently used in Greek law courts for cases without
eyewitnesses. They appeal to what the Greeks called *eikos* (probability or
reasonable expectation).

And I'd never dare join people actually doing it.
Test me. Go to the oracle at Delphi
And ask if my report was accurate.
And then, if you prove I conspired   605
With that seer, take my life.
I'll add my vote to yours for death.
But don't you presume me guilty without proof.
"It's not right to think good men are bad,
Or bad men good, if your reasons are worthless."   610
"When you reject a noble friend, you cast
Your very life away, and all you hold so dear."
In time, you will be certain of my innocence.
"It takes time to prove the goodness of a man,
But you'll see evil come to light in one bad day."   615

CHORUS:
A good speech, my lord. Anyone who treads carefully
    will agree:
Decisions made too quickly are dangerous.

OEDIPUS:
When a conspirator moves quickly against me,
Then I must be quick to conspire back at him.
If I hesitate I will lose the initiative,   620
While he will seize the moment and strike.

CREON:
What do you want? To throw me out of Thebes?

OEDIPUS:
No, not exile. I demand your death.

CREON:
When have I done anything to deserve that penalty?   623a

OEDIPUS:
When you showed how much you resented me.

CREON:
Why won't you believe what I tell you?   625

609–15: Sentences in quotation marks—Creon closes with a series of
moral platitudes probably familiar to the audience.

623a: We have supplied this line to fill a gap in the text.

OEDIPUS:
626a   How can I believe a man like you?

CREON:
    I see it now. You've lost your mind.

OEDIPUS:
                              My mind is clear.

CREON:
    Then it should think like mine.

OEDIPUS:
                   Like yours? You're contemptible!

CREON:
    And you could be wrong.

OEDIPUS:
                      Nevertheless, I must rule.

CREON:
    Not if it means ruling badly.

OEDIPUS:
                      Oh, my city, my city . . .

CREON:
630   I belong in this city, it's not only yours!

CHORUS:
    Stop! Please, gentlemen, Jocasta
    Is on her way from the house. This is timely;
    She will surely make you settle your dispute.

          (Enter Jocasta through the great doors.)

JOCASTA:
    What are you thinking? Why this outburst of fighting
       words?
    You should be ashamed, forcing your personal quarrels
       on us
635   When the whole country is suffering from such sickness.
    Why don't you go inside, and Creon, please go home.
    There's no reason to cause this mayhem.

626a: We have supplied this line to fill a gap in the text.

CREON:
> Sister, your husband, Oedipus, wants to throw me out
> Of my own country or have me put to death.   640
> He's on the brink of making a horrible decision.

OEDIPUS:
> Indeed I am. Jocasta, I caught him conniving,
> Hatching malignant plots against me.

CREON:
> If I did anything that you accuse, then may the gods
> Let me die in misery—I put this curse on myself!   645

JOCASTA:
> You must accept his word, Oedipus. He has sworn
> Before the gods. Oaths call for reverence.
> So do I, and so do the people standing before you.

[Strophe a]

CHORUS:
> Take thought, sir. I pray you change your mind . . .

OEDIPUS:
> And why should I yield?

CHORUS:
> He has never been a man to speak lightly.   650
> You must respect the power of this oath.

OEDIPUS:
> Do you know what you are asking of me?

CHORUS:
> I know.

OEDIPUS:
> Then say what you mean!   655

CHORUS:
> He's a part of your family and under his own curse:
> You should not disgrace him with a groundless charge.

649–96: Here, the dialogue moves into a rapid and excited meter more suitable for the occasion than the iambic trimeter used in most of the play for dialogue.

OEDIPUS:
Then you should know that what you want
Will mean my exile or my death.

[Strophe *b*]

CHORUS:
660   No, by the brightest of the gods, Apollo.
If that was ever in my mind, then let me die the death,
Friendless, godforsaken, in agony.
But the wasting of this land eats away my heart,
665   Horror piled on horror,
First the plague and now this deadly quarrel.

OEDIPUS:
Then let him go, though it means death
670   Or dishonor, cast out of my country, forever.
I feel for you, not him; your voice has moved me.
Wherever he goes he'll always have my hate.

CREON:
Look, you're as hateful now as you were fierce before.
Your submission is as painful as your rage. It's in your nature—
675   A kind of justice—that you hurt yourself the most.

OEDIPUS:
Go! Leave me. Go!

CREON:
I will go.
You don't know the truth, but these men knew what was right.

(*Exit Creon through the stage right wing.*)

[Antistrophe *a*]

CHORUS:
Lady, you should help him home.

JOCASTA:
680   First, I want to know what happened.

CHORUS:
Only words—blind suspicion.
But that eats away at a man, even when it's wrong.

JOCASTA:
Words on both sides?

CHORUS:
Yes.

JOCASTA:
What did they say?

CHORUS:
No more, please, no more. This land is full   685
Of agony already. They spoke; now, let it be.

OEDIPUS:
Can you see what you have done, trying
To blunt my edge with your good intentions?

[Antistrophe *b*]

CHORUS:
Sir, I have said it many, many times: You can be sure
I'd have to lose every shred of my good sense   690
Before I'd turn away from you.
You were the one, when our land was tossed
In storms of trouble, who brought us a fair breeze,
And set us straight. Now, I pray again,   695
Be our good steersman—make us safe!

JOCASTA:
By the gods, sir, what is the cause?
Why are you so angry? Please explain.

OEDIPUS:
I will, not for them, but from respect for you, my wife.   700
It is Creon; he conspires against me.

JOCASTA:
Tell me exactly how this fighting started.

OEDIPUS:
He says I am guilty of murdering Laius.

JOCASTA:
Was he a witness? Or is he acting on hearsay?

OEDIPUS:

705   He sent his malevolent soothsayer;
He would never say such things himself.

JOCASTA:

A soothsayer? Then you should dismiss all charges.
Listen. I'll tell you why you can't rely
On any merely human soothsayers.
710   Here, in brief, is my evidence:
An oracle came to Laius once—I won't say
"From Apollo"; it came from priests—
That "Laius would die at the hands of a son
That would be born to him and me."
715   But Laius was killed by strangers
At a place where three roads meet. That's the story.
And our son? He did not last three days.
Laius yoked his feet and had him thrown away—
By other people—into a wilderness of mountains.
720   So Apollo did not make the tale come true:
The boy never came to murder his father;
The father had nothing to fear from his son.
That's the way a soothsayer charts the truth!
Don't trust them. The god knows what's needed:
725   The god himself will speak when he sees fit.

OEDIPUS:

What you're telling me shakes my soul,
Sends my mind reeling one way then another.

JOCASTA:

What's the matter? You're startled. Tell me.

OEDIPUS:

I thought I heard you say that Laius
730   Was murdered where three roads meet.

JOCASTA:

So they say. The tale's still told.

OEDIPUS:

Where exactly did this happen?

JOCASTA:

A place called Phocis, where the road divides,
One road from Delphi, one from Daulis.

OEDIPUS:
   When was this?   735

JOCASTA:
   The news came shortly before you arrived
   And became the master of our land.

OEDIPUS:
   Zeus! What are you conspiring against me?

JOCASTA:
   What is tormenting you, Oedipus? Please tell me.

OEDIPUS:
   Wait! Not yet. Tell me what Laius   740
   Looked like. How old was he?

JOCASTA:
   He was dark, about your size,
   Hair just starting to go gray.

OEDIPUS:
   O gods, no! I think I've cursed myself,
   Called down calamity. I never knew . . .   745

JOCASTA:
   What do you mean? It scares me to look at you.

OEDIPUS:
   A terrifying thought. What if the blind prophet can see?
   It will all be exposed if you can tell me just one more thing.

JOCASTA:
   I'll try. But you frighten me.

OEDIPUS:
   Was he traveling with a small entourage   750
   Or in force at the head of a large column?

JOCASTA:
   He had five men, including his herald;
   There was one carriage, and Laius rode in that.

OEDIPUS:
   Oh, now I start to see!
   Jocasta, who told you about this?   755

JOCASTA:

A slave. The only survivor.

OEDIPUS:

Is he still here, among our household?

JOCASTA:

No. He came and saw that you
Now held the power Laius had
760 Before he died. He touched my hand,
Begging me to send him far away,
To be a shepherd in fields from which
He could not see this city. I did as he asked.
He was a slave, but I owed him more than this.

OEDIPUS:

765 Could he be brought back as soon as possible?

JOCASTA:

He could. But why ask for this?

OEDIPUS:

Jocasta, I fear I've already said too much.
I have to see this man for myself.

JOCASTA:

Very well. But I deserve to know
770 This burden that you find so hard to bear.

OEDIPUS:

I will not keep it from you, not when hope seems
So very far away. To talk to you at a time
Like this means more to me than anything.

My father was Polybus of Corinth and my mother,
775 Merope, a Dorian. I was held in the highest esteem,
A prominent man. Then something strange happened,
Something that shocked me. It wasn't much,
And I should not have worried, but my thoughts raced:
A drunken dinner guest filled with wine
780 Blurted out that I was not my father's son.
It was all I could do that day to control my rage.
But on the next day, I went to my mother and father
Seeking some explanation, and they were furious

That anyone would speak such spurious slander.
I was consoled, but a rumor creeps in stealth,   785
And soon enough it started to grate on my mind.
I left in secret; my mother and father never knew
I went to Delphi. But there, Apollo shunned me,
Denied my questions and sent me away,
But not before he revealed what was to come.   790
Such tormenting horrors! He said I would
Mate with my mother and reveal a race
Too vile to stand in the sight of man.
He said I would kill my father.
I heard Apollo's word, and I ran,   795
Tried to flee a universe from Corinth,
To reach some place that would never see
The fulfillment of that revolting prophecy.
On and on until I reached the region
Where you say your ruler met his death.   800
You, dear wife, you shall know the truth:
I traveled to a place where three roads meet
And saw a herald coming toward me
Followed by a horse-drawn carriage,
And seated inside, a man, just as you said.   805
We met, then the herald and the old man
Ordered me out of their way, forcing ahead.
Run off the road, I furiously struck the driver,
The old man saw this and as his carriage passed
He cracked his two-pronged goad down on my head   810
And I swiftly smashed my walking stick square
Across his shoulders; he spun headlong out of his carriage,
And I killed every last one of them, there and then.
But if this stranger bled the blood of Laius,
Who could be as contemptible as I?   815
What man could be more heaven-hated?
Neither foreigner nor citizen could shelter me;
I would be shunned in silence,
A pariah, hounded from humanity.
Condemned by a curse called down   820
By no one else but me.
If these hands that touched her killed him,
I have defiled a dead man's bed. Am I so foul?
So hopelessly unholy? Then I'll be banished,

An outcast, never to see my family,
825 Never to set foot in the land I called my home.
Or I'll be yoked in marriage to my mother
And forced to murder my own father,
Dear Polybus, who brought me into the world.
Some malicious spirit bears down on me—
What man in his right mind could say otherwise?
830 No, no, never, great gods above,
Never let me see that terrible day,
Wrench me from the human race, obliterate me!
But never let me see myself so disgraced.

CHORUS:
That would be horror for us all. But keep hope alive
835 Until you've heard from the man who was there.

OEDIPUS:
I will await the herdsman;
He is now my only hope.

JOCASTA:
And when he arrives, what then?

OEDIPUS:
Let me tell you; if what he says agrees
840 With your story, then I will escape this crisis.

JOCASTA:
What did you hear me say?

OEDIPUS:
You said he explained how Laius was killed
By several thieves. If he still says thieves,
Then I could not have killed him.
845 How can one be the same as many?
But if he should speak of just one lone man,
Then the guilt will clearly fall on me.

JOCASTA:
Don't worry, I told you exactly what he said.
It's too well known for him to take it back.
850 The whole city heard it, not just me.
But even if he tries to change his tale,
He cannot make the oracle prove true.

Laius' death was not the one that was foretold:
He did not die by his son's hand,
That wretched child never killed him;   855
He was dead himself, long before the murder.
So much for soothsayers. After that they'll never
Have me looking for answers, here, there, and everywhere.

OEDIPUS:
You are right, of course, but I still want
That herdsman here. Send for him now.   860

JOCASTA:
I'll send for him the quickest way.
Let's go inside. I want what's best for you.

   (Exit Oedipus and Jocasta through the great doors.)

Third Chorus (Second Stasimon)

CHORUS:

[Strophe *a*]

Be with me always, Destiny,
And may I ever sustain holy
Reverence in word and deed,   865
According to the Laws on high,
Brought to birth in brightest sky
By Heaven, their only father.
These Laws were not made by men;
Men are born to die.   870
But the Law shall never sleep forgotten;
Great among gods, it never ages.

[Antistrophe *a*]

Hubris grows from tyranny,
Hubris overflowing, a monstrous waste,
Loss without measure: 875
It climbs high,
It rushes to a precipice jutting out—

873: "Hubris grows from tyranny"—a corrected text. The manuscripts
read, "Hubris begets a tyrant." See endnote.

The end, no foothold saves it now.
880   And so I pray the god will not dissolve
What is good for the city, our wrestling for power.
May god protect us always.

[Strophe *b*]

If a man moves in lofty pride
His hands or tongue
885   Fearless of injustice—
No reverence for holy places—
I pray he meet an evil fate
To pay for his miserable excesses.
If he piles wealth on wealth, without justice,
890   If he does not shrink from fighting reverence
And puts his hand to what may not be touched,
Then may his efforts be wasted,
And may there be no shield
To save his mind from blows.
895   But if gods give honor to a life like his,
Why should I dance in prayer and praise?

[Antistrophe *b*]

No longer will I go in reverence
To the sacred navel of the world—
Not to Delphi, not to Abai,
900   Or the temple at Olympia,
If the oracles do not come true
For all humanity to see.
Ruler of all, O Zeus our lord,
If that be your name, do not let this escape
905   Your notice or your undying power:

881: "Our wrestling for power"—the repeated contests for power that mark democracy. The chorus here seems to be speaking for Athens against tyranny.

899–900: Delphi, Abai, Olympia—important shrines with oracles. For Delphi, see note on line 70. Abai was the site of a sanctuary of Apollo in northwest Phocis, a region of central Greece to the east of Mount Parnassus. Olympia was the great sanctuary of Zeus in the western Peloponnesus.

Apollo's word to Laius long ago
Is fading, it is already lost.
Now Apollo's fame and honor die away,
And everything divine departs.   910

> *(Enter Jocasta and an attendant through the great
> doors. She is holding wreaths and a small container
> of incense.)*

JOCASTA:
  I thought that I should go to the temple, sirs,
  And bring these gifts to the gods—
  Incense and ritual wreaths.
  Oedipus is chafing his mind too much,
  One agony after another. It makes no sense: 915
  He weighs this strange news
  Against old prophecies and lets anyone who speaks
  Frighten him. Nothing I say can raise his hopes.

> *(Jocasta makes her offerings at the altar.)*

  Apollo, nearest god, to you I pray:
  I have come with offerings,   920
  I entreat you for relief, light out of darkness.
  The captain of our ship has lost his wits,
  And we are all so very afraid.

> *(Enter an elderly Corinthian from the stage left
> wing.)*

CORINTHIAN:
  I am a stranger here. Please, tell me,
  Where is the house of Oedipus Tyrannus.   925
  Or better yet, where is the man himself?

CHORUS:
  This is his house, and he's at home.
  But here is his wife and mother of his children.

CORINTHIAN:
  Blessings on her and her family:
  She is a perfect wife for him.   930

---

913 ff.: Jocasta is bearing the offerings of a suppliant, a mortal who seeks
the protection of the gods.

JOCASTA:
The same to you, sir, thanks for your kind greeting.
Tell me, now, what brings you here?

CORINTHIAN:
Good news for your house, lady, and for your husband.

JOCASTA:
935   What is it? Who sent you?

CORINTHIAN:
I came from Corinth. My news . . .
Well, it might please you, or it might make you sad.

JOCASTA:
What is it? Why such ambivalence?

CORINTHIAN:
I hear that the people of Corinth
940   Will make him ruler of their land.

JOCASTA:
What! Is old Polybus no longer in power?

CORINTHIAN:
No. He's dead and buried.

JOCASTA:
What are you saying? Polybus is dead?

CORINTHIAN:
On my life, it's true.

JOCASTA: *(To her attendant.)*
945   You, go at once and tell this to your master.
These oracles from the gods—
Where are they now? Oedipus was so afraid
Of killing Polybus that he ran from home.
And now look: He was killed by chance, not Oedipus.

(Enter Oedipus through the great doors.)

OEDIPUS:
950   Jocasta, dear wife,
Why call me from our house?

JOCASTA:
>   Listen to this man. He'll make you doubt
>   The truth of "holy oracles from the gods."

OEDIPUS:
>   Well, who is he? What is he saying?

JOCASTA:
>   He's from Corinth. He has news   955
>   That your father, Polybus, is dead.

OEDIPUS:
>   What's your message? Speak for yourself.

CORINTHIAN:
>   If I must tell him that first,
>   Yes, he is dead and gone. It is true.

OEDIPUS:
>   Was there foul play, or did he die of natural causes?   960

CORINTHIAN:
>   A small push lays an old man down to sleep.

OEDIPUS:
>   So sickness sapped the poor man's life.

CORINTHIAN:
>   Yes. That and old age.

OEDIPUS:
>   Why? Why, dear wife, should we observe the oracle
>   At Delphi, or strain to see signs from birds screeching   965
>   In the sky? They led me to believe that I would kill
>   My father, yet he's dead and buried deep in the earth.
>   And here am I, who never raised a hand against him,
>   Unless my absence made him die brokenhearted.
>   Then, I suppose, I could be called his killer,   970
>   But not the kind contained within these worthless oracles.
>   Polybus has taken those with him to Hades.

JOCASTA:
>   Exactly what I said in the beginning.

OEDIPUS:
>   You did, but fear misguided me.

JOCASTA:

975   And now you mustn't worry about these things any more.

OEDIPUS:

But I should still shun my mother . . . her bed.

JOCASTA:

Why be afraid? Chance governs human life,
And we can never know what is to come.
Live day by day, as best you can.
980   You must not fear this marriage to your mother:
Many a man has slept with his own mother
In a dream. But these things mean nothing
If you bear life's burdens easily.

OEDIPUS:

This would all be well and good
985   If my mother were dead, but she's still alive
And I still fear her, whatever you say.

JOCASTA:

But this is spectacular—your father's dead!

OEDIPUS:

A great comfort, but it's the living that scare me.

CORINTHIAN:

Who is the woman you are worried about?

OEDIPUS:

990   The wife of Polybus, old man, Merope.

CORINTHIAN:

But why are you so afraid of her?

OEDIPUS:

A terrifying prediction, stranger, given by a god.

CORINTHIAN:

May I hear? Is it permitted for you to speak of it?

OEDIPUS:

It is. My fate was revealed by Apollo.
995   He said I would lie with my own mother
And stain my hands with my father's blood.
From then on I shunned Corinth, kept well away,

And all seemed well, except I always knew
I would never again see my parents' kind faces.

CORINTHIAN:
　And this was the fear that made you leave your home?   1000

OEDIPUS:
　So I could not kill my father.

CORINTHIAN:
　Why don't I relieve you of this fear?
　I came to do you good, after all.

OEDIPUS:
　For that I'd pay you dearly.

CORINTHIAN:
　And that's the very reason I came—   1005
　I'll receive my reward when you come home.

OEDIPUS:
　No! I will not be near my parents.

CORINTHIAN:
　My boy, it's quite clear you don't know what you're doing.

OEDIPUS:
　By all the gods! Explain yourself, old man.

CORINTHIAN:
　If they are the reason you shun a homecoming . . .   1010

OEDIPUS:
　I'm afraid I'll see Apollo's word come true.

CORINTHIAN:
　So you wouldn't have the guilt of a crime against parents?

OEDIPUS:
　You are right, old man, it is my ever-present fear.

CORINTHIAN:
　And you never knew! Really, you had no cause for fear.

OEDIPUS:
　Why? They are my parents; I am their son.   1015

CORINTHIAN:
　Because Polybus is no relation of yours.

OEDIPUS:
What are you talking about? I was born to Polybus.

CORINTHIAN:
The man was no more to you than I am.

OEDIPUS:
How could you equal my father? You are nothing to me.

CORINTHIAN:
1020 He did not father you, and neither did I.

OEDIPUS:
Then why did he call me his son?

CORINTHIAN:
You were a gift, you see, taken from my own hands.

OEDIPUS:
From another's hands? But he loved me like a son.

CORINTHIAN:
He was overcome by the need to have a child.

OEDIPUS:
1025 So you gave me away. Was I bought? Did you find me
somewhere?

CORINTHIAN:
I found you in a tangled ravine on Mount Cithaeron.

OEDIPUS:
Why were you traveling in that region?

CORINTHIAN:
At that time I was grazing sheep in the mountains.

OEDIPUS:
So you were a wandering shepherd, a hired hand?

CORINTHIAN:
1030 Yes, child, and there and then your rescuer.

OEDIPUS:
And when you first held me, was I hurt?

CORINTHIAN:
Your own feet can testify to that!

OEDIPUS:
An old affliction; why speak of it now?

CORINTHIAN:
Because I set you free from a spike that pierced your feet.

OEDIPUS:
A hideous blemish I've carried from the cradle.   1035

CORINTHIAN:
That's how you came to have your name.

OEDIPUS:
Gods! Who did this—my mother? My father?

CORINTHIAN:
I don't know. The man who gave you to me, he'd
    understand.

OEDIPUS:
You took me from someone else? You didn't find me?

CORINTHIAN:
No, another shepherd gave you to me.   1040

OEDIPUS:
Who was it? Do you know? Can you tell me?

CORINTHIAN:
I think I heard he belonged to Laius.

OEDIPUS:
The Tyrannus who used to rule this country?

CORINTHIAN:
Of course. The man was his herdsman.

OEDIPUS:
Does he still live? Can I see him?   1045

CORINTHIAN: (To the chorus.)
You men who live here, you'd know best.

OEDIPUS:
Do any of you gathered here know
Who this herdsman could be?

1036: The name "Oedipus" can be taken to mean "swollen foot."

Is he somewhere out in the country? Is he here?
1050   Make it known! Everything must be exposed.

CHORUS:
I think he's the same man,
The shepherd you wanted to see just now.
Jocasta would have the best answer.

OEDIPUS:
My wife? *(To Jocasta.)* Could the man he means
1055   Be the one we summoned? Do you know?

JOCASTA:
Why ask who it was? Don't listen to this man.
Put his worthless words right out of mind.

OEDIPUS:
I cannot, not while I hold the evidence
That will reveal the truth of my birth.

JOCASTA:
1060   No! By all the gods, if you care for your life,
Stop these questions. Have I not suffered enough?

OEDIPUS:
Be brave. Even if I find my mother was a slave,
Descended from slaves, you would still be noble.

JOCASTA:
Even so, be persuaded, I entreat you. Stop.

OEDIPUS:
1065   You'll never persuade me to give up the truth.

JOCASTA:
But this is for your own good. It is what's best . . .

OEDIPUS:
Then long ago your "best" married me to woe.

JOCASTA:
Your fate is dismal. I pray you never know the man you are.

OEDIPUS:
Now, somebody bring this herdsman here.
1070   Let her bask in the glory of her eminent line.

JOCASTA:
> Your fate is hideous. That is all
> That I can say to you, all I can say forever.

> *(Exit Jocasta through the great doors.)*

CHORUS:
> What is it, Oedipus? What savage grief
> Has hurled your wife away?
> Her silence frightens me; evil will break from it.   1075

OEDIPUS:
> Then it will break! I have to know
> Who I am, however low my birth.
> That woman, with her feminine conceit,
> Is ashamed of my humble origins,
> But I see myself as a child of good-giving   1080
> Fortune, and I will not be demeaned.
> She is my mother, the seasons my kin,
> And I rise and fall like the phases of the moon.
> That is my nature, and I will never play the part
> Of someone else, nor fail to learn what I was born to be.   1085

Fourth Chorus (Third Stasimon)

CHORUS:

[Strophe]

> Tomorrow, if my skill is good
> At soothsaying, Heaven be my witness,
> You, O Mount Cithaeron, will know glory   1090
> Shining in the full moon's light,
> For you have been nurse and mother to Oedipus.
> We dedicate our dance to you,
> For you it was
> Brought joy to our masters.   1095
> Apollo, hear our prayers.

[Antistrophe]

> Who gave you birth, my child?

1088: See endnote.

1100 Was she one of the Nymphs who dallies with Pan
   In the mountains?
   Or was she bedmate to Apollo,
   Lover of high meadows?
   Or Hermes of Cyllene?
1105 Or Dionysus, mountain-dweller—
   Were you his lucky find?
   For he loves to toy with Nymphs,
   And his delight is in their darting eyes.

   (Enter the elderly Herdsman accompanied by
   Oedipus' men from the stage right wing.)

OEDIPUS:
1110 Elders, though I never knew him,
   I believe that this could be the herdsman
   We've so long sought to see.
   He's just as old as this Corinthian,
   And those are my men bringing him in.
1115 Have you ever seen this shepherd?
   For you may know far more than I.

CHORUS:
   Yes, of course I know the man. Laius
   Was his master. No shepherd could be more loyal.

OEDIPUS:
   First of all, tell me, Corinthian, is this the man?

CORINTHIAN:
1120 Yes, he is the man you see.

OEDIPUS: *(Addressing the Herdsman.)*
   You there! Old man, come here and look at me.
   Answer me this: Did you once belong to Laius?

HERDSMAN:
   Aye, but not a boughten slave; I grew up in this house.

1100: Pan was a deity of rustic pursuits and remote regions. He was depicted as half man, half goat. Nymphs are minor female divinities of woods and streams.

1104: Cyllene was the name of a mountain in northeast Arcadia, a region in the central Peloponnesus and the birthplace of Hermes, the messenger god, divine guide, and herdsman.

OEDIPUS:
What was your job, your livelihood?

HERDSMAN:
Tending flocks, most of my life.   1125

OEDIPUS:
Where did you usually work?

HERDSMAN:
Mount Cithaeron—that general area.

OEDIPUS:
Was this man ever there—did you know him?

HERDSMAN:
What has he done? Which man do you mean?

OEDIPUS:
This man. Have you met him before?   1130

HERDSMAN:
Couldn't say, offhand. Can't call him to mind.

CORINTHIAN:
That's not surprising, sir. But I am sure,
Though he's forgotten, I can bring his memory back.
I knew him well in those days on Mount Cithaeron,
When he had two flocks and I had one.   1135
We were neighbors for three full seasons,
Six months each, from spring to fall.
Come winter, I'd drive my herds home,
And he'd take his to Laius' barns.
(To the Herdsman.) Am I not right?   1140

HERDSMAN:
It's true, but so long past!

CORINTHIAN:
Then tell me this: Do you know a child
You gave to me to bring up as my own?

HERDSMAN:
What about it? Why look into this?

CORINTHIAN:
Because, my friend, this is the man who was that boy.   1145

HERDSMAN:
Damn you! Can't you keep your mouth shut?

OEDIPUS:
Don't scold him, old man,
It is you that deserves the scorn.

HERDSMAN:
Master, when have I ever done wrong?

OEDIPUS:
1150   When you refused to answer him about the child.

HERDSMAN:
He doesn't know what he's saying; he's wasting our time.

OEDIPUS:
If you won't speak willingly, you'll speak through pain.

HERDSMAN:
No, by all the gods! I'm too old for torture!

OEDIPUS: *(To his attendants.)*
Lock his arms behind his back!

> *(Oedipus' men take hold of the Herdsman's arms and
> force him to his knees.)*

HERDSMAN:
1155   Gods, no! What more do you need to know?

OEDIPUS:
Did you give him a child as he said?

HERDSMAN:
Yes. I should have died that day.

OEDIPUS:
It may come to that, unless you start telling the truth.

HERDSMAN:
I'm more likely to die if I do.

OEDIPUS:
1160   I think he's trying to play for time.

1153: In fifth-century Greece, evidence from a slave was considered trust-
worthy only if it had been obtained through torture.

HERDSMAN:
Not me. I said, ages ago, that I gave the child to him.

OEDIPUS:
Where did you get it—your own home, or from someone else?

HERDSMAN:
It wasn't mine. From someone else.

OEDIPUS:
Which citizen was it? Whose house?

HERDSMAN:
No, by all the gods, master. No more questions!   1165

OEDIPUS:
If I have to ask you again, you'll die.

HERDSMAN:
Laius. It was born in his house.

OEDIPUS:
A slave child, or one of his own?

HERDSMAN:
No! I'm on the edge of saying terrible things.

OEDIPUS:
And I of hearing them. But hear them I must!   1170

HERDSMAN:
I heard the child was his—but she's inside:
Your wife's the one who'd answer best.

OEDIPUS:
She gave it to you?

HERDSMAN:
                    She did, sir.

OEDIPUS:
For what reason?

HERDSMAN:
                    So I would destroy it.

OEDIPUS:
Her own baby? So callous.

HERDSMAN:

1175   She feared an oracle.

OEDIPUS:
   That said what?

HERDSMAN:

                          That it would kill its parents.

OEDIPUS:
   Then why did you give him to this old man?

HERDSMAN:
   I took pity on him, sir. I meant to deliver him abroad,
   To the place where this man came from, but his rescue
1180   Was a disaster. If you are the same as the man
   He speaks of, then truly you were born for a hideous fate.

OEDIPUS:
   Oh! Oh! It all comes clear!
   Light, let me look at you one last time.
   I am exposed—born to forbidden parents, joined
1185   In forbidden marriage, I brought forbidden death.

         (Exit Oedipus, rushing through the great doors.
         Exit the Herdsman stage right and the Corinthian
         stage left.)

Fifth Chorus (Fourth Stasimon)

CHORUS:

                          [Strophe *a*]

   Oh, what a wretched breed
   We mortals are:
   Our lives add up to nothing.
   Does anyone, anyone at all
1190   Harvest more of happiness
   Than a vacant image,
   And from that image fall away?
   You are my pattern,
   Your fortune is mine,
1195   You, Oedipus, your misery teaches me
   To call no mortal blessed.

[Antistrophe *a*]

You aimed your arrow high, and struck happiness,
You self-made lord of joy.
Zeus knows, when you killed
The snag-clawed maiden, the riddling Sphinx—
Then between death and my land   1200
There rose a fortress, and it was you.
For that, we call you king,
Our king of highest glory,
Lord of mighty Thebes.

[Strophe *b*]

Now is there a sadder story to be heard?
Madness so cruel? Pain so deep?   1205
You have shared your home with catastrophe.
O, Oedipus,
One harbor served you as a child
And as a father sailing into marriage.
How, oh how, could the field your father plowed   1210
Bear you so long in silence?

[Antistrophe *b*]

Time found you out, all seeing,
And brought you to the judgment you can't bear:
This marriage is not a marriage,
Wherein the maker of children is a child.   1215
Oh, child of Laius,
I wish, I wish
I'd never seen you.
I mourn you above all others, crying out
Truly, you gave me breath,   1220
And now through you I close my eyes in sleep.

(Enter a Messenger through the great doors.)

MESSENGER:
    Most honored elders of this land,

1202: "For that, we call you king"—This is the first time in the play that
anyone has called Oedipus "king" (*basileus*).

The things you will hear! The things you will see!
1225   The burden you will carry! It is grief.
That is, if you care for this family as kin.

No river is great enough, not the Danube,
Not the Phasis, to wash this house clean.
So deep is the stain of evil hidden here.
1230   Soon it will come to light:
The worst pain is self-chosen, deliberate.

CHORUS:
Nothing could be heavier than what we know
Already. How can you add anything to that?

MESSENGER:
As brief a message as you could hear:
1235   She is dead. The queen, Jocasta, is dead.

CHORUS:
Poor, poor woman. What happened?

MESSENGER:
She killed herself.
It's horrible, but you weren't there.
You won't see the worst of it.
Listen, you'll find out how much she suffered,
1240   If I have any power to tell a tale.

Well, then. She was in a terrible state.
She went inside and ran straight to the bedroom,
To her marriage bed. She was tearing at her hair
With both hands, and she slammed the doors
1245   As soon as she was inside, then called a dead man's name—
"Laius! Do you remember making love, making the child
That later killed you, that left me to give birth
To the children of your child, children of the curse?"
And she was wailing at the bed where she had conceived,
1250   A double misery: a husband from her husband,
And children from her child. Then she died.

1228: The Danube is named *Istros* in the Greek. The Phasis was the name
of a river in Colchis, the modern-day Rioni, which flows into the Black
Sea. These rivers lie at the extreme edge of the Hellenic world.

I don't know more, because Oedipus plunged in,
Shouting so loud we could not think about her troubles.
We kept our eyes on him dashing up and down,
Raving about, roaring, "Bring my sword.   1255
And where's my wife—no, not my wife,
Mother of two crops, myself and my children."
He was in a frenzy, and some spirit led him—
It wasn't any one of us servants—
He went charging at the doors and bent them inward   1260
With a terrible shout, as if someone guided him,
Plunged through the doors, fell inside the room.

She was hanging there, his wife. We saw her
Hanging in a noose of braided rope.
Then he saw her. He howled in misery,   1265
Loosened the hanging rope, and laid her down
On the ground, poor woman.
Then a horrible sight: he tore out the long pins
Of beaten gold that had adorned her clothes,
Lifted them up, and plunged them into his eyes,   1270
Crying out, "Now you may not see the evil,
Not the evil I have done—or suffered.
From now on, you must gaze in darkness
On forbidden faces, while the ones you should have seen
You'll never know." That was his litany.   1275
Again and again he chanted it and struck his eyes.
Blood was running down from the sockets,
Staining his cheeks red, an unstoppable flood
Dashing down, a dense hail of gore.
And so the storm has broken on them both—   1280
Husband and wife, their suffering commingled.
It used to be happiness that they shared,
Happiness indeed, but now, today:
Grief, unseeing madness, death, disgrace,
Every horror that we know how to name.   1285

CHORUS:
Poor man. Is there no relief for him?

MESSENGER:
He shouts for someone to unlock the gates
And show all Thebes the father-killer,

The mother- (I cannot say what is unholy),
1290   And then he'll cast himself out from this land
And not stay on to be a curse at home,
For he bears the curse that he called down.
He begs for strength, and for someone to lead him,
For he is sick beyond what he can bear.
1295   He'll show you, himself. The doors are opening now.
What you will see is loathsome; pity him.

> (Exit Messenger through the stage right wing. Enter
> Oedipus through the great doors. The gruesome
> effects of his blinding can be seen clearly.)

CHORUS:
Amazing horror!
Nothing worse can come upon a man.
Was it madness that struck your mind?
1300   Or was it a god great bounds away,
Who leapt upon your life,
Bringing disaster?
Cry, cry misfortune! I cannot bear to look.
Many things I wish to ask
1305   I wish to learn, I wish to see,
But you are blinding me with horror.

OEDIPUS:
Ai! Ai! My suffering!
Where on this earth am I going, led by misery?
1310   My voice? It is scattered on the wings of the wind.
How far Destiny has leapt.

CHORUS:
To terrors beyond what we can hear or see.

OEDIPUS:
Oh, darkness!
Hideous clouds engulf me, swept in
1315   By ill wind! Inescapable, unspeakable!

1297: The actor playing Oedipus may have changed his mask while offstage, or the blinding may have been depicted on his existing mask with
the addition of red paint or of ribbons representing blood.

1297–1311: The meter again is excited out of the usual iambic trimeter
into a form suitable for great emotion (see lines 649–96 with note).

Ohhh!
Again and again, so much agony!
Memories stabbing, piercing me with pain!

CHORUS:
Do not be amazed: Your agony's so great,
You feel it twice, first in body, then in soul.   1320

OEDIPUS:
A friend? Here?
You'd stay, for me? Solid in support.
You'd help a blind man, care for me?

    (He sighs.)

This I see, despite the darkness.   1325
I hear you, I know your voice.

CHORUS:
Ah, what a dreadful thing you've done! How could you bear
To put out your sight? Which god spurred you on?

OEDIPUS:
Apollo! It was Apollo, my friends.   1330
Agony after agony, he brought them on.
But I did this . . .
By my own hand.
Why should I have eyes
When there is nothing sweet to see?   1335

CHORUS:
I cannot disagree with what you say . . .

OEDIPUS:
Now,
What can I ever see to love?
What greeting can ever please me to hear?
Cast me out of this place, my friends,   1340
Quickly, cast me out:
I am the destroyer, the curse,   1345
The man the gods loathe most of all.

CHORUS:
Now your mind is just as wretched as your fate;
I wish I'd never known you.

OEDIPUS:
Damn that man, whoever he was,
1350   Who freed my feet from the shackles
And rescued me from death.
Call it cruelty, not kindness!
I should have died there and then
1355   And spared them all this pain.

CHORUS:
It would have been for the best.

OEDIPUS:
Then, I would have never killed my father,
Nor been known as the man
Who married his mother.
1360   Now, I am the godless son of shame,
Who slept in the same bed where he was bred.
1365   What evil could there ever be
That could surpass the fate of Oedipus?

CHORUS:
I can't agree with what you did:
Better to die than to be blind.

OEDIPUS:
Don't tell me that what I did was not for the best.
1370   I do not want opinions, I do not need advice.
If I had eyes, how could I bear to see my father
When I die and go down to the depths of Hades,
Or face my wretched mother? My crimes
Against them could not be cured by suicide.
1375   Could I ever long to see my children, born
As they were born, and enjoy that sweet sight?
My eyes could not bear to look at them!
The finest man raised by Thebes
Has deprived himself of his city, her walls
1380   The sacred idols of the gods. Wretch!
I gave the order: Cast out the curse!
The gods have exposed the impiety,
And so stand I, the son of Laius, defiled.
Now that my vile stain glares out,
1385   Could I ever meet the eyes of my people?
Never! If only I could stem the stream of sound,

Then I'd shut away my broken body
Hearing silence, seeing nothing:
Sweet oblivion, where the mind
Exists beyond the bounds of grief.   1390

Cithaeron, why did you accept me?
Why did you not let me die, there and then?
Why show the world my birth? Why?
Polybus! Corinth! You were my home.
You raised me, covered me in kindness.   1395
But evil festered beneath my skin,
Erupting in me, evil born of evil.

The three ways at that hidden gully,
The narrow track through the woods
Where I spilled my father's blood,   1400
My own blood! Do you remember?
The triple path witnessed what I did.
Do you see where you have led me?
Marriage! The marriage bond bred me,
Brought me up to wed my own blood.   1405
Kin created kin: fathers, brothers, sons
Mixed with mothers, brides, and wives.
Humanity's foulest deeds!
I cannot speak of such abhorrent acts.
By all the gods, you must let me hide away,   1410
Cast me into the sea, kill me, shun me from sight.

> (Oedipus moves toward the chorus; they shrink back
> in fear.)

Come closer, I am not untouchable,
You should not fear the wretched.
My affliction cannot cause you any harm;
No one but me is able to endure my pain.   1415

> (Enter Creon and attendants from stage right wing.)

CHORUS:
The man you need for what you ask is here:
Creon. Ready for action or decision,
He alone remains our guardian in your place.

OEDIPUS:
What could I ever say to him?
1420 Why would he believe a word I say,
Now I've been shown to be so very wrong?

CREON:
Oedipus, I have not come to jeer at you
Or cast any blame for past wrongs.

(To the attendants, who are afraid to go near Oedipus.)

Now, perhaps you've no respect for human
1425 Beings, but at least show reverence
To the fiery sun that feeds us all:
Do not openly display this cursed thing
That earth and rain and light can't bear to touch.
Take him quickly inside our house.
1430 Close relatives alone may see and hear,
With all due holiness, such evil in the family.

OEDIPUS:
O gods! My fears dispelled,
You are the best of men and I the worst.
Just one thing, for your sake, not for mine.

CREON:
1435 What do you want, that you ask so earnestly?

OEDIPUS:
Cast me out, quick as you can, to a place
Where I will never speak to another human.

CREON:
I would have already done so, without fail, but first
I had to discover what the god wished me to do.

OEDIPUS:
1440 But that is clear, it was ordained:
The father-killer is defiled and so must die.

CREON:
Yes, so we all heard. But in a time of great need
We should know for sure what we must do.

OEDIPUS:
You would seek divine guidance for my sake?

CREON:
    Yes, and this time you should believe the god.   1445

OEDIPUS:
    I only ask this of you, I beg you:
    Do right by her, your sister. Give her
    A proper burial, a final place to rest.
    But do not sentence my father's city
    To the curse of caring for me while I live.   1450
    I will go to the mountains, to Cithaeron,
    My mountain, where my mother and father
    Long ago marked out my tomb.
    There they wanted me dead. There I will die.
    Now I know that no ordinary end waits   1455
    For me. There was a reason I was spared
    From death, some other daunting destiny.
    Let fate guide where I go, and what will be will be.
    My children? Creon, don't spare a thought
    For the boys. They are grown men now;   1460
    Wherever they go, they will survive.
    But my poor unhappy girls,
    They've never known another table.
    Everything I touched was theirs to share.
    Take care of them, Creon—please.   1465
    If only I could hold them one last time,
    Let our tears fall together . . .
    O lord, my lord . . .
    Noble Creon . . . could I hold them in my arms?
    I can imagine them . . . as I used to see them.   1470

        (Enter Ismene and Antigone from the stage right
        wing.)

What's this?
    I can hear them, yes, by all the gods, my darlings!
    They're crying, crying . . . Creon, you took pity,
    You sent me what I love more than anything . . . anything.
    Tell me that I'm right.   1475

CREON:
    You're right. I brought them here.
    I knew how much they'd gladden you now, as always.

OEDIPUS:
Oh, bless you. May the gods guard your way.
May your journey be so much better than mine.
My children, where are you? Come here,
Take my hands, the hands of your brother.
1480 Do you see what they did to your father,
Who once looked at you with gleaming eyes?
But, children, I saw nothing, I knew nothing,
I fathered you in the soil where I was sown.
I grieve for you, though I cannot see your faces.
1485 I can imagine how this cruel world
Will make you lead the rest of your lives.
What people will share their city with you?
What festivals will you ever enjoy? Shut away
Out of sight, no more celebrations, only tears.
1490 And when the time comes for you to marry,
Who can he be? Who, my daughters,
Would ever dare to take on the disgrace
That blights the children of this family?
They won't spare a single insult:
1495 Your father killed his father!
Your father is your brother!
Your brother is your father!
Your father fucked his mother!
You'll hear it all. Who would marry you?
1500 No such man exists. No, you'll waste away
Dry wombed, sterile, barren,
Unmarried and all alone.

Creon, son of Menoeceus, you are now
Their only father; they are orphans,
1505 Their parents lost in one cruel stroke.
Don't let them become impoverished
Spinsters, wandering vagrants, outcasts.
Take pity on them. Look at these lost
Children; they have nothing else but you.
1510 Swear it, noble Creon. Give me your hand!

(Creon reels back, and Oedipus turns to his children.)

Oh, children, there was so much I wanted
To say to you, but now I can only ask this:

Pray that you always lead measured lives,
Better lives than lived by your own father.

CREON:
Enough tears! It's time to go inside. 1515

OEDIPUS:
If I must, though it gives me no comfort.

CREON:
For good measure it is best.

OEDIPUS:
Then I'll go, but know my terms.

CREON:
I'll know them when I hear them.

OEDIPUS:
Exile. Banish me from this land.

CREON:
That is for the god to decide.

OEDIPUS:
The gods have come to hate me more than anyone.

CREON:
Then perhaps you'll get what you want.

OEDIPUS:
So do I have your word?

CREON:
I'm always as good as my word; I don't speak before I think. 1520

OEDIPUS:
Then lead me away from here.

CREON:
Come, then, but leave your children.

OEDIPUS:
No! You cannot take them away from me!

CREON:
Still you try to take control of everything.
Go; your power has not followed you through life.

(Exit Creon and children through the great doors.
Exit Oedipus, alone, through the stage left wing.)

CHORUS:

 Behold, all you who dwell in Thebes: This is Oedipus.
1525 He knew the riddle's answer, he held great power,
 And we all looked on his success with envy.
 Now a terrible wave of trouble sweeps over him.
 Therefore, always look to the last day,
 And never say a man is happy
1530 Until he's crossed life's boundary free from grief.

(Exit the chorus through the stage right wing.)

–END–

1524–30: The authenticity of this speech has been doubted by some editors. See endnote.

Oedipus at Colonus

Oedipus at Colonus: Cast of Characters

OEDIPUS	
ANTIGONE	daughter of Oedipus
LOCAL	man from Colonus
CHORUS	elders from Colonus
ISMENE	daughter of Oedipus
THESEUS	king of Athens
CREON	brother-in-law of Oedipus
POLYNICES	son of Oedipus
MESSENGER	

Nonspeaking Roles

ATTENDANT	to Ismene
GUARDS	to Creon
ATTENDANTS	to Theseus

Peter Meineck's translation of Sophocles' *Oedipus at Colonus* was first performed at the Burrows Theatre in New York by New York University's Tisch School of the Arts Department of Drama in November 2000: directed by Brian Parsons; set design by Nicodemus Lopez Gonzalez; costume design by Martin Lopez; light design by Elizabeth Gaines; sound design by Matthew Ezold. Original cast (in order of appearance): *Oedipus,* Kishan L. Redding; *Antigone,* Lindsey Sanna; *Local Man,* Zack Calhoon; *Chorus,* Alexander Crowder-Gaines, Edwina Findley, Danny Brink-Washington; *Ismene,* Katherine Proctor; *Theseus,* Alex Gedeon; *Creon,* Matt Harrington; *Guard,* Ben Fox; *Polynices,* Justin Blanchard; *Messenger,* Haley E. Channing.

Oedipus at Colonus

SCENE: *A sacred grove near the village of Colonus on the out-*
skirts of Athens. The central doors of the scene building
are closed, and the stage directly in front of them repre-
sents a sacred area called the "bronze steps." Leading
from the stage to the orchestra are a set of steps, center
stage. There are two wing entrances, one stage left and
one stage right.

(Enter Oedipus and Antigone from the stage left
wing.)

OEDIPUS:
—Child?
—Where are we?
—I'm old and blind.
—Antigone?
—Who lives here?

And today? Who'll give his pittance
To this beggar, Oedipus?   5
"Give me a little," I get even less.
Pain, time, and dignity: three
Excellent teachers of sufficiency.

Let me rest somewhere, child.
Wait. Are we near a shrine? Is this holy land?   10
Stop! Here! Let me sit down!

(They stop at the grove.)

Opening: The area known as Colonus was situated one-and-a-half miles
north of the Athenian Acropolis. The actor playing Oedipus would have
worn a tattered costume and a mask depicting an older, disheveled blind
man. He may have also held a walking stick. The character of his daughter Antigone would have been played by a male actor wearing the lighter
skin-toned mask of a young woman and costumed in simple women's
clothing.

We're outsiders,
We need guidance.
There must be people here.

ANTIGONE:

15 Oedipus—Father, I can see city walls
Off in the distance but I think this place
Must be sacred; laurel, olives,
And vines thrive, and the air is feathered
With the sweet song of nightingales.
Here's a rock where you can rest.
20 You've come so far for one so old.

OEDIPUS:
Let me sit, but keep watch! I'm blind.

(Antigone helps her father sit down.)

ANTIGONE:
After all this time, I hardly need to be told.

OEDIPUS:
Then can you tell me where we are?

ANTIGONE:
Somewhere near Athens, but I don't know this place.

OEDIPUS:
25 The travelers we met said the same thing.

ANTIGONE:
Shall I go and find out where we are?

OEDIPUS:
Yes. See if anyone lives here.

(Enter Local—a man from Colonus—from the stage right wing.)

ANTIGONE:
Somebody must, but there's no need to go,
I can see a man, not far off.

OEDIPUS:
30 Is he coming this way?

ANTIGONE:
He's very near. Consider what to say.
He's here.

OEDIPUS:
Stranger, this girl sees for me and says
That, luckily, you've come to guide us   35
Out of our darkness.

LOCAL:
I'll not answer anything until you get up and leave!
It is forbidden to tread on this sacred ground.

OEDIPUS:
A god's ground. What god?

LOCAL:
The spirits of the Earth, daughters of darkness:
It must not be touched, no one can stay here.   40

OEDIPUS:
Then tell me their names so I may pray to them.

LOCAL:
We call them the "All-Seeing Gracious Ones,"
They have other names in other places.

OEDIPUS:
Then may they offer me kind sanctuary;
Here I've come to rest, forever.   45

LOCAL:
What's this?

OEDIPUS:
My destiny.

42: The "Eumenides," also known as "Erinyes" and "Furies," were
female Underworld spirits that avenged familial bloodshed, protected
the sanctity of sacred oaths, and restored the natural order. According to
legend, they were given a shrine and worshiped as benevolent protectors
of the city of Athens and its people. This myth is encapsulated in the
third play of Aeschylus' *Oresteia* trilogy, *The Furies.*

45: The Greek term *hedras* has the sense of "seat," "resting place," and
"established place." This term is used again by the chorus at line 176 and
alludes to the foundation of a cult of Oedipus at Colonus.

LOCAL:
>   I can't move you myself. I'll go to the city
>   And tell them what's happening here.

OEDIPUS:
>   Please, stranger, I know I'm a beggar,
>   You can see that—but don't dishonor me,
50 >   Don't deny me the things I have to know.

LOCAL:
>   I won't dishonor you, ask your questions.

OEDIPUS:
>   Where are we?

LOCAL:
>   Listen then, and I'll tell you everything I know:
>   This is sacred territory, all of it.
55 >   Dreaded Poseidon rules here
>   With Prometheus, the bringer of fire.
>   The ground where you tread
>   Is called the "Bronze Way,"
>   The Threshold of Athens. This region
>   Claims the knight Colonus as forefather,

55: Poseidon—the god of the sea, also known as "Earthshaker," the deity who caused earthquakes and tremors. Poseidon was specifically identified with Athens, a maritime power, as the city's second patron deity after Athena. Poseidon was also worshiped at Colonus and one of his titles, *"hippius"* ("horse-breaker"), was attached to the hero Colonus.

56: Titans were powerful, primordial creatures that once battled the gods for supremacy over Olympus. Prometheus was originally loyal to Zeus but was eternally punished after stealing fire from Olympus and giving it to mortals. Prometheus had a sanctuary near Colonus in fields known as the Academy.

57: "The 'Bronze Way'"—an entrance to the Underworld where Theseus and Perithous descended in search of Persephone. This may have been a natural chasm or deep cave.

59: Colonus—one of the ten Athenian eponymous heroes that gave their names to the tribes of Attica. Colonus was a small district of Attica over eleven miles to the north of the Acropolis. It was famous for its natural beauty and for the many shrines to Poseidon, Athena, Demeter, the Eumenides, and hero shrines to Theseus, Oedipus, Perithous, and Adrastus.

And we are named for him.   60
Now you know everything, stranger,
And this is not just a legend
But an honor for all that live here.

OEDIPUS:
So this place is inhabited?

LOCAL:
Yes, by the namesakes of Colonus.   65

OEDIPUS:
Is there a leader, or do the people speak for themselves?

LOCAL:
We are ruled by a king from the city.

OEDIPUS:
And who holds that power?

LOCAL:
His name is Theseus, the heir to Aegeus.

OEDIPUS:
Could you send someone to him?   70

LOCAL:
Is there a message? Something he should do?

OEDIPUS:
Just one small thing. He'll gain much.

LOCAL:
How could a blind man help him?

OEDIPUS:
What I will say will have sight.

LOCAL:
Then wait here and keep safe.   75
You seem a good man in a bad way.
Stay where you first appeared.

69: Theseus—a legendary king of Athens, famed for taming and uniting
Attica, slaying the Cretan Minotaur, and battling the Amazons. The
Aegean Sea was named for his father, who drowned himself after mis-
takenly believing that his son was dead.

I'll not go to the city, but I will speak
To the men of this district.
80   They'll decide if you can stay or not.

(Exit Local through the stage right wing.)

OEDIPUS:
Antigone, has he gone?

ANTIGONE:
He's gone, it's only me.
You can say what you want.

(Oedipus prays.)

OEDIPUS:
Spirits! Terrifying goddesses,
85   Have mercy. In all this land
I found your shrine first,
Apollo guided me here, he foretold
An end to evil, said after so long
That I would come to this place . . . and rest.
He told of a land lived in by dread spirits
90   And of sanctuary, somewhere safe
Where all my sufferings would stop.
There I'd be a blessing to those
That took me in, a curse to the ones
That cast me out. He said there'd be signs—
95   Tremors in the earth, thundering skies,
Or even the lightning bolts of Zeus.
I know it was you who helped me here
Guiding me along the path to this sacred site,
And for the first time I felt I'd arrived.
100   I, with no wine to offer,

86: Apollo was the son of Zeus and a god associated with many functions including prophecy, healing, and music. In *Oedipus Tyrannus* (OT), Sophocles relates how Oedipus as a young man first consulted Apollo's shrine at Delphi, where he was told that he would murder his father and marry his mother. Here Oedipus relates yet another important oracle from Apollo.

96: Zeus—the ruler of Olympus. Zeus wielded the thunderbolt, seen as a flash of lightning.

And you who receive no wine!
So I placed myself here on this ancient rock.
Spirits! Apollo foretold it all,
Release me, let my life end here.
I know how I seem—a slave to suffering,   105
No man has ever felt more pain.
Hear me, sweet Daughters of Darkness,
Hear me Athens, most honored of them all.
Pity me, poor Oedipus, a ghost,
A mere shadow of what was once a man.   110

ANTIGONE:
   Quiet! Someone's coming.
   It's the elders, here to see for themselves.

OEDIPUS:
   I'll be quiet. Quickly, hide me out of sight
   Somewhere in the grove where we can hear them.
   I need to know what they intend to do   115
   Before we make any decisions.

   *(Oedipus and Antigone hide in the grove. Enter the
   chorus of elders from Colonus from the stage right
   wing into the orchestra.)*

Parodos

[Strophe *a*]

CHORUS:
   Do you see him?
   Where is he?
   He's scurried away—
   He's hiding.
   Insolence!

101: The libation offering of poured wine was in recognition of divine
power and a representational act of submission. The poured libation can
never be retrieved. Libations to the dead and chthonic forces were often in
larger quantities and did not include wine. Oedipus refers here to both his
poverty and his status as a religious and social outcast, as a wine offering
was used to ritualize social events and make a connection to the divine.

117: The chorus consisted of twelve to fifteen chorus members wearing
masks and costumes indicating their age and status as elders of Colonus.

120   Outrage!
       Look about, find him, seek him out.
       He's some kind of vagrant—
       A tramp!
       Not from here.
125   Couldn't be, or he'd never dare
       To tread sacred earth—
       Don't ever say their name!
       And never stare, nor speak,
130   Only say a quiet prayer.
       Someone said there was an intruder—
       Shameless!
       Search the sanctuary,
135   Where could he be?
       He must be found!

             (Oedipus and Antigone reveal themselves.)

OEDIPUS:
       I'm the one you want—
       They say the blind see by sound.

CHORUS:
140   Sacrilege! To see someone here. To hear a voice!

OEDIPUS:
       You think I'm a violator? I've done nothing wrong.

CHORUS:
       Zeus protect us! Who is this old man?

OEDIPUS:
       No one whose fortune could be envied
145   I can assure you gentlemen of that;
       See how I need the eyes of another to find my way
       And how I lean my weight on such a small support.

                  [Antistrophe *a*]

CHORUS:
150   A blind man!
       But blind from birth?

126: It was considered impious to enter certain sacred shrines, since the
entry would bring ritual pollution.

You seem to have suffered so much
In your long unhappy life.
Now no more curses,
You've gone far too far and trespassed 155
On a sacred grove where water blends
With liquid honey and flows from lustral bowls.
Beware, stranger, go no further—
Stop now and back away. 160
Do you hear?
Decrepit beggar.
If you've something to say, say it
But not on sacred land.
Speak to us from a place, 165
Where words are allowed.
Keep silent until
You have left forbidden ground.

OEDIPUS:
Antigone, what should we do? 170

ANTIGONE:
Father, we must respect their ways
And listen to what they want.

OEDIPUS:
Then, hold on to me.

ANTIGONE:
I have you.

OEDIPUS:
Stranger, I will trust you, but promise
That you'll not wrong me and force me out. 175

[Strophe *b*]

CHORUS:
No one will move you from your refuge,
Old man, not against your will.

OEDIPUS:
Where should I go?

CHORUS:
Come toward us.

OEDIPUS:
180 To you?

CHORUS:
The girl understands.
Lead him toward us.

ANTIGONE:
Father, trust your sightless steps
To me and follow closely.

(Antigone leads Oedipus toward the chorus.)

CHORUS:
A stranger in a strange land, poor man,
185 But he must learn
What offends our city
And what we hold dear.

OEDIPUS:
My child, lead me where we
Can stand in reverence
And communicate freely.
190 We cannot fight necessity.

CHORUS:
There. No further. Do not step
Beyond the sacred rock. Stay by the edge.

(Oedipus and Antigone stop.)

[Antistrophe *b*]

OEDIPUS:
Here?

CHORUS:
That's far enough.

OEDIPUS:
195 May I sit?

CHORUS:
At the very edge of the rock

182: "Lead him toward us"—Three lines representing an exchange between Antigone and Oedipus seem to have been lost here.

There's a ledge, sit there.

ANTIGONE:
   Father, let me do it.
   Gently, follow me now.

OEDIPUS:
   My, oh my.

   (Oedipus, in great pain, tries to sit.)

ANTIGONE:
   You're old, let me help you.   200
   Hold onto me, I'll take you.

OEDIPUS:
   My life. My terrible life!

   (Oedipus sits on the ledge.)

CHORUS:
   Rest, old man, catch your breath
   And tell us who you are.
   What happened to you?
   Where are you from?   205

OEDIPUS:
   I am an outcast. But please don't . . .

                        [Epode]

CHORUS:
   Don't what?

OEDIPUS:
   Don't ask me who I am.   210
   No questions! Nothing more!

CHORUS:
   Why not?

OEDIPUS:
   My very being is repulsive.

213: "Very being"—*phusis*, the essential character of a human, which the
Greeks believed was marked from birth. Here Oedipus means his essential spirit is tainted.

CHORUS:
> Speak!

OEDIPUS:
> Antigone, what should I tell them?

CHORUS:
215   What is your bloodline? Who was your father?

OEDIPUS:
> Oh gods! Child, how can I tell them?

ANTIGONE:
> You must; you have no choice.

OEDIPUS:
> There's no way to hide it; I'll speak.

CHORUS:
> It's about time. Speak up.

OEDIPUS:
220   Have you heard of the son of Laius?

CHORUS:
> What?

OEDIPUS:
> The royal family of Thebes?

CHORUS:
> Zeus!

OEDIPUS:
> And the accursed Oedipus?

CHORUS:
> Is it . . . you?

OEDIPUS:
> But, don't be afraid . . .

217: Some editors give this line to the chorus.

220: Laius—the king of Thebes and father of Oedipus, unknowingly killed by his son.

222: "The royal family of Thebes"—The Greek has "The family of Labdacus." Labdacus was the father of Laius and a descendant of Cadmus, the legendary founder of Thebes.

CHORUS:
  No! No!

OEDIPUS:
  Antigone, what's happening?   225

CHORUS:
  Get away! Get out of our land!

OEDIPUS:
  You promised! How can you break your oath?

CHORUS:
  A wrong for a wrong, Destiny
  Would never punish that.   230
  Deception is checked
  By deception,
  And betrayal is paid back by pain,
  Not gratitude. Now go! Get out!
  Before you cause something   235
  Horrendous to happen to our city.

ANTIGONE:
  Please, you are god-fearing men;
  You have heard what my father did,
  And even though he knew nothing
  You refuse to tolerate him at all.   240
  But at least feel sorry for me, please,
  And let me plead my father's case.
  I am not blind; look into my eyes
  And imagine your own child begging
  For you to be treated with dignity.   245
  You are the only people we can turn to,
  It's as if you were now our gods,
  Dare we hope to have your good grace?
  For the sake of everything that you love,   250
  Your children, wives, possessions—or the gods.
  The gods guide us all. Can anyone
  Escape the paths they set for us?
  There's not a man on earth who can.

229: This is *moira,* Destiny or Fate, meaning one's appointed share, a
reciprocal force rather than an agent of inevitability.

CHORUS:
> You are Oedipus' daughter, and we pity
255 > Both of you equally for all you've suffered.
> But we fear what the gods might do—
> There is simply nothing else to be said.

OEDIPUS:
> Then what's the point of kudos and acclaim
> If they only drain away leaving nothing?
260 > They say Athens is a most reverent city
> Where any outsider in adversity
> Can turn for sanctuary and protection.
> But how can this be when you
> Tear me from my one place of refuge
> And force me from your land?
> And all because you fear a name—my name.
265 > What else could it be? All I did was suffer!
> Because of what my mother
> And father . . . it's unspeakable.
> Is that what you find to fear in me?
> If so, you tell me what I did wrong—
> Yes, I struck him, after he had struck me,
270 > And even if I had known who he was
> You still could not call it an evil act.
> I could not have known where my way would end,
> But they did, my destroyers, they knew.
275 > So I beg you strangers, by all the gods,
> You moved me from my refuge. Now you should
> Protect me. You cannot say you revere the gods
> And simply turn your back on them now.
> You know they see all—the reverent
280 > And the impious—there's nowhere to hide:
> The godless man never escapes.
> Let the gods guide you and prevent
> The dimming of Athens' brilliant light
> With this sacrilegious act.
> You swore me an oath, I accepted your protection,

257: As far as the chorus are concerned, Oedipus has committed acts of murder, incest, and parricide, making his presence an affront to the gods.

And now you have an obligation to keep me safe.   285
My disfigured face should not blind you to kindness,
I have come in sanctity and reverence
And bring great good for your people.
When your ruler arrives, all will come clear;   290
Until that time you must not do me any wrong.

CHORUS:
This is a serious matter. What you say
Makes sense and carries great weight.
We cannot take this responsibility alone:
A decision can come only from the king.   295

OEDIPUS:
And where is he now?

CHORUS:
In Athens, his father's city. The man
Who brought us here has gone for him.

OEDIPUS:
Do you really think he will come
Just to hear what a blind man has to say?   300

CHORUS:
He'll be here once he hears your name.

OEDIPUS:
But how will he know that?

CHORUS:
Rumors run quickly and news travels fast.
When he hears for himself he'll come.
Your name is known everywhere, old man: 305
Not even sleep will keep him away,
Once he knows who it is that's here.

OEDIPUS:
His arrival will be a blessing for your city
And for me, for a good man is his own best friend.

(Antigone sees someone in the distance.)

285: Oedipus states that whereas he was ignorant of the acts he committed, the gods were not. He claims sanctuary and reminds the chorus that
the gods protect suppliants.

ANTIGONE:
O Zeus! Father! I don't know what to say,
310   What to think!

OEDIPUS:
What's wrong? Antigone?

ANTIGONE:
There's a woman coming,
Riding a Sicilian horse
I can't quite make her out,
Her face is covered by a broad-brimmed hat,
315   But she looks like . . .
It can't be . . .
Is it?. . .
What am I thinking!
320   It is her, I can see her now, she's smiling
And waving. It *is* her! Ismene!

OEDIPUS:
What are you talking about?

ANTIGONE:
Your daughter, my sister!
You'll recognize her voice.

(Enter Ismene and Attendant from the stage
left wing.)

ISMENE:
Father! Sister!
This is wonderful!
325   It was so hard to find you,
Now I see you, I can't help but cry.

OEDIPUS:
Child, is it really you?

313: Sicily had a reputation for breeding fine horses. The horse may not
have appeared onstage as the text implies. Ismene has entered on foot
and left the horse in the care of her servant, who also may not have
appeared. To protect themselves from the sun, travelers often wore a
broad-brimmed hat. The description of Ismene's entrance riding an
expensive mount and dressed in appropriate clothes stands in stark contrast to the disheveled appearance of Oedipus and Antigone.

ISMENE:
   It makes me so sad to see you like this.

OEDIPUS:
   Ismene, you're here!

ISMENE:
   It was difficult, but I'm here.

OEDIPUS:
   Let me touch you. My dear child.

ISMENE:
   Both of you hold me.

   (Oedipus, Antigone, and Ismene embrace.)

OEDIPUS:
   My own flesh and blood.   330

ISMENE:
   What a wretched existence.

OEDIPUS:
   Hers and mine.

ISMENE:
   All three of us share this despair.

OEDIPUS:
   My child, why did you come?

ISMENE:
   Because I care about what will happen to you, Father.

OEDIPUS:
   You came to see me?

ISMENE:
   I have a message that I had to bring in person.
   I came alone, with just one trusted servant.

OEDIPUS:
   And your brothers? Where are they when we need them?   335

ISMENE:
   Where they are things are very bad.

OEDIPUS:
    Like a couple of blasted Egyptians!
    That's how they've decided to live their lives
    Pussyfooting around, sitting at home, sewing
340   While they send the women out to do all the work!
    They should be the ones here caring for me,
    Instead they hide at home like little girls
    And you two shoulder the heavy burden
    Of your poor old father's pain.

        (Indicating Antigone.)

345   And this one, ever since she was old enough,
    She's cared for me, shared all my travels,
    Poor girl, wandering around the wilds
350   Barefoot and starving, drenched by rough rain
    And scorched by the fierce sun. She scorned
    The comforts of a home, all to care for her father.
    And you, Ismene, you have always sought me out,
    Sneaking away from Thebes to bring me word
355   Of the latest prophecies that spoke my name.
    The exile's very own secret spy.
    And what now? Some new mission?
    You've not come for nothing, I can tell.
360   This is serious, you're afraid of something.

ISMENE:
    I won't even describe the trouble I took
    Trying to find out where you had taken refuge—
    I don't want to suffer it all over again
    A second time in the telling.
365   I came because of your unfortunate sons
    And the terrible things that have happened.
    They decided at first to let Creon rule Thebes.
    Knowing that our family was scarred
    By an affliction that had seized your house,
    They hoped this would free the city from defilement.

337: Herodotus notes several distinct differences between the customs of
Greece and Egypt; among them, he writes, "women engage in trade, the
men remain at home and weave" (2.35).

366: Creon—the brother of Jocasta, Oedipus' mother and wife.

But then one of the gods got involved					370
And corrupted their twisted minds
With a lust for power and bitter rivalry.
Then, your youngest son deposed
His older brother, Polynices,
Stripped him of all his authority					375
And banished him into exile.
Rumor has it that he has fled
To the Argive lowlands, forged
A new alliance, and called up
A whole entourage of fighters					380
Sworn to conquer Thebes or die trying.
Father, these are not mere stories:
These terrible things are happening now,
And what the gods will decide to do,
If they feel any pity for you, I just don't know.

OEDIPUS:
What makes you think that the gods					385
Might hear me, even save me?

ISMENE:
Father, we have had new prophecies!

OEDIPUS:
Oracles! What did they say?

ISMENE:
That the people will need you, whether you are alive
		or dead,					390
To grace Thebes with great blessings.

OEDIPUS:
What could a man like me ever do for them?

ISMENE:
It is said that all their strength
Will rest in you.

OEDIPUS:
I'm nothing, how could I ever be that man?

378: Argive lowlands—a region of the eastern Peloponnese also known
as the Argolid.

ISMENE:
   The gods that destroyed you will raise you up.

OEDIPUS:
395   Worthless! Raise up an old man after crushing him in youth.

ISMENE:
   Creon will come because of this,
   He won't be far behind.

OEDIPUS:
   What does he want?

ISMENE:
   To see you placed near Theban soil where he'll possess
400   Your power but keep you out of the city.

OEDIPUS:
   What use am I, lying in no-man's-land?

ISMENE:
   If your grave is neglected, Thebes will suffer your curse.

OEDIPUS:
   I don't need a god to tell me that!

ISMENE:
   That's why they want you near them, under control,
405   In a place where you will do their bidding.

OEDIPUS:
   Will I be buried in Theban soil?

ISMENE:
   That's forbidden, you've killed your own kin.

OEDIPUS:
   Then they'll never have me in their power!

ISMENE:
   Then Thebes will be cursed.

OEDIPUS:
410   When will all this happen?

394: "Will raise you up"—*Ortho-* carries the sense of "restore," "set straight," or "raise up." An apt restoration for the crippled Oedipus.

ISMENE:

>   When they gather near your grave
>   They'll come to know your anger.

OEDIPUS:

>   Who told you these things?

ISMENE:

>   The men Thebes sent to the oracle at Delphi.

OEDIPUS:

>   Apollo spoke of me?

ISMENE:

>   That's what they said when they returned.   415

OEDIPUS:

>   And my sons, have they heard this too?

ISMENE:

>   Both of them, and they understand its meaning.

OEDIPUS:

>   Bastards! They heard this and put their craving
>   For power ahead of their own father?

ISMENE:

>   It's painful to hear, but I have to endure it.   420

OEDIPUS:

>   If this battle is to be, then let no god
>   Prevent it. If I had my way
>   Neither of them would win anything;
>   The usurped throne would be lost,

411: The prophecy implies that the Thebans will one day invade Attica and be defeated somewhere near the final resting place of Oedipus. In 410 or 407 B.C.E., just prior to the staging of this play, the Spartan King Agis led an attack on Athens that involved units of Boeotian cavalry (Thebes is a city in Boeotia). This cavalry raid was defeated somewhere to the north of Athens, and it may well have been at Colonus. This outcome would give great political weight to this line.

413: Delphi—Apollo's oracular sanctuary on the slopes of Mount Parnassus.

419: "Power" here is *turranida,* the same term used in OT.

425   And the exile would never return.
        I was their father, and they both did nothing
        To prevent my cruel banishment.
        They stood by as I was made a pariah,
430   Hounded out of my own city and exiled forever.
        Some said that I got exactly what I wished for,
        But I wanted to die that day.
        My soul burned in agony, and I wished
        That they had stoned me to death there and then.
435   But they refused me even that.
        As time went by my anguish cooled,
        I realized I had been hard on myself
        Unleashing such rage to punish my mistakes.
        But by then my city had cast me out,
440   And my sons, who should have helped me,
        Did nothing and said even less.
        So I became an outcast,
        A beggar, homeless.
445   Only my two daughters stood by me,
        They did all that was humanly possible
        To support me—food, care, and shelter.
        Their brothers traded their father for a throne.
450   I'll never side with them, never,
        And no good will come from their tyranny!
        Now I know. I have heard the prophecies,
        I understand these oracles from Apollo.
455   So let Creon come,
        Send the strongest men in Thebes!
        Strangers, if you grant me the protection
        Of your region's sacred spirits,
        You'll inherit a guardian for your city
460   And a reckoning for all our enemies.

CHORUS:
        Oedipus, we pity you
        And your daughters. We are sympathetic.
        Now that you have offered to be a blessing to us
        I can tell you something that will help you.

OEDIPUS:
465   Befriend me, and all will be fulfilled.

CHORUS:
> The goddesses demand ritual purification
> For trespassing on their holy ground.

OEDIPUS:
> What must I do? Tell me.

CHORUS:
> Cleanse your hands in the sacred spring
> And return here with the holy water.   470

OEDIPUS:
> Yes, a pure offering, what then?

CHORUS:
> There you'll find the finest-crafted vessels;
> Cover the brims and wrap the handles.

OEDIPUS:
> With wool or olive sprigs?

CHORUS:
> Use the fleece from a young lamb.   475

OEDIPUS:
> How do I complete the offering?

CHORUS:
> Pour the libation as you face the rising sun.

OEDIPUS:
> Should I pour from the same vessels?

CHORUS:
> Yes, three streams, but drain only the third.

OEDIPUS:
> What does the third contain?   480

467: Oedipus must atone for treading on sacred ground, in order to remain under the protection of the men of Colonus.

475: Woolen wreaths or twigs festooned with wool were the symbol of the suppliant.

477: "Pour the libation"—The libation is to be poured on the ground as an offering to Underworld spirits, in this case the Furies. The east, as the direction of the rising sun, was considered the direction of new light and purification. Statues of the gods often faced the east.

CHORUS:
Water mixed with honey, but no wine.

OEDIPUS:
And the cool earth will drink
My offering. Then what?

CHORUS:
Take three bundles of nine olive sprigs;
Use both hands to place them. Pray.

OEDIPUS:
485   This prayer is important, let me hear it.

CHORUS:
Pray that the spirits we call benevolent
Will come and care for you with kindness,
Receiving you as their sacred suppliant.
Speak softly; do not raise your voice,
490   Leave quickly, and never look back.
Perform these rites correctly and we
Can support and defend you fearlessly.
If not, all hope for you is lost.

OEDIPUS:
Daughters, did you hear what they said?

ISMENE:
Yes, but what should we do?

OEDIPUS:
495   Perform these rites, I'm too old

481: "Water mixed with honey"—Oedipus must pour fresh water from each of the first two vessels but not empty them. Only the third should be drained, and its water must be mixed with honey. A triple libation to the dead can also be found in Homer's *Odyssey*, where Odysseus pours water, wine, and honey to summon the spirits of the dead (*Odyssey* 10.518–26). It seems that wine was never offered to the Eumenides (see note on line 101).

484: The number three and its multiples such as nine were regarded as sacred. This view may be derived from the three-way division of the cosmos into air, land, and sea. The olive sprig is the symbol of the suppliant, and the tree was sacred to Athens (lines 700–6). The specific instruction regarding placing the sprigs may mean that Oedipus should start and end with the lucky right hand.

And weak, I'll not be able to see.
But one of you could go instead,
One pure heart can represent
A multitude and atone for all.
Quickly now, one of you must do it,   500
The other needs to stay here with me—
I'm far too feeble to be left alone.

ISMENE:
I'll go, but where?

CHORUS:
To the other side of the grove—   505
The guardian there will help you.

ISMENE:
Antigone, stay here and keep watch over Father.
I'll do this. It should be second nature
To want to help our parents.

(Exit Ismene through the stage right wing.)

CHORUS:
I've no wish to open old wounds,   510
But can you tell us . . . ?

OEDIPUS:
Tell you what?

CHORUS:
How did you bear it?
The suffering, the horror?

OEDIPUS:
Please, for the sake of hospitality
Don't dredge up all my painful memories.   515

CHORUS:
We want only to know the truth.
We have all heard the stories.

OEDIPUS:
Oh no!

510–48: Here the play breaks into an excited lyric meter appropriate to
the disturbing memories it brings up, in striking contrast to the iambics
of the dialogue and speeches. Such a passage is called a *kommos.*

CHORUS:
  Please understand.

OEDIPUS:
  No, no!

CHORUS:
520 We did what you asked of us, be persuaded.

OEDIPUS:
  I have suffered the most disgusting evils,
  All of them against my will.
  The gods know I had no choice.

CHORUS:
  What happened?

OEDIPUS:
  A marriage made by the city
525 That matched me to destruction.

CHORUS:
  I've heard it said that you married your . . . own mother.

OEDIPUS:
  Every time I hear that, it sounds like death.
530 These girls, they are mine, yes, but . . .

CHORUS:
  But what? What are you saying?

OEDIPUS:
  My daughters—my curses.

CHORUS:
  Zeus!

OEDIPUS:
  Born to me from the womb of my mother.

CHORUS:
  Then they're your daughters and your . . .

OEDIPUS:
535 Sisters. They are their father's sisters.

521: "All of them against my will"—We follow the mss. Some modern editors choose to correct the line to read "I was willing to bear them."

CHORUS:
   No!

OEDIPUS:
   Why must these evils always
   Return to haunt me? Why? Why?

CHORUS:
   What you suffered . . .

OEDIPUS:
   I suffered so much.

CHORUS:
   But what you did . . .

OEDIPUS:
   I did nothing.

CHORUS:
   How could that be?

OEDIPUS:
   My city gave me a gift—my reward.
   Gods! Why did I ever accept it?   540

CHORUS:
   But there's more, isn't there? You murdered . . .

OEDIPUS:
   What? What else must I tell you?

CHORUS:
   Your father.

OEDIPUS:
   Another blow. Again and again,
   Pain after pain.

CHORUS:
   But you did kill him?   545

OEDIPUS:
   Yes, I killed him, but . . .

540: Oedipus' reward for answering the riddle of the Sphinx and lifting
the plague on Thebes was the throne and his marriage to Jocasta, the
queen—and unbeknown to him at that time—his mother.

CHORUS:
But what?

OEDIPUS:
It was justifiable . . .

CHORUS:
Justifiable?

OEDIPUS:
Let me explain! I did kill him,
After he tried to kill me.
Under any kind of law I'm innocent,
I never knew who he was!

CHORUS:
The king is coming! The son of Aegeus,
550   Theseus has heard you are here.

(Enter Theseus from the stage right wing.)

THESEUS:
The son of Laius, I know all about you,
How you put out your own eyes,
I've heard all the gruesome details.
I'm sure it's you—your face,
555   Your tattered clothes, it can be only
Oedipus.
I've come out of compassion
To ask what exactly you and your poor
Daughter want from us here in Athens.
560   You can speak freely without shame.
There is nothing you can say so unspeakable
That could deny you a fair hearing.
You should know that once I too
Was an exile and had to struggle to survive,
565   So how could I ever allow myself to ignore

547: "After he tried to kill me"—Here we follow Jebb's (1899/1962) correction of a corrupt manuscript.

548: A man in a chariot accompanied by a small retinue forced Oedipus off the trail from Delphi. A fight ensued, and Oedipus killed them all. He later learned that the man in the chariot was in fact his father, Laius (OT, lines 795–813).

The pleas of one so lost in desperation?
I know that I'm just a man and that tomorrow
May hold nothing more for me than you.

OEDIPUS:
Theseus, such kindness, and eloquence.
You know me, my family, and where I'm from,   570
All that remains is for me to explain
Why I've come and what it is I want.

THESEUS:
Tell me everything.   575

OEDIPUS:
I have a gift to give you:
My own broken body—not much to look at,
But appearances can deceive,
And it has the power to bring you great good.

THESEUS:
What kind of power?

OEDIPUS:
Have a little patience, it will all come clear.   580

THESEUS:
When?

OEDIPUS:
When I'm dead and gone and you have buried me.

THESEUS:
So you want me to perform the last rites,
But what about your life, is that worth nothing?

OEDIPUS:
I want nothing else.
This death would make sense of my life.   585

THESEUS:
This is a small thing you have asked me to do.

OEDIPUS:
Yes and no . . . It could bring conflict.

THESEUS:
Between your sons and me?

OEDIPUS:
They'll force you to send me back to Thebes.

THESEUS:
590   Don't you want that, an end to your exile?

OEDIPUS:
Once, but they refused me.

THESEUS:
Be reasonable, anger only makes matters worse.

OEDIPUS:
Don't chastise me until you've heard it all.

THESEUS:
You're right. I shouldn't rush to judgment.

OEDIPUS:
595   Theseus, I have suffered so many wrongs.

THESEUS:
Are you talking about what happened to your family?

OEDIPUS:
No, let everyone else in Greece talk about that.

THESEUS:
Then what makes you suffer more than any man could bear?

OEDIPUS:
My own sons cast me out of my country!
600   And I can never return;
I am stained with the blood of my father.

THESEUS:
Then why bring you back if it is forbidden?

OEDIPUS:
The oracle forces them to do it.

THESEUS:
A prophecy? What are they so afraid of?

OEDIPUS:
605   Their destruction, here in this land.

THESEUS:
But what could cause a conflict between us?

OEDIPUS:

Son of Aegeus, dear boy, only the gods
Can defy old age, they'll never know death,
Everything else is ravaged by time:
A country's power wanes, a body weakens,   610
Devotion decays, and duplicity flourishes.
The essence of friendship is constantly shifting,
Never remaining the same. Two cities are like
Two friends, and everything changes in the passage
Of time—love turns to hate, hate can turn to love.
Now the skies between Athens and Thebes   615
Are bright and fair, but time brings on
The countless days and nights, and on just one
A spear can shatter a delicate pledge   620
And smash all sense of reason.
On that day my old cold corpse
Will be nourished by their thick warm blood.
Mark me, if none of this occurs,
Zeus is not Zeus, and Apollo is a liar.

I've said quite enough for now—
Some things should be kept silent.
I'll end where I began, asking for your word,   625
And if I am not being duped by the gods,
You'll never regret that you welcomed
Oedipus into your land.

CHORUS:

Sir, this is what he's been telling us too.
I think he means to be true to his word.   630

THESEUS:

I must show respect for such good intentions,
Not just for the sake of hospitality
But because he has sought sanctuary with the spirits.
Reverence forbids me to throw away this gift;   635
Therefore I am inclined to allow him to stay
And incorporate him within our city.

(*Addressing the chorus.*)

636–7: See endnote.

If he wants to remain here, then you
Will be responsible for his well-being,
640   Or, he may come with me to Athens.
Oedipus, I'll support whatever you decide.

OEDIPUS:
Oh, Zeus bless you!

THESEUS:
Do you want to come with me?

OEDIPUS:
It is not right. This is the place.

THESEUS:
645   All right, but what can you do here?

OEDIPUS:
This is where I will defeat those who banished me.

THESEUS:
You said that your being here would prove beneficial.

OEDIPUS:
If you are true to your word and do what I ask.

THESEUS:
Don't worry, I won't deceive you.

OEDIPUS:
650   Then this pact will not need an oath.

THESEUS:
My word is my bond.

OEDIPUS:
Then what will happen when . . . ?

THESEUS:
What are you afraid of?

OEDIPUS:
They'll come for me.

THESEUS:
These men will protect you.

OEDIPUS:
Are you leaving me?

THESEUS:
You don't need to tell me what I need to do.

OEDIPUS:
But . . . I'm afraid.   655

THESEUS:
There's no reason to be.

OEDIPUS:
You don't know their threats.

THESEUS:
I know this: No one will take you away
Against my will. I don't care for threats—
They're just angry, bloated boasts,
A sound mind evaporates a threat.   660
These Thebans can brag and gloat
About how they'll come and seize you,
But I think they'll find their journey
A little rougher than they imagine.
Don't worry; you are in my care now,
And it seems Apollo has plans for you.   665
Even though I can't be by your side
My name will be enough to keep you safe.

(Exit Theseus through the stage right wing.)

First Stasimon

CHORUS:

[Strophe *a*]

Stranger, this is gleaming Colonus,
Horse country, beautiful meadows,
Where the mournful trills of nightingales   670
Haunt the shadows of green glades
Garlanded in the god's ivy,

668: "Gleaming"—The Greek has *arghta,* meaning "gleaming-white."
This color was associated with the rituals of death and the Underworld.
Two small knolls of distinctive light soil stood in the sanctuary of Colo-
nus. One knoll was known as Colonus Hippius; the other was sacred to
Demeter.

The deep color of dark wine.
Here intricate berry-filled briars
675   Twist around lush vines,
Never scorched by the sun
Nor struck by storms.
The wreathed reveler,
Dionysus walks this earth
680   Circled by his nurturing Nymphs.

[Antistrophe *a*]

Here, every dawn, heaven-sent dew feeds
The bloom of exquisite narcissus,
Ancient crown of the Great Goddesses.
Here the crocus glistens golden

679: Dionysus—the god of wine, ecstasy, and certain fertility rites. The ivy and the vine are his symbols. His other title *"Bacchus"* is derived from the word meaning "to consecrate with garlands," a poetic link between the god himself and the vivid description of the glade at Colonus. Mystery cults associated with Dionysus promised a blessed afterlife and tranquillity.

680: As a child, Dionysus was nursed by the Nymphs of the mythical eastern region of Nysa.

682: The Mediterranean narcissus (*narcissus poeticus*) has brilliant white petals, with a golden center trimmed with red; it is another Greek symbol of death. Its fragrance was believed to have narcotic powers, and in mythology it is the flower that Persephone is reaching for at the moment she is seized by Hades and taken down to the Underworld. According to legend, Narcissus was a handsome young man who fell in love with his own reflection in the river, gazing on it until he died, whereupon he was turned into the narcissus flower.

683: The goddesses are Demeter and Kore (Persephone). Demeter is the Earth Mother and goddess of vegetation. The winter was caused by the annual disappearance of her daughter Persephone into the Underworld. The cults of Demeter and Kore are connected with death and renewal, the most famous being the Eleusinian Mysteries that promised an afterlife to initiates. The second white hill at Colonus was sacred to Demeter Euchlous (spirit of new plant life). Wreaths made of the narcissus and flowers belonging to the narcissus family were worn by devotees of the two goddesses.

684: The yellow crocus flower was also associated with the myth of Demeter and Kore and with death rites.

Along the banks of Cephissus,   685
His eternal waters threading
Across the fertile fields,
Bathing the broad earth,
Birthing abundant crops.
The Muses grace this place   690
With their heavenly presence,
And Aphrodite rides here
With gleaming golden reins.

[Strophe *b*]

And here is a miracle like nothing else
In all of Asia or the Land of Pelops.   695
Growing wild,
Self-perpetuating,
Terrorizing all our enemies,
It thrives in our soil, eternal,
The nurturing gray-green olive.   700
Neither young nor old
Can blight its sacred crop,
Watched by the all-seeing
Gaze of Zeus   705
And Athena's olive-eyes.

685: In mythology, Cephissus was the name of the father of Narcissus. It is also the name of a river in Attica to the west of Colonus.

690: "Muses"—These nine deities of music and poetry had a shrine in the Academy near Colonus.

692: Aphrodite was the goddess of erotic love, and her mythological companion Eros did have a small shrine at the entrance to the Academy. In Euripides' *Medea* (line 835), King Aegeus tells Medea how Aphrodite blessed Athens after drawing water from the river Cephissus.

695: "Land of Pelops"—the Peloponnese, in southern Greece.

697: "Self-perpetuating"—Herodotus (8.55) tells of Athena's sacred olive tree on the Acropolis sprouting again after the Persians cut it down during their occupation of Athens in 480 B.C.E.

698: "Terrorizing all our enemies"—There was a tradition that during the early phases of the Peloponnesian War, the invading Spartans under Archidamus had spared the sacred olive trees in the Academy.

706: There were an altar to Zeus Morios (protector of the sacred olive) in the Academy and a shrine to Athena nearby.

[Antistrophe *b*]

Two magnificent gifts
The great god Poseidon
Gave our mother-city:
710 The power of horses
And command of the sea.
The son of Cronus,
He himself gave us glory,
And on our roads
715 First bridled the wildest colts.
He fashioned the sleek oar-blade
That trims and sweeps the oceans
Chasing the sea nymphs'
Hundred dancing feet.

(Antigone sees Creon and his guards approaching.)

ANTIGONE:
720 Now land praised beyond all compare,
Prove your brilliance with action.

OEDIPUS:
What is it now, child?

ANTIGONE:
Father, Creon is coming with armed guards.

OEDIPUS:
My friends, elders, now I need you
725 To prove that you will keep me safe.

711: "The power of horses and command of the sea"—A well of saltwa-
ter was situated in the Erectheum on the Acropolis adjacent to Athena's
sacred olive tree. The well and the tree were representations of the gifts
that each god had bestowed on the city as they competed to become its
patron.
712: "The son of Cronus"—The Titan Cronus was the father of the first
generation of Olympians, including Zeus and his brother Poseidon.
717: Poseidon was credited with introducing the training and breaking
of horses, and his connection to the shrine of the horseman Colonus is
apparent. The god also introduced rowing and crafted the first oar-blade.
719: "Sea nymphs' hundred dancing feet"—The Nereids, ocean-dwelling
daughters of the sea-spirit Nereus. Hesiod names fifty in the *Theogony*
(lines 246–65), hence the epithet "hundred footed."

CHORUS:
Don't be afraid, we'll protect you.
We may be old, but this land's still strong.

(Enter Creon accompanied by Theban guards from the
stage left wing.)

CREON:
Gentlemen, citizens of Colonus,
My arrival seems to have made you
Apprehensive. There's no need to be,   730
I've not come to cause an argument,
And I'm certainly not going to provoke a fight.
I'm an old man myself and here I am
In a city as strong as any in Greece.
Despite my age, my city sent me
To persuade Oedipus to return   735
With me to the land of Thebes.
I'm not here at the behest of any one man,
No, all of my citizens urged it,
After all, I am his nearest living relation,
And back home in Thebes I've borne
The bulk of the burden of his pain.

Oedipus, you've suffered enough,   740
Listen to me now and come back home.
Everyone in Thebes wants you back
But no one more than me.
What kind of man would I be
If I could stand to see you in such despair   745
And not be completely heartbroken?
Look at you, a wandering vagrant
With just this little girl to help you.
Poor, poor child, I could never have   750
Imagined that her life would come to this.
Scratching out a living, begging for scraps
Without a husband to keep her safe.
We must all take the blame, Oedipus,
Both you and I, our entire family,

728: Creon is depicted as an old man dressed in royal robes and accompanied by a retinue of armed Theban soldiers.

755   The shame. It's all out in the open now.
Oedipus, please just listen to me,
In the name of our ancestral gods
Return with me to your father's city.
Say your kind good-byes to this place;
It has certainly treated you very well,
But home is where you should be,
760   Home in Thebes, the city of your birth.

OEDIPUS:
There's nothing you wouldn't sink to!
Perverting a seemingly honest plea
To suit your twisted schemes.
What do you hope to achieve
With this feeble attempt to lure me
Into your trap? More torment for me?
765   I remember pleading with you to drive
Me away when I couldn't bear the pain,
But you refused to do that for me.
When my anguish began to ease
And seclusion at home brought some comfort,
You drove me out and forced me away!
770   Where were your family values then?
So, here you are again, and you find
A city that has extended me a welcome
And all you want to do is drag me away,
Shrouding your spite in flattery.

775   Do you actually enjoy forcing
Your "favors" on people?
Suppose you were desperate and you had to ask
Someone for help and he constantly
Refused. Later when you had found
Happiness, he gladly offered charity.
780   Do you think you'd be grateful to him?

756: "In the name of our ancestral gods"—The Theban royal family was descended from Poseidon, whose son Agenor was the father of Cadmus, the legendary founder of Thebes. See Theban Royal Family Tree.

766: At the end of OT (line 1518), Oedipus pleads with Creon to banish him. Creon refuses, citing the need to consult the gods for advice.

That's all the good your offer will do me!
These men will witness your chicanery;
Yes, you've come for me, but not
To take me home, but to dump me
Out on the frontier to protect Thebes   785
From fighting a war against Athens.
You'll never get away with it!
But what you can have is my curse
Festering deep down in this earth, forever!
As for my sons, they'll both inherit
Theban soil, just enough to cover their corpses.   790

I think I see the affairs of Thebes more clearly
Than you, but how could that possibly be?
Because I hear the true words
Of Apollo and his father, Zeus.
You'll find that your politician's perjured
Tongue and conniving doublespeak   795
Will bring you nothing but trouble.
Oh, I know I'll never convince you of anything.
Go; leave me alone to live as I want,
I have made my choice, now let me be content.

CREON:
    And who do you think will suffer more   800
    From your resolution, you or I?

OEDIPUS:
    I'll just enjoy the fact that you'll never
    Convince me or anybody else here.

CREON:
    It's a shame. All these years and still so unwise:
    You're a disgrace, even in your old age.   805

OEDIPUS:
    Yes, you're very clever in your eloquence.
    An honest man would never be so proficient.

CREON:
    Verbosity doesn't win arguments.

OEDIPUS:
    When do you ever speak plainly?

CREON:

810   Never to a man with a mind like yours!

OEDIPUS:

Then I'll speak for all of us here—go!
Take your spying eyes and leave me alone,
This is where I have decided to stay!

CREON:

I call on everybody here, including my own men,
Everybody except you, to witness your insults.
If you were in my custody, you . . .

OEDIPUS:

815   Try it! See if my allies here would let you.

CREON:

I'm warning you, I'll find a way to make you regret this.

OEDIPUS:

Threaten away! What could you do?

CREON:

This. I've already apprehended one of your daughters,
And she's on her way back to Thebes. It's merely
820   A matter of time until I take the other one.

OEDIPUS:

No!

CREON:

I warned you.

OEDIPUS:

What have you done with my child?

CREON:

The same thing I plan to do with Antigone.

OEDIPUS:

Friends! Help me! I need you now.
Force this defiler from your land.

CHORUS:

You must leave. Your actions are impious;
825   We'll not tolerate such behavior here.

CREON:
Guards! Get the girl—if she won't come
Of her own accord, use force.

(Creon's guards move toward Antigone.)

ANTIGONE:
Oh Gods no! Help me!

CHORUS:
What do you think you're doing?

CREON:
I'll not touch him, but she's mine. 830

OEDIPUS:
Guardians of this land!

CHORUS:
Stranger, you have no right to do this.

CREON:
I have every right.

CHORUS:
How can you?

CREON:
She is rightfully mine.

OEDIPUS:
Help me, Athens!

CHORUS:
Stop this, let her go
Or this will come to blows. 835

CREON:
Keep away from me!

828: It was considered impious to remove suppliants from a sanctuary by force, because they were under divine protection.

830: Creon considers himself the legal guardian of Antigone and Ismene. In OT (line 1506), Oedipus asks Creon to adopt them after he has blinded himself.

833–43: "Help me, Athens!"—Here the play returns to lyric meters appropriate to the excitement of the moment. An exact metrical parallel occurs at 876–86, the other abduction scene.

CHORUS:
If you continue, you'll leave us no choice.

CREON:
Lay a hand on me and it will be war.

OEDIPUS:
Just what I predicted.

> *(Creon's guards seize Antigone.)*

CHORUS:
Release the girl.

CREON:
Who do you think you are to give me orders?

CHORUS:
Let her go.

CREON:
840   Why don't you hobble away?

CHORUS:
Come on! Help! To arms!
Defend your city, our home
Is under attack! To arms!

ANTIGONE:
Friends! Friends! Stop them.

> *(Oedipus desperately reaches for Antigone as the guards drag her away.)*

OEDIPUS:
845   Child, where are you?

ANTIGONE:
Father! They're forcing me away.

OEDIPUS:
Take my hand!

ANTIGONE:
I can't! I can't!

843: "To arms!"—Creon and his guards have violated a sacred shrine, which could represent an act of war.

CREON: *(To his guards.)*
  Take her away.

> *(Exit the guards with Antigone through the stage
> left wing.)*

OEDIPUS:
  No! This is unbearable.

CREON:
  From now on you'll walk alone
  Without the aid of these two crutches.
  You want to betray your own country   850
  And turn against your former friends.
  Well, I'm here because they commanded it
  Even though I reign as their king.
  You may have won your victory for now,
  But one day you'll learn that your temper
  Has turned you against your own.
  Your rage has always been your downfall.   855

> *(Creon starts to leave, and the chorus move to
> stop him.)*

CHORUS:
  Stop! Go no further!

CREON:
  Don't you dare touch me.

CHORUS:
  You're not going anywhere
  With these two girls.

CREON:
  You'll regret this, it will be bad
  For your city; you'll force my hand.

CHORUS:
  What are you talking about?

CREON:
  I'll take him hostage.   860

CHORUS:
  You wouldn't dare!

CREON:
    And who's going to stop me—your king?

OEDIPUS:
    You can't touch me, it would be sacrilege.

CREON:
    Shut up!

OEDIPUS:
865   I will not! Let the spirits here
    Witness my curse. You scum.
    I've been blind for so very long,
    And you've stolen from me
    The last light of my life,
    My own dear eyes.
    Let the eternal eye itself,
    The blazing sun in the sky
870   Inflict an old age on you just like mine!

CREON:
    Do you people here see this?

OEDIPUS:
    They've seen everything and know
    That you forced me to curse you.

CREON:
    I've had just about enough of this as I can bear;
875   I'm taking him, even if I have to do it myself.

    (Creon enters the sanctuary and approaches Oedipus.)

OEDIPUS:
    Help me!

CHORUS:
    This is outrageous!
    You'll never get away with it.

CREON:
    Watch me.

876–86: "Help me!"—Here the play returns to lyric meters appropriate to
the excitement of the moment. An exact metrical parallel occurs at 833–
43, the other abduction scene.

CHORUS:
  You think our city has no laws?

CREON:
  When a man is right, the weak can beat the strong.   880

OEDIPUS:
  Listen to him!

CHORUS:
  He wouldn't dare! Zeus would know.

CREON:
  Zeus knows what you don't!

CHORUS:
  But this is . . . hubris!

CREON:
  Hubris you'll have to bear.

CHORUS:
  Citizens! Leaders!
  Come quickly!
  We need your help.   885
  This has gone far enough.

  *(Enter Theseus and attendants through the stage
  right wing.)*

THESEUS:
  What is going on here?
  You're interrupting the rites of Poseidon,
  Who is the guardian of Colonus.
  Someone raised the alarm and I came
  As fast as my feet could carry me.   890

OEDIPUS:
  I know that voice, Theseus!
  My friend! This man wrongs me.

THESEUS:
  Who? Tell me.

883: Here "hubris" has the sense of a moral outrage.

OEDIPUS:
Creon! You must be able to see him.

895 He's taken my children away from me.

THESEUS:
What is this?

OEDIPUS:
I'm telling you the truth.

THESEUS:
Quick as you can, someone run to the altars,
Tell them to abandon the sacrifice,
Mount their horses, and ride
900 With all speed to the place
Where the two roads meet.
At all costs they must prevent
These girls from leaving our territory;
Otherwise this foreigner will
Get the better of us all
And make me look ridiculous.
Now go, as fast as possible!
905 If I were to let my emotions rule,
This man would barely escape
With his life. Well, he came here
Citing certain laws, let us
Therefore enact them now.

(To Creon.)

You're staying right here, until
910 These girls are returned to me
And I see them with my own eyes.
What you've done appalls me
And dishonors you and your country.
You see, this is a city that respects
Justice and holds the law in high regard.
915 Yet you just barge your way in,

901: This reference to the Athenian cavalry may have been political. The
sanctuary of Poseidon may have been where the members of the well-to-
do, land-owning Athenian cavalry class (the *hippeis*) met and enacted a
coup in 411 B.C.E. that overthrew the existing democratic government,
which they considered to be out of control.

Grabbing at whatever you want,
Thinking you can dictate your terms
With barbarity and brute force!
Did you think Athens devoid of citizens?
Perhaps you consider us a slave state
Where you can get away with anything.
Am I, too, beneath your contempt?
It certainly can't be Thebes that taught
You to behave so abhorrently,   920
Surely that city does not produce
Such detestable inhabitants.
I cannot believe Thebes would condone
Your ransacking of my country.
Capturing poor defenseless suppliants,
You steal not only from me, but also the gods.
What if I came to your country,   925
Even if I had right on my side,
Ignored the rule of law there,
And simply started abducting people?
Inconceivable! Because I know how a foreigner
Is supposed to behave as a guest abroad.
But you, you're a disgrace to Thebes,
That city hardly deserves the likes of you.
Clearly the years have only served   930
To bring you old age, not wisdom.

So I'll repeat my words:
These girls must be returned quickly,
Otherwise, you'll stay here yourself
As our reluctant guest.
And I tell you this—I mean what I say.   935

CHORUS:
Can you see what you have done?
A man of your station should know better.

CREON:
Son of Aegeus, I did not think Athens
Backward or weak in any way whatsoever.   940
I never imagined that your people
Would care quite so much
For the fortunes of my hapless family

To offer asylum to one of them, against me.
I was certain that they would never
945 Accept a man who murdered his father,
And committed incest—a foul pariah,
An outcast with a monstrous brood.
I had heard that the Areopagus council
Refused admission to godforsaken derelicts
950 And so I was sure I would get what I wanted.
You know, I would have let him go
If he hadn't called down curses on me.
Was I wrong to want to set things right?
Yes, I'm old, but anger still surges—
955 Only death can calm that rage.
I am at your mercy, I have no power here
Even though I believe I am in the right.
But old as I may be, I can still oppose you
And will find a way to seek redress.

OEDIPUS:
960 This man is contemptible! Have you no shame?
I don't know who you abuse more,
Me in my old age or you in yours.
You rant on about taboo killings,
Foul marriages, and vile incest.
It was I who suffered these things
965 But the gods made it so,
Exorcising some ancient grudge
Through my bloodline.
I cannot be blamed for the crimes
I inflicted on myself and my family,
You won't find a single reason
Why I deserved any of it.
How was it my fault
That my father received
A prediction that he would
970 Be killed by his very own son?

948: Areopagus council—This court convened on the Hill of Ares northwest of the Acropolis in Athens. Prior to the reforms of Ephialtes in 461
B.C.E. it had far-ranging judicial powers, but these were reduced to primarily judging cases of homicide and some religious cases, as well as
acting as an advisory body to the Athenian council.

That happened before I was born—
I had not even been conceived!
But I was born, unluckily,
And yes, I did fight and kill my father,
But I had no idea who he was—
I didn't know what I was doing.   975
How can you call me guilty
When I knew nothing . . . nothing!
And my mother? How dare you
Make me speak of that marriage.
She was your sister—shall I go on?
Yes, you've gone far beyond the bounds
Of decency, why then should I keep quiet?   980
She gave birth to me, a cursed birth,
But she too was ignorant of it all.
My mother also bore my children:
It is disgusting, her everlasting shame!
Yet you seem to delight in degrading   985
Her name and defaming me.
I don't want to talk about it any more
Except to say that I will not be blamed
For that union nor the killing
Of my father, and yet here you are
Continuing to hurl abuse at me.   990
Just tell me this: if a man approached
You right now and threatened your life,
What's the first thing you would do?
Would you defend yourself from harm
Or stop to ask if he might be your father?
Unless you have some sort of death wish,
I'm sure you'd meet his assault, like for like,
Without considering the future at all.   995
That was exactly my situation out on that road.
It was all decided by the gods, and if
My father could be brought back to life,
He'd agree with everything I said.
However, you have no respect for Justice: 1000
You'll say and do anything if it suits your
Purpose, and you spout your filth
At anyone who will listen to you.

I heard you just now fawning on Theseus
And praising the government of Athens,
1005 But the qualities you pay your lip service to
Are all too real, as you will soon discover.
The Athenians respect the laws of the gods
More than any other people in Greece.
You chose the worst place to try
And steal a suppliant from a sanctuary
And abduct his two dear daughters.
1010 So I will pray to the spirits here
To stand by my side as allies,
And soon enough you'll see
The mettle of the men who guard this city.

CHORUS:
This man is our honored guest-friend;
1015 Though his life has been horrendous
He has been given our protection.

THESEUS:
We're just wasting time standing here talking,
The criminals are escaping.

CREON:
There's nothing I can do now.

THESEUS:
You can lead the way and take me
1020 To the place where you are holding
Those two girls and return them to me.
But if your men have already fled for Thebes,
They'll not make it home
And ever get to thank the gods;
My horsemen will cut them off.
1025 Now let's go. The tables are turned:
The hunter has become the prey,
And a prize won by deceit, lost.
No one will help you now,
I know you would never have dared
1030 This aggressive incursion
Without strategy or support.

1031: "Without strategy or support"—This phrase most likely refers to

Something certainly made you so bold.
I'll see to this myself and not commit
Any more of my men to this mission
In case I weaken the defense of Athens.
Do you understand the implications   1035
Of what I'm saying to you,
Or like the lies you spun in pursuit
Of your plot, do they mean nothing?

CREON:
While I'm here I can only agree
With everything that you tell me.
But once I have returned home . . .

THESEUS:
Idle threats! Now start moving.
Oedipus, stay here in safety.
I'll return your children to you,   1040
Or die trying. You have my word.

OEDIPUS:
Bless you, Theseus, you're a just man.
You have already done so much for us.

Second Stasimon

*(Exit Creon, Theseus, and attendants through the
stage left wing.)*

[Strophe *a*]

CHORUS:
I wish I were there
Against the enemy,   1045
Turning the line
And marching into
The battle-clash of Ares.
At Apollo's seacoast,

Creon's military force; however, some scholars have seen a reference to
an Athenian accomplice (Jebb 1899/1962). This seems unlikely, and such
an important point is never developed anywhere in the play.
1049: "Apollo's seacoast"— This may be a reference to the bay of Eleusis
about six miles from Colonus. A temple to Apollo stood there near the

1050 The sacred shore ablaze,
     With brilliant lamps
     Illuminating holy rites.
     Deep mysteries
     Locked tight by priests
     With the golden key
     Of Eleusinian silence.
1055 Theseus is there
     Forging ahead,
     Forcing the fight,
     Screaming for war,
     Rescuing the sisters
     From the frontier.

[Antistrophe *a*]

     Soon they'll be here
1060 Racing the western plain,
     Charging horses leaving
     The snow peak behind,
     Chariots hurtling on.
     Victory will come;
1065 The heart of Ares beats
     In the breasts of our men.
     Bridles glinting, reins flashing,
     The Cavalry charges on.
1070 Knights of Athena,
     Followers of Poseidon,
     Planet Shaker,
     Son of Mother Earth.

---

pass of Daphni. The most direct route from there to Athens was along the
Sacred Way, and the reference to "brilliant lamps" suggests the annual
torchlight procession of the rites of Persephone and Kore. These sacred
rites were concerned with death and renewal, a constant theme in this play.

1054: "Eleusinian silence"—The Greek has "Eumolpidae," the Eleusinian
clan and priests of the sanctuary named for Eumolpus, the mythical first
Eleusinian *hierophant* (priest or minister).

1060: Western plain—The Greek refers to a place called "Oa." Scholars
are divided as to where this is: perhaps the western end of Mount Parnes
to the north of Athens en route to Boeotia, or Mount Aigaleos, a peak
southeast of Colonus.

[Strophe *b*]

Has battle begun?
Do they wait to fight?   1075
Can I dare predict
An end to their pain?
This tortured family.
Zeus will end it.
I sense a victory.   1080
If only I had wings
And could soar
Like a dove, high
On the rushing wind
And there behold the battle.

[Antistrophe *b*]

Zeus who sees all,   1085
Greatest god of all,
Grant good fortune
To our defenders.
Lend them your power.
Daughter of Zeus,
Pallas Athena!   1090
Apollo the huntsman!
Artemis, your sister,
Stalker of fleet-footed deer:
Come to our aid!
Help this land,   1095
Help us all!

> *(To Oedipus.)*

Friend, you'll call me a prophet.
I can see your daughters
Coming this way, safe and sound.

OEDIPUS:
Where? Where? What's happening?

> *(Enter Antigone, Ismene, and Theseus from the stage
> left wing.)*

ANTIGONE:
Father! Father!

1100   If only the gods would let you see
        The man who has delivered us!

OEDIPUS:
        My child! Are both of you here?

ANTIGONE:
        Yes, yes. Theseus and his men
        Rescued both of us.

OEDIPUS:
1105   Come here, let me hold you.
        I couldn't wish for more.

ANTIGONE:
        And we want what you wish.

            (Oedipus, Antigone, and Ismene embrace.)

OEDIPUS:
        My dear children.

ANTIGONE:
        All children are dear to their fathers.

OEDIPUS:
        I need you. My supports.

ANTIGONE:
        We've always braced against the pain with you.

OEDIPUS:
1110   Now that you're back I could die a happy man
        Knowing that the both of you are beside me.
        Hold on tight, each take an arm,
        There, a father and his children:
        My comfort in destitution.
        I was so lost without you, so lost.
1115   But come on, tell me everything
        Quick as you can. Briefly though,
        Young girls can say too much.

ANTIGONE:
        Theseus saved us, he should tell it,
        What's more to be said than that?

            (To Theseus.)

OEDIPUS:
>My friend, I'm sorry I've taken
>So long to greet my children, 1120
>I thought that they were lost forever.
>I owe you this moment of joy,
>You brought them back to me.
>Gods bless you and your wonderful city.
>In all my wanderings, this is the only place 1125
>Where I have found truth, honor, and justice.
>I am well aware of how much I stand in your debt,
>Without your help I would have nothing at all,
>Let me shake your hand, dear king,
>And kiss your cheek in deep gratitude . . . 1130

>(*Oedipus suddenly reels back.*)

>But what am I doing?
>I'm a vile wretch!
>You must not touch me,
>I'm stained with indelible evil!
>No, you must never touch me, 1135
>Only those who have suffered with me
>Could ever understand my grief.
>Stay back and let me thank you from here,
>But please continue to care for me.
>You have always been so kind.

THESEUS:
>It's perfectly natural that you
>Would indulge yourself a little
>In greeting your own children. 1140
>I understand, you should think
>About them before me.
>There's nothing wrong in that.
>Actions speak louder than words,
>That's how I try to live my life,
>And I promised you that I would 1145
>Return these girls to their father.
>And here they are, in good health
>Despite the threats we endured.
>As for the way we won the fight,

I've no need to gloat about that.
Your daughters will tell you everything.

1150   But there is something I have heard,
A small thing, but strange,
It's prudent to be cautious, I think.
Would you give me your opinion?

OEDIPUS:
What is it, Theseus?
1155   We've not heard of anything here.

THESEUS:
A man has sought sanctuary
At Poseidon's shrine,
Where I was sacrificing
Before I came here.
I'm told he claims to be your kin
Yet says he's not from Thebes.

OEDIPUS:
Then where does he come from,
1160   And why does he need sanctuary?

THESEUS:
All I know is that he says he needs
A little time to speak with you.

OEDIPUS:
Why? It's no "little" thing to claim sanctuary.

THESEUS:
I'm told he has asked just to speak to you
1165   And then go on his way again in safety.

OEDIPUS:
But who can this suppliant be?

THESEUS:
Do you have any family in Argos
Who might want something from you?

OEDIPUS:
No! No more!

THESEUS:
What's wrong?

OEDIPUS:
   Don't ask.   1170

THESEUS:
   What is it?

OEDIPUS:
   I know exactly who this is.

THESEUS:
   Who is he? An enemy?

OEDIPUS:
   He is to me. It is my son.
   To hear him would torture me.

THESEUS:
   Can't you at least listen to what he has to say—   1175
   He can't force you to do anything.
   What harm could there be in hearing him out?

OEDIPUS:
   I hate that voice! Loathsome to a father.
   King, do not force me to do this.

THESEUS:
   But you have a sacred obligation
   To a suppliant, that's heaven's law.   1180

ANTIGONE:
   Father, I know I'm too young
   To give you advice, but please listen
   To me now. Let the king have what he wants;
   At least then you will do right by the gods,
   And this is our brother—we want to see him.
   There's nothing he can say or do   1185
   That could shift you from your resolve.
   If his intentions are dishonorable,
   His words will betray them.
   You are still his father, and even
   If he had committed the worst offenses   1190
   Against you, it is simply not right
   To meet them wrong for wrong.
   Show him some kindness.
   You are not the only father

To have had a prodigal son
Who has provoked anger.
Let your friends pacify you,
Forget the here and now
1195   And consider things past;
Remember what you were forced
To endure on account of your parents.
You know very well how rage
Only serves to breed evil.
1200   Your own blind eyes testify to that.
Do this for us and don't be so harsh,
You have been treated so kindly here,
Return their generosity and show compassion.

OEDIPUS:
My dear child, it is too hard not to be
1205   Persuaded by you; I'll do what you want.
But if that man comes here, Theseus,
Promise you'll keep me free from harm.

THESEUS:
There's no need to tell me again.
I don't make idle boasts:
As long as the gods give me life
1210   I will keep you safe.

(*Exit Theseus through the stage right wing.*)

Third Stasimon

CHORUS:

[Strophe *a*]

One who craves
Ever more time,
As life slips
Through his fingers,
1215   Can only be called a fool.
As the years stack up,
The agonies abound.
Happiness subsides

When life is lived
Long past due.   1220
But in the end,
Hades comes to all
Delivering Death
Unsung, quiet. Still.

[Antistrophe *a*]

The best is never   1225
To have been born
Or, once alive, die young
And return to oblivion.
The joys of a thoughtless
Youth are only a prelude   1230
To every kind of pain;
Jealousy turns to hatred,
As anarchy breeds adversity,
Destruction, death, and war.
Then sad old age;   1235
Feeble, lonely,
Neglected, and despised.
Now he's living these years,
But it happens to us all.
Like an ancient crag
Blasted by northern winds,   1240
Lashed by relentless seas,
The bitter tide of ruin.
Angry waves breaking,
Crashing down. Blasted
From where the sun rises   1245
To the place the sun sets,
From the noon's still waters
And the mountains shrouded by night.

1248: Sophocles envisages the tides of trouble coming from all four
points of the compass. The east is the source of the sunrise, and the west
is the location of the sunset. The southern wind was said to blow from
the place of the "noontide ray," an area of heat and stillness rather like
the Doldrums near the Equator. The north is described as the Rhipaean
Mountains, a mythical range believed to lie to the far north of Scythia.

ANTIGONE:
> There's someone coming—
1250 > A stranger, he seems to be alone.
> And Father, he's crying.

OEDIPUS:
> Who is it?

ANTIGONE:
> The man on our minds—Polynices.

> *(Enter Polynices from the stage right wing.)*

POLYNICES:
> What can I do? Where to begin,
1255 > My despair, my sisters' or my father's?
> To see him like this, an outcast, reviled,
> Homeless, with only you to help.
> Clothed in tattered shreds rotting
> On his aged, ragged body.
1260 > The hair on his old blind head
> Windblown and unkempt,
> The meager scraps he must be forced
> To feed on just to survive day to day.
> It's too late! Too late! I've not done enough
1265 > And only now I realize. I'm contemptible!
> This is my fault, I did this to you.
> Who am I to dare to ask you for help?
> All I know is that Mercy
> Stands beside the throne of Zeus
> And has her hand in all his work—
> I wish she would stand with my father.
> The harm can be healed;
1270 > The hurt cannot get worse.

> *(Oedipus ignores him.)*

1267: "Mercy"—*Aidos*, Compassion or Mercy, was personified as a deity, and like *dike*, or Justice, was said to stand with Zeus as he dispensed his power. There was an altar of Mercy in Athens.

1270: Polynices here refers both to the past pain that he has inflicted on his father and to the mistakes that Oedipus himself has made. In seeking to make amends, Polynices appeals to his father, saying that they cannot possibly suffer anything worse than they have already encountered.

Have you nothing to say? Speak!
Don't turn your back on me
Or send me away in shame.
At least explain your animosity.
Sisters, can't you persuade him?   1275
Make him talk to me, break
This bitter silence. I am a suppliant:
The gods would have him listen,
And he has to respond.

ANTIGONE:

Speak to him yourself. Polynices,   1280
Tell him why you have come,
You may still change his mind.
Words can bring so much happiness
Or such terrible anger, why not pity too?
Why can't they give this silent man a voice?

POLYNICES:

Yes, you're right, I will speak to him
But under Poseidon's protection.   1285
I was at his altar when the king
Granted me safe passage to come
And speak, then hear him out.
My hosts, all I ask is that you
Respect a suppliant's rights,
You too, sisters, and you, Father.

Father, do you know why I came?   1290
I was driven from my own land and exiled
Because, as your firstborn son, I claimed
My birthright—the throne of Thebes.
But my younger brother, Eteoclês, staged   1295
A coup, and the citizens expelled me.
This was never debated, nor could I fight,
As dark prophecies circulated through the city
Raising the specter of the curse on our family.   1300
Eventually I arrived in Argos
Where I was taken in by King Adrastus.

1302: Adrastus—the mythical ruler of Argos, an ancient city in the northeast Peloponnese.

I married his daughter and forged new
Allegiances with the finest fighters
1305   Of all southern Greece, the best of men.
Seven warriors and their men swore
On their lives to overrun Thebes
And drive the pretender out.

And now I'm here, Father, to seek
1310   Your blessing for my allies and me;
Seven armies closing in on Thebes:
One: Amphiarus—as expert with a spear
As he is in prophecy.
Two: Tydeus of Aetolia, son of Oeneus.
1315   Three: Argive Eteoclus.
Four: Hippomedon, fighting in the name
Of his father, Talaus.

1308: The myth of the Seven against Thebes was enshrined onstage by Aeschylus in his play of that name produced in Athens in 467 B.C.E. It was also the subject matter of Euripides' *Phoenician Women* (409 B.C.E) and *Suppliant Women* (422 B.C.E). The myth of the Seven, which was known to Homer's audience, may have had its origins in eastern warrior stories. Thebes was said to have had seven gates (*Iliad* 4.406), and each of the seven warriors fought to take a gate.

1312: Amphiarus—a mythical descendant of the famous prophet Melampus. He knew that the mission was doomed to fail but was honor-bound to go by his wife Eriphyle, who had been tricked by Polynices. Amphiarus died at Thebes by being swallowed by the earth.

1314: Tydeus—a fierce Aetolian warrior who married the daughter of King Adrastus and who fathered Diomedes. Tydeus' brutality in combat at Thebes led to his killing Ismene. He was mortally wounded by the Theban hero Melanippus, and when presented with the dead Theban's head, Tydeus tried to suck out the brains. Athena was so repulsed that she withdrew her offer of immortality.

1315: Eteoclus—the son of the Cypriot Iphis. Eteoclus is not always included in the list of the Seven in earlier versions, though Aeschylus includes him.

1317: Hippomedon is variously described as the son of King Adrastus' sister, or the son of Aristomachus or of the Argive Talaus. According to Herodotus (2.6.6), though, Talaus was the father of Adrastus. The various myths of the Seven never fix a canonical list of combatants. Hippomedon was killed by the Theban Ismarus.

Five: Capaneus, who can't wait
To crush Thebes.
Six: Parthenopaeus, named for Atalanta,   1320
His mother.
Seven: The commander of this enterprise,
Polynices, myself—the son of Oedipus,
Or should I say the son of some ill-fate?

In the name of your daughters,   1325
For the sake of your own life,
For all in my army—I beg you—
Repress the rage you feel for me
As I move against my brother's regime.
He stole my country from me.   1330
If the predictions come true, the winner
Will be the one who has your benediction.
Father, for the love of our land
With its sparkling streams,
For the love of all our gods,
Please relent and do what I ask.   1335
Now both of us are homeless beggars
Forced to live from hand to mouth,
While that tyrant sits in our house
Scorning the both of us—how dare he!
But if you give me your help,   1340
My mission will surely succeed,
And he will reign no more.
Then I'll be able to bring you home
And assume my proper place.
With you on my side—victory!   1345
Without you—I am lost.

1318: In one version, Capaneus is struck down outside the walls of
Thebes by Zeus' thunderbolt. See also *Antigone* 131–40.

1320: Parthenopaeus—the brother of Adrastus and the son of Atalanta,
the mythical huntress who would marry only the man who could beat
her in a footrace. Hippomenes finally defeated her and cheated death by
dropping golden apples, which she stopped to pick up.

1324: Polynices' name means "much strife," whereas his brother's name,
Eteoclês, means "true glory."

CHORUS:
>Oedipus, out of respect for Theseus
>You should at least respond.
>Say something, whatever you feel is right.

OEDIPUS: *(To the chorus.)*
>You represent your country and its people well,
>And had it not been Theseus who sent him
1350
>To speak to me, he would have heard nothing.
>So let him leave with some of my words,
>But he'll find no joy in anything that I say.

>   *(To Polynices.)*

>It was you, bastard!
>You had the power and sat
1355
>On the throne where your brother
>Now squats, and what did you do?
>You forced out your own father,
>Denied him house and home,
>Turned him into a tattered old tramp!
>And now you come here
>Crying your eyes out to see me
>In such a state. Are these tears for me—
1360
>Or your own similar predicament?
>I'll bear my pain alone.
>You wanted me dead!
>You forced me into this vagrant's life!
>You denied me my country;
>You made me homeless;
>You taught me how to beg.
1365
>And I would be dead
>If it weren't for my dear daughters
>And their loyal, loving care.
>These girls are more man than you,
>And you are certainly no son of mine!

1370
>Yes, the Fury is watching your armies
>Marching on Thebes.
>She knows you'll never take the city.
>You'll die, you and your brother,
>Both with bad blood on your hands.

I called a curse down on you,   1375
And that curse will fight for me now.
You'll see, you should have honored
Your parents and learned
Respect and compassion
For a father and his blindness.   1380
My daughters never neglected their duties.
According to the ancient, age-old ways
My curse cancels out your supplication
And you cannot claim the throne
While Justice sits by Zeus as law.

Get away from me, you bastard!   1385
You have no father, just his curse:
You'll never occupy Thebes;
You'll never return to Argos;
You'll kill your own brother;
Your own brother will kill you.

I curse you in the name of Tartarus,
Father of never-ending darkness,   1390
In the name of the Furies and Ares
Who infected your brain with violence.
Go and tell that to your confederates
And hear it echo in the streets of Thebes.
This is the blessing that Oedipus   1395
Has conferred upon his sons!

CHORUS:
Polynices, you came with nothing but grief,
Now go back the way that you came.

POLYNICES:
No, not this! Why did I ever come?
They followed me all the way from Argos;   1400
How can I tell them where it will end?
No, there's no turning back now;
I'll never speak of this to anyone:
I'll face Destiny down and keep silent.
Antigone, Ismene, you've heard his curse;   1405

1375–6: See endnote.

If it should come to pass and you ever
Return to Thebes, swear to me now
That you'll remember me, give me
1410   The last rites and a proper resting place.
It will only add to the good you have already done
In caring for your father. Please, dear sisters,
Show me a little of that kindness.

ANTIGONE:
Polynices, please do something for me.

POLYNICES:
1415   What, Antigone? Tell me.

ANTIGONE:
Save yourself before it's too late—
Call back your forces, spare Thebes.

POLYNICES:
I will not. I would lose the army's respect—
No one would follow me then.

ANTIGONE:
1420   Why do you always burst into anger?
What will you gain destroying your own home?

POLYNICES:
How could I stand the shame
Of my brother's jeers if I backed down?

ANTIGONE:
Can't you see, you are fulfilling his curse.
1425   He's already said you are going to die!

POLYNICES:
If that's what he wants; I will not back down.

ANTIGONE:
But who will follow you into battle
Once they have heard of his curse?

POLYNICES:
They'll not hear it from me—

1413: Sophocles alludes to the focal point of *Antigone.* It is Antigone's
insistence that her brother receive burial rites that brings her into conflict
with Creon.

A good general never gives bad news.   1430

ANTIGONE:
  Brother, will nothing change your mind?

POLYNICES:
  Nothing can stop it now.
  I see my way ahead,
  Though my father and his curses
  Make it a harrowing journey.
  I just hope that Zeus will bless you   1435
  With a happier future, especially
  If you honor me with a proper burial
  When I die. Let me go now;
  You'll never see me alive again.

ANTIGONE:
  I can't bear this!

POLYNICES:
  You shouldn't cry over me.

ANTIGONE:
  How could I not mourn for my brother
  When he faces certain death?   1440

POLYNICES:
  If it's to be, then I'll die.

ANTIGONE:
  Please listen to what I'm saying!

POLYNICES:
  You can't prevent this.

ANTIGONE:
  I can't believe I'm going to lose you.

POLYNICES:
  We'll let Destiny decide that.
  I hope to high heaven that you two   1445
  Never face such a fate.
  You, above all, deserve better.

    (Exit Polynices through the stage left wing.)

[Strophe *a*]

CHORUS:
> Now new curses,
> New hostility
1450   From the blind man.
> Or could it be Destiny
> Hitting her mark?
> No one can ever say
> That the gods act in vain.
1455   Time sees everything,
> Turning some upside down,
> Raising others to new heights.

    (The low rumble of thunder is heard.)

Thunder sounds the will of Zeus!

OEDIPUS:
> Children, children? Are you still here?
> Send for Theseus, the best of men.

ANTIGONE:
> Why do you need him, Father?

OEDIPUS:
1460   The voice of Zeus shakes the skies,
> Calling me to my death; you must fetch him.

    (Thunder is heard, louder than before.)

[Antistrophe *a*]

CHORUS:
> The sky shudders!
> Deafening thunder!
1465   I can hear Zeus!
> Dread-bolts electrify the air!
> Static shivers my skin cold!
> Sheets of fire split the sky!
> A thunderbolt will fall!

1447–56, 1462–71, 1478–85: The three episodes of thunder, in which Zeus appears to speak to Oedipus, are in lyric meters, making this passage a *kommos.*

There is a reason for this!   1470
His reasons are ruthless!

(Louder thunder.)

The skies are screaming!
Zeus!

OEDIPUS:
Children, my ordained end has come.
It cannot be avoided.

ANTIGONE:
How can you know—some sign?

OEDIPUS:
I can feel it.   1475
Send for the king.

[Strophe *b*]

CHORUS:
Look! Up there, look!
Earth-shattering bolts!
Spirits protect us!   1480
The darkness is coming!
Earth resounds with rage!
Be compassionate;
We looked on a pariah,
We tried to help!
Spare us, Zeus!   1485

OEDIPUS:
Is he here yet? He must come
Before I die while I can still think.

ANTIGONE:
What do you want him to know?

OEDIPUS:
I swore that I would return his generosity.   1490
I must deliver on my promise.

[Antistrophe *b*]

CHORUS:
Theseus, royal son,

Leave Poseidon's shrine
On sea-cliffs standing high.
1495   Leave the holy rites.
Our guest-friend needs you now
To bestow his blessing.
Come my king, come quickly.

(Enter Theseus and attendants from the stage
right wing.)

THESEUS:
1500   What is it?
Who needs me?
I've heard the thunder.
Was it Zeus,
Or just a sudden storm?
When the gods stir
The elements like this
Anything could happen.

OEDIPUS:
1505   Theseus, I am so glad you are here.
The gods bless me with your presence.

THESEUS:
What is happening, Oedipus?

OEDIPUS:
My life has tipped the scales,
And I want to die knowing
That I did not break my promise.

THESEUS:
1510   Has there been some sign of your death?

OEDIPUS:
The gods have sent me their message.
I understand what was laid down long ago.

THESEUS:
How do you know?

OEDIPUS:
I hear the blasts of thunder;
1515   I feel the lightning crackling in the air.

THESEUS:

    I believe you, Oedipus; you're no false prophet.
    Tell me what you need me to do?

OEDIPUS:

    Listen carefully, Son of Aegeus: I will reveal
    Secrets that your city will hold forever.
    Very soon I will lead you,
    Unassisted, to the place where I will die.   1520
    You must never reveal this to anyone,
    It must remain hidden for the rest of time.
    Then you will inherit a mysterious power
    Far stronger than any kind of military might.
    Keep this confidence sacred, never speak of it;   1525
    Only you may know and you alone.
    You must not tell any of your people,
    Nor my children, even though I love them.
    Guard this mystery with your life,
    And when your end is near bequeath   1530
    This knowledge to your successor, no one else.
    And so it will pass down through the generations.
    Then your city will be protected forever
    From the force of the dragon's teeth
    That sprouted the sown men of Thebes.
    No city is immune from the insanity   1535
    Of aggression, whatever its government.
    But the gods always see, sooner or later,
    When righteousness is choked by the grip
    Of hysteria. I hope that never happens here.
    That's a lesson you could well do without.
    But I know I hardly need to tell you that.

1524: "Far stronger than any kind of military might"—Oedipus offers Theseus and Athens the power of his *kleos*, or fame. As a mortal man, he lived larger than life and endured terrible suffering; and in death, his reputation creates a mythical power as his grave site becomes the location of a mysterious hero-cult capable of protecting the city.

1534: "Sown men of Thebes"—According to legend, Cadmus, the mythical founder of Thebes, killed a dragon that was guarding a well. Cadmus sowed the dragon's teeth in the ground, and each tooth produced a warrior. All these warriors fought each other until only five remained. These five men became the original ancestors of the Thebans.

1540
It is time, we must go now.
I feel the hand of a god guiding me.
The inevitable cannot be delayed.

Come here, children, after a life
Of leading me, let me be your guide,
Be careful, you must not touch me.

1545
I'm on my own now. I'll find my grave;
This land will embrace my bones.

(Oedipus seems to know exactly where he is going and starts to move toward the great doors.)

This is the way . . . this way.
Hermes, are you leading me toward
The Underworld goddess?
Light of the world! I knew you once,

1550
Now I feel your warmth for one last time.
Hades will have the last of my life.
Bless you, Theseus, bless you all,
And bless this land and its people.
You'll have my good grace forever.

1555
I only ask that you always remember
Oedipus.

(Exit Oedipus, followed by Theseus, attendants, Ismene, and Antigone through the great doors.)

Fourth Stasimon

[Strophe]

CHORUS:
Now pray, pray
To the dark goddess

1548: Hermes—the messenger god, crosser of boundaries, and immortal guide to the dead on their way to Hades.

1549: "The Underworld goddess"—Persephone, daughter of Zeus and Demeter, and wife of Hades. In the minds of the Athenian audience, she was most strongly connected with her mystery cult at Eleusis. The language employed here by Sophocles, such as the "leading" by Hermes and the reference to "light," is strongly reminiscent of the cult practices of Eleusis, where initiates were led on a torchlight procession.

And the Underworld king.
Aidoneus! Aidoneus!   1560
Welcome him to your death house
Free from further suffering.
He has already endured enough.
Let the spirit of Justice
Resurrect his memory.   1565

[Antistrophe]

Underworld goddesses
And the infernal Hellhound,
Standing sentinel, howling
Through the catacombs   1570
At the dread jaws of death.
Death, son of Mother Earth
And Dark Tartarus,
Let him pass away softly,   1575
A stranger slipping past
On the shallow breath
Of deep eternal sleep.

(Enter a Messenger through the great doors.)

MESSENGER:
Citizens! My message is simple;
Oedipus has gone.   1580
But to tell how it happened—
How to find the words . . . ?

CHORUS:
Finally laid to rest?

MESSENGER:
His days on this earth are over.

1560: Aidoneus—a poetic form of the name of the god Hades.

1566: Underworld goddesses—the Furies (see note on line 42).

1571: "Jaws of death"—This is Cerberus, the three-headed (though in some myths he has fifty heads) guard dog who patrols the gates of Hades.

1574: "Death" is Thanatos, though in mythology he is usually the son of Night. Tartarus was the name of an elemental god, a son of Earth and Sky, and also the name for the deepest part of the Underworld.

CHORUS:

1585   Did the gods allow him to die peacefully?

MESSENGER:
    It was awe-inspiring. I'll tell you:
    You all saw how he left,
    Refusing any help, leading the way
1590   Alone; we followed him to the edge of the gorge
    Where the bronzed steps descend deep down below.
    Then he stopped at a fork in the winding track
    By the sunken crater where Theseus' pledge
    To Perithous was cast in stone.
1595   He stood there facing the Rock of Thoricus,
    Then sat himself down under the hollow pear tree
    By the granite tomb. He removed his tattered
    Old clothes and told his daughters to fetch
    Freshly drawn river water to cleanse
    Himself and pour the libations.
    They found a lush stream at the foot
1600   Of Demeter's hill, returned quickly,
    And carried out the proper rites of ritual,
    Bathing as if they were cleansing a corpse.

1591: "Bronzed steps"—This was a gorge or deep cavern in the region of Colonus (see note on line 57).

1592: This fork in the road is a vivid reminder of "the place where three roads meet" (OT 716) in Phocis. It was here that Oedipus unknowingly killed his own father.

1594: Perithous was a Thessalian king, whom Theseus joined in a descent to Hades to try to abduct Persephone. Hades captured both of them, and Heracles later rescued only Theseus. The feature described was either a natural hollow in the ground or some sort of ritual sacrificial bowl.

1595: Thoricus—a town of Attica about forty miles from Colonus. The mention of Thoricus here may be that in mythology it was said to be the place where Eos raised Cephalus up to heaven. Like Oedipus, Cephalus had been involved in a crime against his family when he accidentally killed his wife. His punishment was exile. After living as a huntsman, he became a founder of the cities of the island of Cephallenia.

1596: "Pear tree"—This may be the site of the abduction of Persephone, according to local legend.

1600: There was a shrine to Demeter Euchloos (mother of new crops) near Colonus.

Just when he seemed content that all was ready,   1605
The skies cracked with thunder, the very voice
Of Zeus! The two girls fell at their father's feet,
Shaking and crying, beating their breasts in anguish.
When Oedipus heard these mournful cries,   1610
He opened his arms up wide and said:
"Children—this is the day. I have to go.
All things come to an end, and you are now free
From the burden of caring for me. I know
How difficult this is for you,   1615
But there is one small word that can soothe—
And that is 'love.' I loved you more than
Anyone else could ever love, but now
Your lives must go on without me."
They fell into each other's arms and wept,   1620
Crying their eyes out until they had no more tears,
Then silence, complete stillness, not a sound . . .
Suddenly we heard a voice, huge and booming—
The sound of it shook us to the core, and we
Shuddered in fear. It must have been a god   1625
Calling over and over again:
"Oedipus—Oedipus,
It has been too long,
Now is our time."
He knew right away that this was a summons
From some god, and he immediately asked
For King Theseus, saying, "Dearest friend,   1630
Take my daughters' hands and swear to them
That they will be forever in your care
And will always receive your kindness.
Daughters, you must promise the same."
Theseus, being a true noble, fought back his grief   1635
And gave his word that he would do all his friend
Had asked of him. Then Oedipus drew his daughters
Near to him and told them: "Children, be brave,
You must go now, it is not permitted for you   1640
To see the sacred secrets or to hear the holy words.
Go now, leave, as quickly as you can. Only Theseus
May stay alone to know what will happen here."
We all cried when we heard this and left.
After we had gone a short distance,   1645

We chanced a glance behind, but Oedipus
Had completely vanished. Only the king remained
1650   Standing alone and covering his eyes with his hands
As if he had just seen something so terrifying
That it had almost blinded him.
Then he knelt down and kissed the ground
And stood up and stretched his hands to heaven,
1655   Offering his salute to the gods above and below.
Theseus is the only man on earth who can explain
How Oedipus passed away. We saw no thunderbolts,
1660   There were no great waves surging in the sea
·   That could have swelled up and engulfed him.
Something else, not human, came down from above
And led him up high into heaven, or else the ground
Opened up and received him deep down in the earth.
Whatever happened, he is at peace. There was no pain,
No suffering, we have no reason to mourn.
For a mere mortal, his death was truly wondrous.

1665   What I've said might seem to make no sense.
Don't believe me if you think I'm some kind of fool.

CHORUS:
What happened to his daughters and the rest of your
    party?

MESSENGER:
They're close behind. Listen,
You can hear their sorrow.

> (Enter Antigone, Ismene, and attendants from the
> great doors.)

[Strophe *a*]

ANTIGONE:
1670   No! No! There is nothing left!
All we can do is cry for him
And mourn for the infection
Of our father's curse in our blood.

1670–1750: Carrying the reaction to Oedipus' death, these lines are a *kommos* in lyric meter.

We withstood so much for Father.
Now that he's gone there is only confusion.   1675

CHORUS:
   What happened?

ANTIGONE:
   There is no way of ever really knowing.

CHORUS:
   He's gone?

ANTIGONE:
   Yes, as you would have wanted,
   Not struck down in battle,
   Nor swept away by the sea,   1680
   But something mystical that carried
   Him to the shores of infinity.
   Sister, our lives will be cloaked
   In deep dark night, where do we go—   1685
   Wandering aimlessly in lands unknown
   Or drifting on a hopeless sea?

ISMENE:
   I don't know! I wish I were dead
   So I could go down to Hades with him!   1690
   I have no future.
   I have no life.

CHORUS:
   Dear daughters, you must accept
   What the gods have decreed.
   Don't stoke the fires of grief.   1695
   You're blameless, you've done nothing wrong.

[Antistrophe *a*]

ANTIGONE:
   I had no idea what his death
   Would mean to me. Our lives
   Were hard, but to be near him
   At least brought me some happiness.
   Father, though you are shrouded deep   1700
   In the earth, you will know our love forever.

CHORUS:
> He rests in peace now.

ANTIGONE:
> At least he had his heart's desire.

CHORUS:
1705
> What was that?

ANTIGONE:
> To die abroad
> In a land he loved
> Buried in the shadows
> Under the cool earth.
> To be mourned tenderly—
1710
> My eyes will always cry for him,
> My grief will be unending.
> Buried in a foreign land,
> But death has taken him
> So very far away from me.

ISMENE:
1715
> What will happen to us
> Now that we have no father?

CHORUS:
> At least he is quiet now.
> You must remember
1720
> That no one lives a life
> Free from pain and suffering.

[Strophe *b*]

ANTIGONE:
> Ismene, we must go back!

ISMENE:
> What?

ANTIGONE:
> Back! Back!

ISMENE:
> Why?

ANTIGONE:
1725
> I have to see his grave.

ISMENE:
  But . . .

ANTIGONE:
  I can't leave Father.

ISMENE:
  It is taboo. Can't you see that?

ANTIGONE:
  Why are you against me?   1730

ISMENE:
  Don't you know . . .

ANTIGONE:
  What! What!

ISMENE:
  His death was secret, there is no grave.

ANTIGONE:
  Then take me where he went and let me die!

ISMENE:
  Then you'd leave me all alone.   1735
  How would I survive?

[Antistrophe *b*]

CHORUS:
  Don't be afraid.

ANTIGONE:
  But where can we go?

CHORUS:
  Whatever happens,
  You will always be safe here.   1740

ANTIGONE:
  But . . .

CHORUS:
  But what?

1734: There seems to be a missing line between 1733 and 1734, another
exchange between the sisters.

ANTIGONE:
> Will we ever be able
> To go home to Thebes?

CHORUS:
> You shouldn't even try.

ANTIGONE:
1745
> Wherever we go, there will be trouble.

CHORUS:
> You must put all that behind you now.

ANTIGONE:
> I fear there is worse to come.

CHORUS:
> You've been cast adrift on a sea of suffering.

ANTIGONE:
> Yes, yes. But what now, Zeus?
> What lies in our future?
1750
> Where will Destiny take us?

(Enter Theseus from the great doors.)

THESEUS:
> There is no need to cry, children,
> Death was a great gift for Oedipus.
> The gods would not want us to grieve.

ANTIGONE:
> Theseus, please do one thing for us.

THESEUS:
1755
> What is it you want?

ANTIGONE:
> Let us see our father's grave.

THESEUS:
> It is forbidden.

ANTIGONE:
> But why? You're the king!

1751–79: These lines are in anapests, a meter most often used for entrances and other fast-moving passages such as this one.

THESEUS:

    Your father wanted it that way.   1760
    No one can ever go there,
    Nor can I ever speak of the sacred
    Site where his body lies.
    He told me that if I kept true to my word,
    Athens would never know suffering.
    This was my sacred pledge   1765
    Sworn before Zeus, god of oaths.

ANTIGONE:

    If that was his last desire,
    Then I must accept his wishes.
    Send us back home to Thebes.
    We must try to stop the slaughter   1770
    And save both of our brothers.

THESEUS:

    I will do what you ask.
    It is my duty to serve you
    Out of respect for Oedipus   1775
    Who now lies beneath our soil.

CHORUS:

    No more tears.
    Grief is at an end.
    Instead remembrance
    Forever.   1779

       (Exit all.)

—END—

1778–9: See endnote.

Endnotes

A. Antigone

Recent editors differ widely on how to read certain lines in *Antigone*. The new Oxford Classical Text of Lloyd-Jones and Wilson (1990a), supported by their *Sophoclea*, is fairly free with emendation. Griffith's Cambridge edition is more conservative, and so is the excellent new translation by Blundell (1998). On the whole I have followed a conservative policy, translating the manuscript readings wherever possible. In the following notes I comment on passages for which different readings give significantly different results. LJW stands for Lloyd-Jones and Wilson.

Line 10: The Greek text allows three fairly literal translations: (1) "Evils from our enemies are advancing against our friends" (Lloyd-Jones 1994 and Griffith 1991, whom I follow): (2) "Evils that are appropriate to our enemies are advancing against our friends" (Blundell); (3) "Evils inflicted on our enemies [i.e., the dead Argives] are advancing against our friends." In the first reading, Antigone takes Creon to be her enemy. In the second, she presupposes the principle that it is right to cause harm (such as non-burial) to one's enemies (on which see Blundell 1989). That principle has a place in ancient Greek tradition, but it has already been challenged by poets (including Homer) and does not appear to be supported elsewhere in this play. The general wisdom seems to be that Achilles goes too far in punishing Hector's corpse, and that Creon will err in the same way with the remains of Polynices. The third reading refers to the punishment already inflicted on the Argive corpses according to the story that none of the Argives were granted burial—a story that Antigone does not elsewhere seem to know.

Line 157: The text is faulty here; the word "ruler" is a conjecture, and the word translated as "new" is thought by some editors to be a mistake by a copyist. It is unparalleled in this usage.

Lines 167–8: LJW suspects a gap in the text in which we should supply a line such as "With my sister as his wife, you always served them faithfully." This provides an antecedent for "their" in "their sons" (line 168).

Line 369: "If he honors the law." Along with most editors, I translate an emended text. LJW and Blundell (1998) follow the manuscript reading "If he inserts the law . . . ," probably meaning "If he weaves the law into the fabric of his life, or of the city."

Lines 582–625: Second Stasimon. Although the general ideas are clear, the manuscripts are not; and editors have proposed a number of changes. I have kept as close as possible to the manuscript readings, while trying to convey a clear meaning to the audience or reader.

Line 601: "Claimed by the dust." Some editors emend the text to read "It is harvested by a bloody chopper."

Line 607: "Sleep, that weakens everyone"—so in the manuscripts. Most editors reject the manuscript reading, which more literally means "sleep, the all-aging one," because sleep does not by itself cause anyone to age. But the word for old age also connotes infirmity, and any sleeper is more feeble for being asleep.

Line 608: "The untiring months of gods"—so in the manuscripts. Most editors, including LJW, correct "gods" to "years." But the meaning in the manuscripts is fine: For gods, the procession of months goes on forever. "Untiring"—The procession of months never weakens for the gods, nor does it weaken them.

Line 613: "Madness stalks mortals who are great." The text given by the manuscripts is unreadable, but this cliché is the most likely.

Lines 624–5: "Time is very short for them / Leaves no time for disaster." LJW emends the text to read "The small man fares throughout his time without disaster."

Lines 663–71: I have followed the manuscripts, as has LJW; in 669 I translate *de* as "later," to bring out the alternations of power that it implies. Some editors, however, including Griffith (1999), believe that lines 663–7 were transposed by copyists from their original place after 671. Then it is not the appointed leader who is willingly ruled by someone else, but the good citizen who plays his assigned role as leader in some contexts and as follower in others:

The public knows that a man is just	661
Only if he is straight with his relatives.	662
And I have no doubt that such a man will lead well	668
And will cheerfully be led by someone else.	669

In hard times he will stand firm with his spear	670
Waiting for orders, a good, law-abiding soldier.	671
So, if someone goes too far and breaks the law,	663
Or tries to tell his masters what to do,	664
He will have nothing but contempt from me.	665
But when the city takes a leader, you must obey,	666
Whether his commands are trivial, or right, or wrong.	667
But reject one man ruling another, and that's the worst.	672
Anarchy tears up a city, divides a home,	673
Defeats an alliance of spears.	674

Lines 666–7: Some editors find it hard to believe that Creon would demand obedience to orders that are wrong, and so they argue that these lines are not authentic.

Line 687: "Someone else." Some editors emend the line to give the meaning "Still, this [i.e., the job of refuting Creon] could be done in another way"; others, such as LJW, take it to mean "Still, another view might be correct." Some editors consider the line to be inauthentic.

Lines 688–9: "My natural duty"—so the majority of editors, including Blundell (1998) and Griffith (1999). LJW read a variant, "But it is not in your nature to foresee people's words or actions. . . ." But it is not Creon's nature but his job that keeps him from hearing what people say about him (Griffith); Haemon can serve as his ears.

Lines 720–1: "And *I* say that the oldest idea. . . ." I am taking "every" (*panta*) as accusative of respect with "knowledge," rather than as modifying "man," which would give us "And *I* say that the oldest idea, and the best, / Is for every man to be born full of knowledge."

Line 753: "You haven't thought this through." LJW emends the text to yield the meaning "What kind of threat is it to tell you my decisions?" But a decision could well be a threat, and the word LJW would give up ("empty" in "your plans or thoughts are empty") is nicely picked up by the next line, as often in dialogue.

Line 798: Sexual love is "a power to sweep across the bounds of what is Right." I translate an emendation proposed by Griffith (1999), which prepares the way for line 801. The reading of the manuscripts presents metrical difficulties as well as an implausible meaning: that desire is enthroned beside what is Right. "Right" translates "great *thesmoi*," which refers to a concept that is older and more fundamental than law or justice. No tradition gives Aphrodite such a throne; what she stands for is subversive of order.

Line 845: "Chariot-reaches of the plain." Some scholars take *alsos* to mean "grove," but "plain" is more likely in this context (Griffith 1999). Chariots need open space.

Lines 904–20: Some editors reject these lines as spurious because they do not see how they can be consistent with Antigone's position that unwritten law requires all the dead to be buried. Virtually all recent editors accept the lines, however, and Foley (1996) has shown how suitable they are for Antigone. Note that Aristotle cites lines 911–2, alluding to the main argument of the passage, at *Rhetoric* 3.16, 1417a32–33.

Line 980: "Born to be a queen." Here I follow the text as emended by LJW.

B. Oedipus Tyrannus

Lines 376–7: The manuscripts read, "It is not you who will bring down my doom," corrected by an early scholar to the reading we, and most others, follow. Knox (1957/98) defends the original reading with great vigor (1998, pp. xiii and 7–8). In his reading, the lines say that Tiresias' life is in the hands of Apollo because he is a priest. In that case, as Knox points out, there is no line in the text that would treat Oedipus as a victim of the gods. This bears on the issue of whether or not the play should be read as a tragedy of fate.

Line 873: "Hubris grows from tyranny." This is Blaydes's correction, followed by Dawe (1982) and others. The correction is justified by noting that it makes no sense to say that Oedipus became a tyrant because of hubris; he never asked to be tyrant. But it does make sense to claim that his extraordinary power led to hubris, and this is a very Athenian thought.

Most recent editors, however, have followed the manuscripts, which have "Hubris begets a tyrant." In this reading, the line cannot refer to Oedipus, because hubris did not make him a tyrant, though his father's hubris may have caused him to be born. But the lines ought to refer to Oedipus, not to Laius.

Every scholar who writes in detail about the play has discussed this line. We follow the careful analysis of Winnington-Ingram (1980), who accepts the corrected line. But see also the discussions in Knox (1957/98), Carey (1986), Segal (1995), and Edmunds (2002).

Lines 1088–91: On the complexity of this passage, see Segal (1995, p. 264, n. 42).

Lines 1524–30: Dawe (1982) rejects these lines as spurious, but most other editors retain them. The lines contain traditional Greek wisdom

(Herodotus 1.32), which may be found in virtually the same form in a number of classical tragedies. The thought is echoed in Aeschylus, *Agamemnon* 928–9; Sophocles, *Women of Trachis* 1–3; and Euripides, *Trojan Women* 509–10, *Children of Heracles* 865–6, *Iphigenia at Aulis* 161–3, and *Andromache* 100–2.

C. Oedipus at Colonus

Lines 636–7: "Therefore I am inclined to allow him to stay / And incorporate him within our city." The text has been emended long ago to give a reading that seems to imply that Theseus is promising full citizenship in Athens to Oedipus. This is unlikely, however, on three grounds: the text need not be emended, the new reading would not imply citizenship in any case, and Oedipus does not need to be a citizen. Oedipus comes as a hero bringing a gift to Athens, and his grave, becoming part of Athens, will be a powerful defense for the city. Oedipus would not want the rights and duties of an ordinary citizen at this point. The issue is thoroughly reviewed in Vidal-Naquet (1990, pp. 329–59) and in Wilson (1997, pp. 63–90).

Lines 1028–33: These lines appear to be out of order in the manuscripts; we translate the corrected order in LJW, which places them after 1019.

Lines 1375–6: "I called a curse down on you, / And that curse will fight for me now." The Greek includes the word *prosthe*, which simply indicates "a time before now." Scholars differ as to whether Oedipus refers to the curse delivered earlier in the play (lines 421–7, 450–1, 787–90) or a curse delivered before Oedipus left Thebes (a curse that caused the rift between the sons, as was reported in the older poetic tradition). Lewis Campbell (1879) in the 19th century and Bernard Knox (1982) in the 20th lead the group who believe that Oedipus cursed his sons before he left Thebes; Jebb (1899/1962) argues that the curse must have been brought about by Ismene's news when it reached Oedipus at Colonus. Wilson argues well for the same conclusion (1997). Jebb and Wilson are almost certainly right. Sophocles generally shows onstage the human causes for the actions that we will see, and thus gives unity to his plays. The point, as Jebb says, "is more than a detail: it must affect our estimate of the play as a work of art."

Lines 1778–9: "Instead remembrance / Forever." English has no good equivalent for the last line of the Greek text. A literal reading would be the meaningless sentence "For these things have authority in every way." That might mean that "Theseus will keep his promise," but that would be a weak ending. Jebb proposes "'These events have assuredly been ordained past recall' (by the gods)." But the past is always beyond recall, so this would be a tautology. We think the line refers to the establishment of this sacred place as a permanent reminder of Oedipus, along with the establishment of Oedipus, the hero, as protector of Athens.

Appendix: Hegel on *Antigone*

Hegel presents so many difficulties to the reader that "he is cited much more frequently than he is read and discussed far oftener than he is understood" (Wood 1991, p. xxvii). Although Hegel's influence on subsequent readings of *Antigone* has been powerful, many readers (such as Bradley 1950) overlook the importance of *Antigone* to Hegel's phenomenology. As a result, they miss the subtlety of Hegel's account of the play. Hegel's theory does not lend itself to summary, but here is a sketch of the main points that bear on *Antigone*.

Reading *Antigone* is not merely an aesthetic exercise for Hegel. Its heroine provides him a clear statement of the absoluteness of right. The unwritten laws that Antigone cites simply *are*; they are beyond human investigation and evaluation: "If they are supposed to be validated by my insight, then I have already denied their unshakeable, intrinsic being. . . ." (Miller 1977, 437, references by paragraph number).

Nature has assigned different ethical concerns to women than to men. Women guard the divine law on which family bonds depend; men guard the human law that supports community and government. But men grow up within the family, and women reside in the larger community, so the assignment by gender does not free either group to follow its own law without attention to the other. In any event, both laws are believed to be supported by gods, and, in Hegelian terms, both laws belong to the same ethical substance. But it is only by action—the kind of action taken in a tragic play—that a superior ethical consciousness comes, through suffering, to recognize this.

Because of her conscious action, Antigone is Hegel's clearest instance of ethical consciousness. "Ethical consciousness must recognize its opposite as its own actuality . . . it must recognize its guilt" (Shannon 2001, p. 24; Miller 1977, p. 469). Antigone, Hegel says, commits her crime knowingly—or, more accurately, her knowledge comes with her action. In the case of Oedipus, Hegel says, "A power that shuns the daylight lies in wait for the ethical self-consciousness, and sallies out and catches it red-handed when the deed is done. . . ." (Shannon, p. 24; Miller, p. 469). The power that ambushes a tragic character is the ethical power that he or she has been unable to recognize before committing the deed that brings it out into the open, represented by the god who is neglected by that character. Like her father, Antigone has been ambushed.

"Because we suffer, we recognize that we have erred," she says, according to Hegel, who is following Hölderlin's version of lines 925–6: "If this truly has now come before the gods, then we suffer and ask to be forgiven our past sins" (quoted in Shannon, p. 24, n. 41). Hegel must suppose that Antigone infers her error from her suffering and that she understands this as an error of her entire community.

Antigone's admission of guilt—not just for herself, but for her community—is crucial to Hegel's appreciation of her. She is "the prophet of her epoch." Her recognition of error is "a death sentence on both herself and her community" (Shannon, p. 172). In her admission there is a kind of reconciliation of the two laws, because both are recognized. But the conflict remains, and it remains destructive to Antigone and her people. There remains no hope of redemption while the conflict is understood only as a contest between divine and human law. The ancient world and its fundamental conflict must be superseded by the modern world and its conflict between faith and reason. This supersession, however, does not leave Spirit, the subject that realizes itself in history, untouched by tension between the two laws; that tension continues to animate the movement by which Spirit comes to understand itself.

Such is the background theory against which this play takes on special meaning for Hegel. *Antigone* is not merely the perfect tragedy; its heroine is the ideal embodiment of a principle "recognizing its opposite in its own actuality."

Hegel's reading of the play may be better philosophy than it is scholarship. There are two main points of friction between his theory and the play Sophocles wrote. First, the true representative of community in *Antigone* is not Creon but the chorus of elders, who constitute the council of state and who show some measure of sympathy for Antigone. Creon's edict is not a law of the community (though it is intended to secure the community), and his actions truly represent community values only when they arise from genuine consultation with the council of elders. Second, Antigone is not really acknowledging her guilt at lines 925–6. I have rendered the same lines "If the gods really agree with this [Creon's judgment], / Then suffering should teach me to repent my sin." But nothing in the play suggests that the gods do agree with Creon's judgment, and nothing Antigone says implies that she believes suffering implies guilt. Her last lines, after all, are "Look what these wretched men are doing to me, / For my pure reverence!" (942–3).

Selected Bibliography

See also Suggestions for Further Reading on page lxxii.

For General Readers
On Sophocles and His Age

Blundell, Mary Whitlock. *Helping Friends and Harming Enemies: A Study in Sophocles and Greek Ethics*. Cambridge: Cambridge University Press, 1989.

Bowra, C. M. *Sophoclean Tragedy*. Oxford: Clarendon Press, 1944.

Buxton, R. G. A. *Sophocles. Greece and Rome: New Surveys in the Classics*, No. 16. Oxford: Clarendon Press, 1984.

Ehrenberg, V. *Sophocles and Pericles*. Oxford: Basil Blackwell, 1954.

Euben, Peter, ed. *Greek Tragedy and Political Theory*. Berkeley: University of California Press, 1986.

Gardiner, C. P. *The Sophoclean Chorus*. Iowa City: University of Iowa Press, 1987.

Goldhill, Simon. *Reading Greek Tragedy*. Cambridge: Cambridge University Press, 1986.

Guthrie, W. K. C. *The Sophists*. Cambridge: Cambridge University Press, 1971.

Jones, John. *On Aristotle and Greek Tragedy*. New York: Oxford University Press, 1962.

Kitto, H. D. F. *Form and Meaning in Drama: A Study of Six Greek Plays and Hamlet*. London: Methuen, 1956.

Knox, Bernard. *The Heroic Temper*. Berkeley: University of California Press, 1964.

Lloyd-Jones, Hugh. *The Justice of Zeus*. Berkeley: University of California Press, 1971.

Nietzsche, Friedrich. *The Birth of Tragedy*. 1872. Trans., with commentary, by Walter Kaufmann, with *The Case of Wagner*. New York: Random House, 1967.

Reinhardt, Karl. *Sophocles*. 3rd ed., 1947. Trans. by Hazel Harvey and David Harvey. With an introduction by Hugh Lloyd-Jones. Oxford: Blackwell, 1979.

217

Seaford, Richard. *Reciprocity and Ritual: Homer and Tragedy in the Developing City-State*. Oxford: Oxford University Press, 1994.

Segal, Charles. *Tragedy and Civilization: An Interpretation of Sophocles*. Cambridge, Mass.: Harvard University Press, 1981.

———. *Sophocles' Tragic World: Divinity, Nature, Society*. Cambridge, Mass.: Harvard University Press, 1995.

Silk, M. S., ed. *Tragedy and the Tragic*. Oxford: Oxford University Press, 1996, pp. 49–73.

Vernant, Jean-Pierre, and Vidal-Naquet, Pierre, eds. *Myth and Tragedy in Ancient Greece*. Trans. by Janet Lloyd. New York: Zone Books, 1990.

Waldock, A. J. A. *Sophocles the Dramatist*. Cambridge: Cambridge University Press, 1951.

Whitman, C. H. *Sophocles: A Study of Heroic Humanism*. Cambridge, Mass.: Harvard University Press, 1951.

Winnington-Ingram, R. P. *Sophocles: An Interpretation*. Cambridge: Cambridge University Press, 1980.

Woodruff, Paul. "Ancient Greece: The Way of Being Human." In *Reverence: Renewing a Forgotten Virtue*. New York: Oxford University Press, 2001, pp. 81–101.

On Ancient Theatre

Carpenter, Thomas H., and Christopher A. Faraone, eds. *Masks of Dionysus*. Ithaca: Cornell University Press, 1993.

Easterling, P. E., ed. *The Cambridge Companion to Greek Tragedy*. Cambridge: Cambridge University Press, 1997.

Pickard-Cambridge, A. W. *The Dramatic Festivals of Athens*. 3rd ed. Oxford: Oxford University Press, 1990.

Winkler, John J., and Froma I. Zeitlin, eds. *Nothing to Do with Dionysos? Athenian Drama in Its Social Context*. Princeton: Princeton University Press, 1990.

Translations

Blundell, Mary Whitlock. *Sophocles'* Antigone: *With Introduction, Translation, and Essay*. Newburyport, Mass.: Focus Publishing, 1998.

Fagles, Robert. *The Three Theban Plays*. Introduced by Bernard Knox. New York: Viking Press, 1982.

Grene, David. *Sophocles II (Oedipus the King, Oedipus at Colonus, Antigone)*. 2nd ed. Chicago: University of Chicago Press, 1991.

Lloyd-Jones, Hugh. *Sophocles I (Ajax, Electra, Oedipus Tyrannus)* and *Sophocles II (Antigone, The Women of Trachis, Philoctetes, Oedipus at Colonus)*. Cambridge, Mass.: Harvard University Press, 1994.

On *Antigone*

Gilligan, Carol. *In a Different Voice: Psychological Theory and Women's Development*. Cambridge, Mass.: Harvard University Press, 1982.

Goheen, Robert. *The Imagery of Sophocles'* Antigone: *A Study of Poetic Language and Structure*. Princeton: Princeton University Press, 1951.

Loraux, Nicole. *Tragic Ways of Killing a Woman*. Trans. by Anthony Forster. Cambridge, Mass.: Harvard University Press, 1987.

Mogyoródi, Emese. "Tragic Freedom and Fate in Sophocles' *Antigone:* Notes on the Role of the 'Ancient Evils' in 'the Tragic.'" In Silk, M. S., ed. *Tragedy and the Tragic* (1996), pp. 358–76.

Nussbaum, Martha. "Sophocles' *Antigone:* Conflict, Vision, and Simplification." In *The Fragility of Goodness: Luck and Ethics in Greek Tragedy and Philosophy*. Cambridge: Cambridge University Press, 1986, pp. 51–82.

Steiner, George. *Antigones: How the Antigone Legend Has Endured in Western Literature, Art, and Thought*. Oxford: Oxford University Press, 1984.

On *Oedipus Tyrannus*

Bloom, Harold, ed. *Modern Critical Interpretations:* Oedipus Rex. New York: Chelsea House Publishers, 1988.

Burkert, Walter. *Oedipus, Oracles, and Meaning: From Sophocles to Umberto Eco*. The Samuel James Stubbs Lecture Series. Toronto: University College, 1991.

Bushnell, Rebecca W. *Prophesying Tragedy*. Ithaca: Cornell University Press, 1988.

Dodds, E. R. "On Misunderstanding the *Oedipus Rex*." *Greece and Rome* 13 (1966): 37–49. Reprinted in Bloom (1988), pp. 35–47.

Edmunds, Lowell. *Oedipus: The Ancient Legend and Its Later Analogues*. Baltimore: Johns Hopkins University Press, 1985.

———. "Oedipus as Tyrant in Sophocles' *Oedipus Tyrannus*." *Syllecta Classica* XIII (2002), pp. 63–103.

Freud, Sigmund. *The Interpretation of Dreams*. Trans. by James Strachey. New York: John Wiley & Sons, 1961, pp. 261–7.

Griffith, R. Drew. *The Theatre of Apollo: Divine Justice and Sophocles'* Oedipus the King. Montreal: McGill-Queens University Press, 1996.

Hawkes, Terence. *Structuralism and Semiotics.* Berkeley: University of California Press, 1977.

Johnson, Allen, and Douglass Price-Williams, eds. *Oedipus Ubiquitous: The Family Complex in World Folk Literature.* Stanford: Stanford University Press, 1996.

Knox, Bernard. *Oedipus at Thebes: Sophocles' Tragic Hero and His Time.* 1957. New ed., augmented, New Haven: Yale University Press, 1998.

Lear, Jonathan. *Open Minded: Working out the Logic of the Soul.* Cambridge, Mass.: Harvard University Press, 1998.

Lévi-Strauss, Claude. *Structural Anthropology.* Trans. by Claire Jacobson and Brooke Grundfest Schoepf. New York: Basic Books, 1963.

Mullahy, Patrick. *Oedipus: Myth and Complex; A Review of Psychoanalytic Theory.* New York: Grove Press, 1948.

Pucci, Pietro. *Oedipus and the Fabrication of the Father:* Oedipus Tyrannus *in Modern Criticism and Philosophy.* Baltimore: Johns Hopkins University Press, 1992.

Segal, Charles. Oedipus Tyrannus: *Tragic Heroism and the Limits of Knowledge.* New York: Twayne Publishers, 1993.

Vernant, Jean-Pierre. "Ambiguity and Reversal: On the Enigmatic Structure of *Oedipus Rex.*" Orig. 1970. In Vernant, Jean-Pierre, and Pierre Vidal-Naquet, *Myth and Tragedy in Ancient Greece.* Trans. by Janet Lloyd. New York: Zone Books, 1990, pp. 113–40.

———. "Oedipus without the Complex." Orig. 1967. In Vernant, Jean-Pierre, and Pierre Vidal-Naquet, *Myth and Tragedy in Ancient Greece.* Trans. by Janet Lloyd. New York: Zone Books, 1990, pp. 85–112.

On *Oedipus at Colonus*

Knox, Bernard. Introduction in Fagles, Robert, *Sophocles: The Three Theban Plays.* New York: Penguin, 1982, pp. 255–77.

Vidal-Naquet, Pierre. "Oedipus between Two Cities: An Essay on *Oedipus at Colonus.*" In Vernant, Jean-Pierre, and Pierre Vidal-Naquet, *Myth and Tragedy in Ancient Greece.* Trans. by Janet Lloyd. New York: Zone Books, 1990, pp. 329–59.

For Scholars

On Sophocles' Plays

Campbell, Lewis. *Sophocles, Edited with English Notes and Introduction.* 2nd. ed., revised. Oxford: Clarendon Press, 1879.

Dawe, R. D. *Studies in the Text of Sophocles.* Leiden: E. J. Brill, 1978.

Jebb, Sir Richard. *Sophocles: The Plays and Fragments, with Critical Notes, Commentary, and Translation. Part 1, The Oedipus Tyrannus.* 2nd ed., 1887. *Part 2, The Oedipus Coloneus.* 1899. *Part 3, The Antigone.* 3rd ed., 1900. Reprinted, Amsterdam: Hakkert, 1962.

Kamerbeek, J. C. *The Plays of Sophocles.* Leiden: E. J. Brill, 1967.

Lloyd-Jones, H., and N. G. Wilson. *Sophoclis Fabulae.* Oxford: Oxford University Press, 1990a.

———. *Sophoclea: Studies on the Text of Sophocles.* Oxford: Oxford University Press, 1990b.

On *Antigone*

Bennett, Larry J., and William Blake Tyrrell. "Sophocles' *Antigone* and Funeral Oratory." *American Journal of Philology* 111 (1990): 441–56.

———. *Recapturing Sophocles'* Antigone. Lanham, Md.: Rowman and Littlefield, 1998.

Brown, Andrew. *Sophocles:* Antigone. *With Translation and Notes.* Warminster: Aris & Phillips, 1987.

Cropp, Martin. "Antigone's Final Speech (Sophocles, *Antigone* 891–928)." *Greece and Rome* 44 (1997): 137–60.

Else, Gerald F. *The Madness of Antigone.* Heidelberg: Carl Winter, 1976.

Foley, Helene P. "Tragedy and Democratic Ideology: The Case of Sophocles' *Antigone.*" In Goff, Barbara, ed., *History, Tragedy, Theory: Dialogues on Athenian Drama.* Austin: University of Texas Press, 1995.

———. "Antigone as Moral Agent." In Silk, M. S., ed., *Tragedy and the Tragic* (1996), pp. 49–73.

———. *Female Acts in Greek Tragedy.* Princeton: Princeton University Press, 2001.

Griffith, Mark. *Sophocles:* Antigone. Cambridge: Cambridge University Press, 1999.

———. "Antigone and Her Sister(s): Embodying Women's Speech in Classical Athens." In Lardinois, André, and Laura McClure, eds., *Making Silence Speak.* Princeton: Princeton University Press, 2001, pp. 117–36.

Lewis, R. G. "An Alternative Date for Sophocles' *Antigone.*" *Greek, Roman and Byzantine Studies* 29 (1998): 35–50.

Murnaghan, Sheila. "*Antigone* 904–920 and the Institution of Marriage." *American Journal of Philology* 107 (1986): 192–207.

Neuburg, Matt. "How Like a Woman: Antigone's 'Inconsistency.'" *Classical Quarterly* 40 (1990): 54–76.

Ormand, Kirk. *Exchange and the Maiden: Marriage in Sophoclean Tragedy.* Austin: University of Texas Press, 1999.

Ostwald, Martin. "Was There a Concept of ἄγραφος νόμος [Unwritten Law] in Classical Greece?" In Lee, E. N., et al., eds., *Exegesis and Argument.* Assen, Netherlands: Van Gorcum, 1973, pp. 70–104.

Oudemans, Theodorus C. W., and A. P. M. H. Landinois. *Tragic Ambiguity: Anthropology, Philosophy, and Sophocles' Antigone.* Leiden: 1987.

Seaford, Richard. "Tragic Money." *Journal of Hellenic Studies* 118 (1998): 119–39.

Segal, Charles Paul. "Sophocles' Praise of Man and the Conflicts of the *Antigone.*" *Arion* 3 (1964): 46–66.

Sourvinou-Inwood, Christiane. "Assumptions and the Creation of Meaning: Reading Sophocles' *Antigone.*" *Journal of Hellenic Studies* 109 (1989): 134–48.

Trapp, Michael. "Tragedy and the Fragility of Moral Reasoning: Response to Foley." In Silk, M. S., ed., *Tragedy and the Tragic* (1996), pp. 74–84.

Zeitlin, Froma. "Thebes: Theater of Self and Society in Athenian Drama." In Winkler, John J., and Froma I. Zeitlin, eds., *Nothing to Do with Dionysos?* (1990), pp. 130–67.

Hegel on *Antigone*

Bradley, A. C. "Hegel's Theory of Tragedy." Oxford Lectures on Poetry (London 1950). In Paolucci, Anne and Henry, eds., *Hegel on Tragedy* (1962), pp. 367–88.

Harris, H. S. *Hegel's Ladder II: The Odyssey of Spirit.* Indianapolis: Hackett Publishing Company, 1997.

Miller, A. V. , trans. *Hegel's Phenomenology of Spirit.* Oxford: Oxford University Press, 1977.

Mills, Patricia Jagentowicz. "Hegel's Antigone." *The Owl of Minerva* 17 (1986): 131–52.

Paolucci, Anne and Henry, eds. *Hegel on Tragedy.* New York: Anchor Books, 1962.

Shannon, Daniel E., ed. *G. W. F. Hegel: Spirit; Chapter Six of Hegel's* Phenomenology of Spirit. Indianapolis: Hackett Publishing Company, 2001.

Westphal, Kenneth R. *Hegel's Epistemological Realism: A Study of the Aim and Method of Hegel's* Phenomenology of Spirit. Dordrecht: Kluwer Academic Publishers, 1989, pp. 177–8.

Wood, Allen W., ed. *Hegel: Elements of the Philosophy of Right.* Cambridge: Cambridge University Press, 1991.

On *Oedipus Tyrannus*

Bollack, Jean. L'Oedipe roi *de Sophocle: Le texte et ses interprétations.* Four volumes. Lille, France: Presses Universitaires de Lille, 1990.

Carey, C. "The Second Stasimon of Sophocles' *Oedipus Tyrannus.*" *Journal of Hellenic Studies* 106 (1986): 175–9.

Dawe, R. D., ed. *Sophocles:* Oedipus Rex. Cambridge: Cambridge University Press, 1982.

Knox, Bernard. "The Date of the *Oedipus Tyrannus* of Sophocles." *American Journal of Philology* 77 (1956): 133–47. Reprinted, with other fine essays, in his *Word and Action: Essays on the Ancient Theater.* Baltimore: Johns Hopkins University Press, 1979, pp. 112–24.

LIMC: Lexicon Iconographicum Mythologiae Classicae. Zurich: Artemis Verlag, 1981.

March, Jennifer. "The Creative Poet: Studies in the Treatment of Myth in Greek Poetry." University of London: *Bulletin of the Institute for Classical Studies,* Supplement 49, 1987.

On *Oedipus at Colonus*

Burian, Peter. "Suppliant and Savior: *Oedipus at Colonus.*" *Phoenix* 28 (1974): 408–29.

Dunn, Francis M. "Introduction: Beginning at Colonus." *Yale Classical Studies* 29 (1992): 1–12.

Easterling, P. E. "Oedipus and Polynices." *Proceedings of the Cambridge Philological Society* 13 (1967): 1–13.

Edmunds, Lowell. *Theatrical Space and Historical Place in Sophocles'* Oedipus at Colonus. Lanham, Md.: Rowman and Littlefield, 1996.

Tanner, R. G. "The Composition of the *Oedipus Coloneus.*" In Kelley, Maurice, ed., *For Service to Classical Studies: Essays in Honor of Francis Letters.* Melbourne: F. W. Cheshire, 1966, pp. 153–92.

Travis, Roger. *Allegory and the Tragic Chorus in Sophocles'* Oedipus at Colonus. Lanham, Md.: Rowman and Littlefield, 1999.

Wilson, Joseph P. "The Hero and the City: An Interpretation of Sophocles' *Oedipus at Colonus.*" Ann Arbor: University of Michigan Press, 1997.